Winter Galley

WINTER GALLEY

The Autobiography of

MONROE E. TROUT

E-mail: smcove@bellsouth.net

Printed in Canada

First Printing: October 2008

ISBN: 978-0-615-25654-2

LCCN: 2008909298

Credits
Production Manager: Jim Wells
Book and Text Design: Barbara Boeing

To Sandy, my wife of 48 years

Contents

· ·

Contents

Acknowledgments

························ ························

This book would never have been written without all the strangers on my highway of life, and also the help and encouragement of the four high school teachers who made the biggest difference in my life: Miss Elva Lippi, Miss Elizabeth Watts, Mrs. Ethel Rolston, and Mr. Tony Wilsbach. Dr. and Mrs. Howard Milliken also played a significant role in encouraging me to go to college.

This book also could not have been written without the very able assistance of my writer, Sarah Maté, and the historical knowledge and help of my brother Chester and my fraternal brothers Tom and Ted Scotes. Bill Nydam has also helped jog my memory about past events. Special thanks to Jim Wells for guiding the book production and bringing together a fine team that included Ronda Robinson, Barbara Boeing, Linda Marion, and Bob Land.

There have been so many individuals and groups who have helped me have a successful career that I would be remiss if I tried to acknowledge them all. Some are named in the book, and I know some have been forgotten and will have to forgive me for their omission.

Last I want to thank Sandra, my wife of forty-eight years who has supported all my endeavors, and even encouraged me in some I was reluctant to engage in but that turned out to make my life more interesting and fulfilling. She also is my computer expert and was instrumental in making the tough job of writing a book a little easier.

My friendship with Monroe Trout spans six decades. Much has happened around the world during that period of time, but despite radical changes and far distances, our ties of fraternal affection and mutual respect have remained unbroken and lasting.

Our early years at William Penn High School in Harrisburg, Pennsylvania, laid the firm groundwork of our enduring relationship. Whether translating together *The Aeniad* under Miss Lippi's inspiring tutelage or writing Chaucerian parodies of each other with Mrs. Rolston's enthusiastic encouragement, Monroe and I spent many challenging and stimulating hours together in the classroom and at home. Many a time was passed in long-winded discussions about history, science, religion, current events, and high school activities and sports, when we were not trying to impress the girls at the weekly "sock hops" and "scruff dances" or during the summer, when we were not striving to win at miniature golf after a swim with the gang at the Hershey Park pool.

While our interactions were usually amicable, this did not mean that we did not have our occasional disagreements, especially over politics. Monroe ardently arrayed himself on the side of the Republicans (long the dominant party in Central Pennsylvania), with me on the side of the Democrats. Our discussions could get quite heated, but always ended with jokes and good-natured ribbing.

Monroe's childhood was difficult and his large, close-knit family often in straitened circumstances. From a young age he had to work after school and weekends. Yet he never complained. On the contrary, he was always positive and optimistic with a good sense of humor and a strong sense of purpose. Once he started to laugh, he would laugh so hard that tears would come to his eyes. I would often try to bring this about and as often succeeded.

Very soon Monroe became, in effect, a member of the Scotes family. We spent many hours around my mother's kitchen table, doing homework and enjoying her good Greek cooking. Monroe was especially fond of the pastries, and particularly the kourambiethes, sugar-powdered cookies.

Along with the food, he picked up some basic Greek phrases and words he would sometimes use at rather inappropriate occasions. For example, he took my parents to New York to see my sister, Anna, off to Greece in the summer of 1956. As the passengers started to board the ship, Monroe began to bid farewell enthusiastically to everyone with the traditional Easter salutation, "Christos anesti" or "Christ is risen," no doubt believing this was a phrase to be used for all events because he had heard us use it so often for weeks after Easter. The boarding passengers were both confused and amused.

In fact, when we celebrated Greek Easter, we always took Monroe with us to church, where the long service and the many collection plates would soon exhaust both Monroe's stamina and meager purse. The latter was quickly replenished with quarters from my father, who was standing by. The former was eventually restored by the giant Easter feast we indulged in after we returned home from church early Easter morning.

In 1949 with both of us winning substantial scholarships, we went on together to the University of Pennsylvania, where we were roommates in our freshman year and then fraternity brothers in Delta Tau Delta the following three years. These, too, were happy and unforgettable times.

As sophomores, Monroe and I both "went out," as the campus term had it, for the Mask and Wig show, staged by the venerable and prestigious undergraduate musical comedy club of the same name. Monroe was counted among the managerial staff and I in the cast. That Christmas we boarded a special Mask and Wig train that took us to many East Coast cities over a ten-day period in what was an unbroken series of performances and parties. What a blast that was!

Monroe, or "Spider" as he became known at Penn (originally for his tall, gangly stature but eventually for his astute and successful political tactics), soon became a BMOC, or Big Man on Campus. As president of the junior class, he was responsible for the organization of Junior Weekend, the big social event always held on the weekend that Penn played Navy. That year a young cadet named Ross Perot was president of the junior class at the Naval Academy. By tradition, Monroe had to find a date for his Navy counterpart. He asked my sister Anna, who was attending nearby Harcum College, if she would agree to be the blind date. She did, and a good time was had by all.

In his senior year Monroe went on to head the Interfraternity Council as well as the Undergraduate Council, the latter being the main governing body for all undergraduate organizations and activities. At graduation in recognition of his service and leadership, he was named by his fellow classmates one of the four honor men of the class of '53.

The following years took Monroe to medical school at Penn and then to law school at Dickinson, with an intermediate Navy stint. Meanwhile, I entered the U.S. Foreign Service and began a career that took me to the Middle East. On June 11, 1960, we both were married, he in Wisconsin and I in Iran.

As the years passed we always stayed in touch, and we

never missed the chance to see each other, either singly or with respective families in New Canaan, Washington, Maine, or California. In January 1975, Monroe made a special effort to be present at my swearing-in ceremony as U.S. ambassador to Yemen, which took place at the American ambassador's residence in Damascus, Syria.

Through good times and bad, Monroe has always been there for the family and me with his words of advice and his expressions of support. It has truly been said that a man is deemed fortunate if he possesses good health, a good family, and good friends. The first two prerequisites can be judged only at the end of a man's life, as Solomon once pointed out. Yet, Monroe's good and steadfast friendship over sixty years already permits me to claim a place among the fortunate.

Thomas J. Scotes

I n the ensuing pages of this book, the reader will be treated to the extraordinary life of a totally self-made man. Monroe Trout is an exceptional example of what one individual can achieve in this great land of opportunity if one has the grit, intestinal fortitude, and determination to succeed.

I have known Monroe for almost sixty-five years. We first met when I was about eight years old. Monroe was just entering junior high school as a thirteen-year-old when he and my brother Tom became seventh-grade classmates at Camp Curtin Junior High School in Harrisburg, Pennsylvania. Monroe, born in 1931 during the depths of the Depression, was one of fourteen children. His family was living at the poverty level due to the Depression, but also because his father, who was an expert carpenter, suffered from alcohol abuse. Because of these circumstances, Monroe started working at a very early age to contribute to the support of his family.

Even though Monroe had to work before and after school, he still managed to maintain the highest levels of academic achievement, graduating from William Penn High School in 1949 as the class salutatorian. During the years from seventh grade through high school, Monroe was a frequent visitor in our home. As my brother's closest friend, Monroe was looked on by my parents as one of their own.

In 1949 Monroe and my brother became freshman roommates at the University of Pennsylvania. They subsequently became fraternity brothers in Delta Tau Delta. During those college years, whenever Monroe came home to Harrisburg, invariably he would be at our house, visiting my parents to tell them of his adventures at the university. While at Penn, because of financial constraints Monroe had to work to supplement the scholarships he had received. Though he had to work his way all through college, when Monroe graduated in 1953 he was an honor man in his class.

Monroe was accepted into the medical school of the University of Pennsylvania in 1953. In 1954 I was accepted as a freshman at the University of Pennsylvania and entered that fall. Monroe was at that time a sophomore in the medical school and a dormitory proctor. Because of the close relationship between Monroe and my family, he acted as a surrogate brother to me during my trying first months as a freshman. To this day, I am convinced that Monroe's interest, advice, and mentoring during the three years that we overlapped at the university contributed significantly to my successful college career. Monroe went on to graduate from medical school.

Upon graduation, he then entered the Navy as a physician. After his internship, he volunteered and was accepted as a regimental surgeon assigned to the Marine Corps. As a career Marine Corps officer, I can attest to the fact that the Navy's best doctors are assigned to the combat Marines–and Monroe was the best. After serving his country honorably, Monroe determined he would enter law school. Not only was he accepted into Dickinson School of Law in Carlisle, Pennsylvania, but he joined the faculty as a lecturer in forensic medicine. All the while at Dickinson, he was practicing medicine to support his family, for by 1961 Monroe had married Sandra and their first son had been born. He was a member of the Order of the Coif and was elected to *Dickinson Law Review*.

During those years, I had a close relationship with Monroe and Sandy. Brother Tom had gone off to the U.S. Foreign

Service, but the link between my family and Monroe's remained strong. I became godfather to his son, and Monroe stood up for me when I married.

Through hard work, Monroe rose steadily in the corporate world, ultimately achieving the position of chief executive officer and chairman of the board of a multibillion-dollar corporation. At every step, his career was marked by his honesty and integrity. What is of great significance to note here is this: Monroe, all his life, has endeavored to balance achievement with benevolence. He acknowledges that it has been his life's goal to raise a billion dollars for charity.

This goal is a major focus in his life, and I believe that he works at it every day. Monroe has established scholarships for needy students. He has established endowments for colleges and hospitals and endowments to support the arts. He has set up funds to build homes for families of Appalachia and quietly helps individuals whom he learns are in need. He has given his time to assist people with medical emergencies or illnesses to get them admitted to medical facilities where their needs can be best met. This list only scratches the surface. A Horatio Alger Award recipient, Monroe has stated, "There is no shame in being poor, but there is great shame in being successful and not helping others."

Being friends for all these years, I regard Monroe as a brother. I am ever proud of him. He has attained great success, yes, but to me, where his greatness lies is in his determination to aid, to encourage, and to provide for people in need. He has given back, and continues to give back, to this great country for providing him the opportunity to reach for–and touch–the stars.

My hat is off to you, Monroe! I salute you!

Theodore J. Scotes
Lt. Col. USMC (Retired)

Chapter 1

Winter Galley Sails to America

My first known ancestor was Balthasar Trout, born in Germany in 1570. He had a son named Hans Leonhardt Trout, who was born in 1620 in Germany and died in 1682 in Switzerland. Hans married a German girl named Elizabeth Koch. They had two children, Hans Velten, born in 1645, and Johannes Trout, born in 1651. Hans Velten married Margaretha Mock in Germany on April 24, 1672. They had one child, Johann Wendell Georg Trout, born in 1689 in Umstadt.

Vintel, as Johann Wendell Georg was called, married Maria Appalonia Steinlin in Pfalz, Bayern, Germany. They had four children together. Maria died giving birth to daughter Anna Maria, and in June 1738 Vintel left Germany with all the children. They sailed in a fleet of fifteen ships on a vessel named the *Winter Galley* to escape possible religious persecution in the Palatine section of Germany to begin a new life in America.

Many of their fellow passengers would never realize a new life in America. On other trips there had been an occasional death or two. But because of disease that year, hundreds of people who left Holland in Vintel's fleet perished on the journey. For that reason, 1738 became known as the "Year of the

Destroying Angels."

In spite of her name, which suggested storms and a poor season for sailing, the *Winter Galley* made good time on the journey from Rotterdam to America. Vintel and his children—George, Nicholas, Michael, and Anna Maria—arrived in Philadelphia on September 5, 1738, in just under three months.

Vintel, who was my great-great-great grandfather, settled in Lancaster County, Pennsylvania, swore allegiance on a Bible to the Commonwealth, and moved to a farm twelve miles from the county seat. His second wife, Maria Magdalena Walter, bore him seven children. He died in 1760.

Sixteen years later in Philadelphia, Congress adopted the Declaration of Independence, promising freedom from persecution for a fledgling nation. Little did Vintel know that, in years to come, his descendants would be living throughout the United States and enjoying the freedom he had sought.

The family line included twins born to Vintel and Maria Magdalena on October 29, 1743, in Strasberg, Lancaster County, Pennsylvania. Wendel or Wintel, one of the twins, married Elizabeth Druckenbrod in Trinity, Lancaster County, Pennsylvania, on March 21, 1780. They were the parents of eleven children, including one named Adam. Wintel, my great-great-grandfather, died in Hopewell, York County, Pennsylvania, on August 31, 1820.

We have had our share of soldiers of one kind or another. Joab Trout, Vintel's relative and soldier of the cross, was a "hellfire and brimstone" Lutheran minister who gave the sermon at Brandywine to George Washington and his troops. While I have a copy of this sermon, I believe the original version is in the Yale University Library.

Several have distinguished themselves in war. One of Vintel's sons, John Wentzel Trout, fought in the Continental Army as a private fifth class, Second Company, Sixth Battalion of the Lancaster County militia, commanded by

Lt. Col. John Huber. Vintel's great-grandson Michael David Trout–the tenth of Adam's eleven children–fought on the Union side in the Civil War. Michael David was my grandfather. His wife, Jemima Davis Trout, bore him fourteen children, one of whom was my father, David Michael. Two of my brothers, David and Bob, served in World War II. David was killed in France in 1944.

While not a soldier, my great-granduncle on my mother's side, Nelson Rehmeyer, was a victim of a violent episode so odd and interesting that books were written about it.

Three men broke into Nelson's home and murdered him. When the case came to trial in York County, the accuseds' defense was that my uncle had put a hex on them. The only way to get rid of the hex was to kill the offender. Actually, the crime was just plain robbery and murder. All three were convicted.

If you go to Pennsylvania Dutch country, you'll see hex signs on many of the barns. Because of the superstition, this case got international attention from the press and inspired the book *Hex. The Pow-Wow Book*, was also written about the murder and reports many of the beliefs of the Pennsylvania Germans. It also contains a prayer my grandmother said when we were children.

My father married into a well-respected family. Florence Kashner was the daughter of Cecilia Rehmeyer and Herman Kashner. Rehmeyer Valley, Pennsylvania, is named after my grandmother's family. The sixth of thirteen sisters and brothers, I was born in Harrisburg, Pennsylvania, on April 5, 1931. I had a stepsister from my father's previous marriage. One sibling died in childbirth, so I always just say I was in the middle of the brood. Nine were brothers, so we had our own baseball team.

Since we are of German ancestry, when we went to visit Grandma Cecilia nearby, she admonished us for not speaking the right language. Maybe this is why I took four years of German in college! She had a ritual in which she would put the children from infancy to about five years old "through the string." Somehow this was supposed to protect them from illnesses and calamities. The ritual was passed down only from a male to a female or a female to a male. While Grandma passed the string over and around all of us in a "special" way, she would say a prayer in German. I watched her perform this ritual on my brothers and sisters. The practice has been lost to the current generation, probably because people considered it witchcraft. However, *The Pow-Wow Book*, mentioned previously, contains the very prayer.

She also insisted that we all swallow a concoction of black molasses and sulfur at least once or twice a year. It was awful. But this was supposed to cleanse us from germs and whatever ailed us. Actually, when we were sick my mother also gave us sulfur and molasses, as well as cod-liver oil, also awful. Maybe it did help, because we survived childhood.

Mother protected us and probably saved many of our lives accidentally by feeding us homemade sauerkraut. In the attic of our house were huge porcelain crocks in which she used to cure the kraut. Of course, it stank up the house, but on top of these crocks a mold would form which, unknown to us, actually contained penicillin. That's how Arthur Fleming first discovered it. I'm not sure it was from the top of sauerkraut, but it was mold. Obviously, you're never going to get all that mold off, so you're going to eat some of it. Literally, it was the first antibiotic, and it only took small doses back then to fight severe bacterial infections such as streptococcus that caused sore throat, rheumatic fever, and severe kidney disease. It takes large doses of antibiotics now because bacteria have become immune to them. But I am quite convinced that a good part of why we survived was the mold in the sauerkraut.

To return to family history, my genealogy research is extensive. I am always interested when I meet or hear of someone named Trout. I was on the board of the Cleveland Clinic for sixteen years from 1970 to 1986 and saw a picture in the clinic paper of a housekeeper named Mrs. Trout. On one of my board meeting visits I asked to meet with her, and she turned out to be a direct relation. There were three branches of the family. Ours stayed in Pennsylvania. One went up to the Buffalo and Erie areas. She was part of that branch. There was another line that went down into Virginia and on into Tennessee in the early 1800s.

In my ancestry, through marriage we had a governor of Pennsylvania (George Leader), a congressman, also from Pennsylvania, and even a distant relation to President James Buchanan. A professional football player for the Pittsburgh Steelers named Trout caught my eye and, sure enough, I was able to trace him back as a relative.

So I run into kinfolk all the time. I did get a phone call from a Trout family in Tennessee asking if we were related. If we were, I couldn't find it in my genealogy. There are Trouts all over the country.

As a baby I made news too in a case of mistaken identity. I was apparently mistaken for the Lindbergh baby, who had been kidnapped. Somebody in a moment of hysteria accused my mother of having the baby. So the police interviewed her, and the mistake was cleared up. It was one of those events that can occur when hysteria sweeps the country.

As for my early childhood, my first five years we lived way out in the country. The main thing I can remember is snakes–snakes all over the place–to the point that I remember seeing them outside my window and on the roads. It was in that remote location I had my first accident. I fell and cut my right forearm so badly that I still have an eight-inch scar to show for it.

Finally my father decided that we needed to move into the

city so he could find work. He was a pretty good barber and carpenter and an excellent cabinetmaker, but his alcoholism kept him out of work for long periods at a time.

He rented a three-bedroom wooden house in a poor neighborhood of Harrisburg. At that point nine children were in the family. Nevertheless, we moved into this house with no central heat, just a pot-bellied stove in the middle room on the first floor. It was supposed to heat the whole house, but of course it didn't. Beds were crammed into each bedroom, and nine children and parents had to sleep in them.

"Winter galley" is a good metaphor for my life–starting out in a bad season, constantly struggling against storms and turbulent waters, then being launched by unexpected headwinds. I think my most important early memories were of deprivation. We were not alone. The Great Depression had the United States by the throat. My father tried his hand at a little bit of everything but was unsuccessful, and many times we went hungry. Unfortunately, the house we lived in was only three doors from a bar, where he usually was, spending what little money we had to live on.

I also remember standing in line many times to get sacks of cornmeal distributed by the government. My mother made what she called "mush." That was the staple of our diet. We all tried to be first at the table.

All the older children had to go to work as soon as they were able. I started working when I was six. I worked for an elderly lady named Mrs. Milliken, whose son was chief of surgery at the Polyclinic Hospital and mayor of the town. I carried out the ashes from the furnace. Nobody had oil back then. Everyone used coal, so if they had central heating, they had big furnaces, and somebody had to carry out the ashes. I also cleaned house for her, mowed the lawn, shoveled the snow from the sidewalk, and did whatever chores she assigned me. I guess I was a pretty good worker. You didn't make much in those days. I started at a nickel an hour.

Her son, Dr. Howard Milliken, quickly became my life role model. He encouraged me to stay in school and study medicine.

Through Mrs. Milliken, I met several neighbors who hired me to do the same kind of jobs for them. Mrs. Rudder, I remember, was one and so was her daughter, Mrs. Minnick. Mrs. Minnick had a son who was killed on Okinawa during World War II. We felt a special bond because I later served in Okinawa from 1958 to1960 with the Marine Corps.

When I was eight or nine, Mrs. Milliken's daughter-in-law asked me to come work for her, and I did so all day Saturday. We went to the farmer's market each week. She had a little red wagon that I pulled for the length of the market, which was about two blocks long. She bought all the fruits and vegetables and meat she wanted.

During the war many things were rationed–sugar, coffee, and what have you. With fourteen children, we had lots of ration books because every citizen got rations. We weren't going to use all that sugar and such, so I gave Mrs. Milliken some of our ration stamps so she could buy things her family wanted. In many ways she helped me a lot, and during the war we helped her. She also gave me hand-me-down clothes from her son's wardrobe.

To get into the movies free during World War II, you brought an old aluminum pot, so everyone was looking for old pots. We also collected tinfoil from cigarette packs for the war effort.

We had lots of blackouts. They seemed to come in waves. You heard the sirens and, if you could, you blacked out your windows; otherwise, you turned off all the lights. Later an all-clear siren sounded.

Our Boy Scout troop was designated as one of the plane spotters for our particular area. We all had to memorize what the enemy planes looked like, and then on certain nights we had plane-spotting duty. Of course, no planes ever flew over.

We did have a big scare when German submarines dropped off spies on the East Coast. However, they were quickly captured and, as I remember, executed.

All of my older brothers and sisters quit school and left home as soon as the law allowed–at age sixteen. As a result, none of them graduated from high school. I was the first one, I think in large part because the Millikens and other people I worked for urged me to continue in school.

In third grade I met the first teacher who encouraged me to graduate, Mrs. Burgoon. She talked to my mother, the stabilizing influence at home, to help keep me in school. She was also the first person who spanked me in school. I think she recognized I had some potential, and she wanted me to learn early on that if I was bad, I would be punished. She actually became a lifelong friend of the family and visited my mother long after all of us were out of grade school.

She was not the last teacher to spank me. Growing up during World War II, I organized an army in grade school. Of course, I made myself the general. We all had ranks. The parents of one of the other students, James Sendi, bought all the army insignia so we could dress up by rank. The bullies in the school didn't like this, so there were many fights on the playground. If you had a fight, you got spanked. The spankings were well deserved and didn't hurt me. In retrospect, they probably helped.

Basically the only pleasure I had as a child, since I worked too much to have time for play, was to attend Boy Scouts one evening a week in a church a block away from our house. I managed to become a star scout, and later an assistant scoutmaster.

It was not an easy childhood–all work and no play–but that was life for many children growing up in the Depression and during World War II.

At the end of sixth grade when we were about to enter

junior high school, we had to decide whether we were going to be in the academic program or take commercial courses or shop. The academics were the smallest section, but those were the ones who had their sights on college. I was considered whatever a nerd was called back then–"square"–because I worked after school and had no time to socialize. Jocks looked on squares with contempt. Commercial students were going into business to be secretaries, clerks, or lower management personnel. The shop students learned how to be auto mechanics, carpenters, and so forth. We all had to take courses from other programs. The academics had to take shop courses and commercial courses. In one of the shop courses I made a table, which I still have in my house. It's an antique now, and I have to say that, looking at it today, I don't know how I made it back then. It is truly beautiful.

The parents who bought the army insignia gave me one of the other early jobs I had when I was a teenager. They owned a little confectionery store, and I worked there as a clerk, making milkshakes and serving ice cream. It was the neighborhood hangout for all the teenagers, a place where they could get together, talk, listen to the jukebox, and laugh, laugh a lot. These would be fond memories of youth.

Years later, I crossed paths again with one of the jocks. Steve Macian was a star of the football team, a nice guy. At that time, high school was sharply divided because of our shop and academic courses. Later, when I became a senior vice president at Sterling Drug Inc., I was visiting our plant in Myerstown, Pennsylvania. There I met Steve's wife, also a member of our high school class, now working on one of our drug lines. She approached me and asked if I could get her husband a better job. Apparently he was working as a janitor in the plant. I talked to the manager, who said he would look into it. We agreed there would be no special favors but, if qualified, Steve would move up.

The war took its toll on many families and added a somber note to my early teen years. My oldest brother, David, was drafted into the army. My second-oldest brother, Bob, enlisted in the Air Force. The third brother, Bill, was exempt because of poor eyesight. My brother-in-law Jerry also served.

I remember the military people came to our house to tell my mother that David had been killed. I don't think there is anything worse for a mother than to hear that her son is dead. He was buried in Epinal, France, at the request of his widow. I think, if it had been up to my mother, she would have brought him home.

Parents hung a flag in their windows which had a blue star if a son or daughter was serving. If a son or daughter was killed, the flag had a gold star. Two of my brothers served at the time, and when David was killed, one star was changed to gold.

I knew Mother was upset, but I never realized how much. She basically had never traveled outside of Harrisburg her entire life. However, at the age of seventy-seven, she had saved up enough money and said, "I'm going to France."

We said, "Who with?"

"I'm going by myself."

So she went to visit my brother's burial place in a foreign country. I think her action shows the impact of a child's death on a parent.

One thing I remember from Dave's letters home was how much The Salvation Army did for the troops at the front, providing hot coffee and other comforts. Remembering that The Salvation Army had been important to my brother, my wife and I have made many contributions to the organization. We received the National Caring Award from The Salvation Army in 1996.

The first job I had working for a business was a paper route. A lot of children had them and delivered papers directly to houses. The one day I made more money than any other day of my paper route career was December 7, 1941. I remember hawking papers on the street corner, "Japan Bombs Pearl Harbor." I quickly sold out my allotment. I was ten years old.

As I grew older, Mrs. Milliken had me haul paper and books off to the junkyard. I kept the books because they were very good, and I was interested in reading many of them and keeping others for reference materials.

When we moved to Knoxville, Tennessee, we visited Tusculum College and saw the rare book section of its library. We were talking to the curator, and I told him that I had a number of very old history books, including a well-known atlas of the Civil War with photographs of the war, published in 1871. The curator was very interested, but I had no connection to Tusculum. At the time I had some good friends at the East Tennessee Historical Society. I later went on the Board of Trustees but resigned very shortly because it was not a good fit for me, and my health was deteriorating. My friends convinced me that I should give the books to the McClung Collection, which is part of the Knox County Public Library system. The director of McClung came to the house, looked at the books, was quite interested, and promised he would restore them. I gave the books to the McClung Collection.

Mrs. Milliken also gave me several old Bibles from the 1800s. I will tell about one of them later.

The other item the Millikens gave me when I went off to college was a microscope. I had worried about how I would ever afford one, they were so expensive. I used it all through college and medical school. My grandson now has that microscope.

Howard Milliken Jr. had used this microscope in medical school. When I moved to California to become chairman and CEO of American Healthcare Systems, he was working in one of the hospitals in our consortium. So we met again, on a more equal footing than when I was one of his family's hired help.

We renewed our acquaintance and became very good friends.

After grade school, I went into Camp Curtin Junior High School. Camp Curtin was named after the governor of Pennsylvania during the Civil War. There I took my first classes in Latin, which later became my favorite subject. In that class I met Tom Scotes, whose parents were Greek immigrants. He was extremely bright, and we hit it off and became lifelong friends.

I nearly didn't graduate from William Penn High School. I was in serious competition for valedictorian with Joe Reuwer, whose father was my oral English teacher. I had straight A's in high school, and it was difficult for him not to give me an A, but the A he gave me was a 90 and the A he gave his son was a 100. I am not disparaging young Joe. He was a great guy, and his father wanted him to have every advantage. Joe and I were, in fact, good friends.

My high school Latin teacher, Miss Elva Lippi, my math teacher, Miss Elizabeth Watts, and my gym teacher, Mr. Tony Wilsbach, all knew what was happening, along with my English teacher, Mrs. Ethel Rolston. They were quite upset over Mr. Reuwer's actions. Miss Lippi, Miss Watts, and Mr. Wilsbach all took great interest in me and encouraged me to apply to different schools, including the University of Pennsylvania, which is where I wanted to go.

I finally couldn't take it from Mr. Reuwer anymore. So I went in on one of the last days before the end of my senior year and lambasted him. I was immediately suspended, of course. The question then was whether I would graduate. If I didn't graduate, I couldn't go to college.

Barbara Loban was a classmate and friend of mine. She went home and told her father everything. He was the assistant superintendent of schools. After checking all the facts, he influenced the high school principal to graduate me.

I graduated salutatorian of my class of three hundred-ten

with the highest score ever given in Latin at our school. In addition, I had a starring role in the school play in both my junior and senior years.

I won the Colonial Dames of America State Essay Contest. My essay was entitled "Seward's Folly." I remember my ending, the closing lines of a poem by Robert Service:

> Above the igloo piteous flies
> Our frayed flag to the frozen skies.

The award was to be given in Philadelphia. It is hard to say which excited me more–the all-expense-paid trip away from Harrisburg for the first time or the $100 prize.

Also, I was awarded the gold watch given to the outstanding senior in the high school. I still have it. It's a Bulova and was engraved on the back.

In 1946 when I was just sixteen, Dr. Milliken gave me a version of the key to the city. It is a big wooden key which I still have. Basically, it named me Harrisburg's most outstanding boy. Of course, I had worked for the family many years and was active in distributing campaign materials for his mayoral runs. Having said that, in high school I had earned enough awards and honors that I believe I was entitled to the key.

I was admitted to the University of Pennsylvania class of 1953 and was awarded two scholarships. One from a local bank was for students who were qualified but could not afford college. The other was a full-tuition scholarship given by a state senator. Since Dr. Miliken was actively involved in politics, he was able to convince Sen. M. Harvey Taylor that I deserved the scholarship, which paid for my tuition both in college and medical school. Dr. Milliken got me summer jobs with the city. I painted parking meters and traffic lines. He also asked a physician at Penn if he needed some help. That is how I got a job cleaning offices, which I did all the way through college.

I mentioned Mr. Wilsbach, my gym teacher. When I went

away to college, he bought me the first new suit of clothes I ever owned. I wore the jacket of that suit until the 1990s!

Years later, I had the opportunity to honor these early supporters of mine. The University of the Cumberlands (formerly Cumberland College) in Williamsburg, Kentucky, has a mountain outreach program we have been supporting since the early 1990s. Dr. Jim Taylor, president of that school, came to visit us in California. He wanted big bucks instead of the small donations we had made in the past.

I said to him, "Dr. Taylor, I have been giving you money for the past ten or fifteen years, and I don't even know if you exist. I just read a brochure about the programs you have to help poor kids in Appalachia go to school."

"Well, why don't you come out and visit?"

My wife and I did, and I must say, we have never been so impressed by a college campus and the students as we were at Cumberland. A couple of years ago, we decided to fund a scholarship there, which we did with a $100,000 endowment.

Then we found out that students, who are almost all on financial aid, build houses or dig wells for poor people in Appalachia. That is how they pay their tuition. It costs about $35,000 for the supplies to build one of these houses, which are like palaces for the residents. Sandy and I decided to give the money to build a house, and at the dedication we added something we had been thinking about for a long time. To honor my four teachers, Miss Lippi, Miss Watts, Mrs. Rolston, and Mr. Wilsbach—because without them I would not be here today—and out of respect for Dr. Taylor and his wife, Dinah, we surprised the college by establishing a $1 million endowment fund to build a house every year forever, each with a brass plaque with my teachers' names.

Chapter 2

The Scotes Brothers and Other Friends

I have been fortunate to have many friends, and they in turn have led me to many others.

Tom Scotes became such a person in my life. He and I had most of our classes together in junior and senior high school and became extremely good friends. We both went to the University of Pennsylvania, where we were roommates our freshman year and pledged the same fraternity. I learned all the Greek swear words because, when he got mad at me, he would swear in Greek.

At the time we entered Penn, the university had a camp in the country outside Philly. It was called Green Lane. All freshman students had to go there for orientation. Tom won the contest for the best class cheer: "'53 has fighting spirit, Pennsylvania will ever cheer it."

That camp is where I got my nickname "Spider" because of my long arms and legs. I am 6'5." The name followed me all through college, and then I tried to abandon it. When I was practicing medicine and too busy to chat on the phone, my wife always knew if a good friend was calling because they would ask for "Spider." Then she would know it was okay to say I was home.

Tom's parents were like second parents to me. Later when I was in medical school and became a junior intern at Polyclinic Hospital, where my mentor Howard Milliken was chief of surgery, the Scotes family lived about a block from the hospital and also owned a restaurant in another part of town. I went to their house at all hours of the night and had coffee and goodies. His mother baked the best kourambiethes and baklava, both Greek pastries and delicious. Tom's brother Ted worked nights in the steel mill at that time, and his mother waited up for him to come home, so I knew someone was always home to greet and feed me.

Ted lives in Knoxville, Tennessee. He and his wife, Thale, along with Kay and Jim Clayton (currently president of Clayton Bank & Trust), were major influences in persuading us to move to Knoxville. I've known Ted for sixty-seven years and still see him a couple of times a week. We swap Marine Corps stories and reminisce about our childhood escapades.

Every year on November 10 in Knoxville, he and Gen. Robert Tiebout have a Marine Corps birthday party, and it's great fun. Ted and Thale and the general organize it and invite all the Marines they know. I am the only Navy man to attend because I treated the Marines in the Far East, plus they like to rib me about my branch of the service. I remind them that the Marine Corps is still a unit of the Department of the Navy.

Tom Scotes is a brilliant guy who speaks eight or nine languages. When he graduated from college, he went to Harvard Law School, didn't like it, and quit. He joined the U.S. State Department. In 1974 he was selected by Secretary of State Henry Kissinger to be his interpreter in his shuttle diplomacy effort between Israel and Egypt.

At the same time, I was serving as an advisor to the State Department on medical affairs and was asked to meet as a private citizen with the minister of health of Egypt to see where any monies we gave them would be spent. We hoped a goodly portion of the billions involved would be used for health benefits. So I went to Egypt and met with the minister, where we discussed various ways of spending this money. Schistosomiasis afflicted about twenty million Egyptians at the time, and since we were doing extensive research at Sterling Drug Inc., on finding cures for it, I was quite familiar with its life cycle. The minister and I discussed ways to prevent the disease and also to cure it. I was extremely pleased with his approach and reported this back to the State Department. The minister was a radiologist and later became prime minister but died suddenly within the year he became prime minister.

At the time I visited Egypt, Anwar Sadat was the president. While there, I met a fellow named Dr. Ahmed Fadl, who was one of the influential advisors on health affairs to the Egyptian government. He was a pharmacologist. We became extremely good friends.

I had to return to Egypt a second time. Christmas was not important there except to members of the Coptic Church, so my meetings with the minister of health were over the Christmas holidays.

While I was there, the U.S. ambassador to Egypt, Herman Eilts, informed me that Kissinger had just named my friend Tom Scotes as the ambassador to Yemen. Tom's swearing-in ceremony was to be in early January in Damascus, Syria. With the help of Eilts, I arranged a flight to Damascus to surprise Tom at the ceremony.

Because he was the highest ranking U.S. diplomat in Syria, Tom had a diplomatic car and gave me a tour of the country. I saw the Golan Heights from the Syrian side and many of the old historic places in Damascus, including the mosque where John the Baptist was buried. It turned out to be a marvelous trip and a real surprise to Tom.

He is now retired. It's funny how things happen over the

years. Tom was probably one of the real experts on the Middle East. He spent his entire career there.

Upon returning to the U.S., I had to go to Washington immediately to report what had happened. Dr. Fadl knew I was staying at the Hilton Hotel in Egypt and told me that, if I wanted to have any private conversations that were important, I should have them outside the hotel because my room was bugged. Later when Sandy and I were living in San Diego, he asked if I would look after his daughter and her husband who were coming to San Diego and expecting a baby. So I helped make arrangements at the hospital.

About a year after my trips to Egypt, Dr. Fadl called and said he had a very important patient whose name he could not reveal who needed to see a liver specialist. He wanted to know if I could arrange it, and I said I would try. I called a professor of gastroenterology at the University of Pennsylvania, Dr. John Senior, whom I knew very well. He said the best liver specialist was in New York at Mount Sinai Hospital and gave me his name. The specialist was obviously Jewish, and Mount Sinai is a Jewish hospital, but I didn't think that was important.

I called Dr. Fadl and said, "Okay, Ahmed, I found a specialist, one of the best in the country right here in New York at Mount Sinai Hospital. I talked to him, and he'll see your patient."

Ahmed said, "Wait a minute. No way. We can't see a Jewish doctor. We can't go to a Jewish hospital. I understand there is somebody at NIH (National Institutes of Health) Hospital. Can you get my friend into NIH Hospital?"

I said, "Ahmed, that's a government hospital and very difficult to get into."

He said, "It would help U.S.-Egypt relations if you do this."

"Okay, but Ahmed, why don't you go through the State Department? That's the easiest way to get into NIH."

"No, no. It has to be private."

So I called my good friend Roger Egeberg, who was the assistant secretary of health. NIH reports to the assistant secretary of health.

"Roger, I don't even know this fellow's name and he won't give it to me."

And Roger said, "Dammit, Monroe. Tell him to go through the State Department."

"Roger, I can't. I've already told him that."

"All right. Let me see what I can do." Fadl was waiting. Roger called me back. "All right. It's arranged. The top liver doctor will see him, and we can have him admitted. But, dammit, I need to know his name!"

So I called Dr. Fadl back and said, "It's arranged. I can get him into NIH Hospital, but Dr. Egeberg, the assistant secretary of health, needs to know who it is. He can't be admitted anonymously."

Well, it turned out that the patient was Sadat's brother, and that's why they didn't want it known. He probably had schistosomiasis of the liver. There is an interesting follow-up to this. About three months after this happened, I received a call from the assistant secretary of health for the Middle East. I don't remember his name because he made me so angry. He had just learned about Sadat's brother and was berating me for making the arrangements for his hospitalization without going through the State Department. He was just upset because he didn't know what the hell was going on. I finally got tired of listening to him and hung up.

Another friend from college, my "little brother" Bart Leach, was a very poor kid from Massachusetts when he came to the University of Pennsylvania on scholarship and later pledged my fraternity. That is how he became my little brother.

Bart became an All-American basketball player at Penn and was inducted into Penn's Hall of Fame in 2005. He was drafted by the Boston Celtics but turned down Red Auerbach to go to Princeton Theological Seminary to become a Presbyterian minister.

He served a church for a while but for some reason left the ministry to go into business. He became an extremely successful businessman in New York City, and we used to get together for lunch. Then he decided he wanted to go back into the ministry. The Presbyterian Church wouldn't take him back because they said they had to focus on helping the young people coming out of the seminary and they just didn't have a position for him.

Bart asked me if I knew anybody who could help him get back into the ministry. Well, I knew Guthrie Speers, who was the minister of the Presbyterian Church in New Canaan, Connecticut. His father, also a Presbyterian minister, was head of the Presbyterian Church (U.S.A.). So I went to see Guthrie, and he gave me the same story Bart had been given.

I finally said, "Guthrie, have you ever heard the story of the prodigal son? This guy is one of the greatest Presbyterian ministers you've ever had. He played All-American basketball in college; he went to Princeton Theological Seminary; he has a graduate degree from Harvard; he was a successful business-man; he's in his forties; and you tell me that you have no place for him?"

Guthrie looked at me, and basically said "touché" and that he would talk to his father. He did, and Bart got an offer from the Third Presbyterian Church in Pittsburgh and later from the First Presbyterian Church, the largest of its denomination in the city.

When Bart visited us in California, I showed him the old Bibles. He said, "I would love to have one of those for my church." I gave him one, which I believe is in the Third Presbyterian Church.

Bart's college roommate and dear friend to both of us was Jack Guest from Canada, who also became a Delt. Both he and

Bart were honor men when they graduated. Jack was a great oarsman who later rowed for the Canadian Olympic team. Ask any Canadian who Jack Guest is, and chances are he'll know. Jack later became vice president of Kodak for all of Canada.

Bart developed Alzheimer's and had to retire from the ministry. When I visited Bart at his home, I was one of the few people he recognized. He told his wife, "This is the guy who kept me in school." Basically, I did, because I talked him out of going home. He was homesick and was not doing well scholastically at that time. I tutored him along with a couple of other athletes. Unfortunately, Bart passed away recently. The Fairhaven High School principal in Massachusetts where Bart was the all-time star basketball player named the school's new gymnasium after him.

A good friend of mine, Jerry McGinley, an All-American end at Penn, later became senior vice president of Paine Webber in New York. We had lunch almost every month and are still in touch. McGinley's son, John, was a star in *Platoon* and also on the TV program *Scrubs*.

Jerry called me about a year ago to tell me that Eddie Bell, also an All-American end at Penn and a friend of mine, was not doing well. His wife had died, and he was in a deep depression. He asked me to call Eddie, which I did. Eddie had numerous health problems himself. He obviously remembered the Pennsylvania days and was happy I called. He is now doing much better, not because of my calls but because of his doctors.

Chapter 3

Crossing Paths with Ross Perot and Mae West

During my college years, I wanted to participate in student activities as much as possible. Even though I was working for a Philadelphia doctor and cleaning offices, I did manage to row on the freshman rowing team, become involved in campus politics, and join a fraternity. I was also busy working as a parking lot attendant for the university. I was later asked to head the entire parking lot operation because I could employ sixty to seventy students every year and still make a profit. I kept this job even through medical school and made the parking lots a profit center for the university, whereas before it had been a losing proposition.

Starting in my junior year, I was also a dorm advisor for a freshman dorm. I received a free room for which I had to be available to freshmen in case they had any problems.

My senior year I also became advisor for a football dorm. One of the football players, Dave Hovey, used to be a little destructive. Dave and I became friends even though I had to discipline him frequently. He became headmaster of a very prestigious preparatory school in New England, where I understand he was very strict.

During medical school, I became a proctor in the dorms, which is what they call advisors for more than one dorm. I was the proctor for three football dorms, although all the students were not necessarily football players. One of the students in my dorm almost died because of acute alcoholism from a who-could-drink-the-most contest. Fortunately, we got him to student health in time.

That summer one of the football players invited me to his wedding in the New York area. I was driving some of the other people to the wedding. The roads were wet, and I flipped the car. It was totally destroyed, but no one was hurt. We all got to the wedding on time and intact, although badly shaken. It was a wedding to remember.

Robert Sebastianelli, a football player from Scranton, was a prankster of the first order and kept us all smiling. In fact, his nickname was Smiley. His father was a coal miner, and his mother worked hard. I became good friends with his parents, who invited me to Scranton to visit. Robert, who married his high school sweetheart, died of lung cancer at thirty-nine. He did not smoke. I later met one of his sons who played football for Penn as well.

My sister Betty had married Gerald Schultz from Macedon, New York, so I spent part of my summers picking sour cherries and digging ditches for construction sites in upstate New York. Pretty good money for school expenses, but the work was hard. I had to become a union member to work as a laborer. I also worked on several overpasses in Rochester, New York.

My sophomore year, I was assistant manager of the Mask and Wig, the men's drama club. At that time, the university pretty much separated men and women, with almost no coed activities. Although this was starting to break down while I was there, as there were some women in my classes, men still took ladies' parts in musical plays. The actors were so good and so funny that they were invited to tour all over the country.

When we were in Buffalo, we were at the same theater with Mae West. We were invited to see her show and had front-row seats. She called me up to the stage. Basically, I was the sex object of her performance and the laughingstock of my colleagues.

I was also active in the Interfraternity Council, which governed the thirty-nine fraternities on campus. There were two factions in the campus political system, and the faction that my fraternity, Delta Tau Delta, was in had consistently lost in previous elections. The president of the Interfraternity Council was automatically a member of the Undergraduate Council. Whoever was chairman of the Undergraduate Council, the supreme governing body on campus, determined where all the student funds would be designated.

I became lifetime friends with Bernie Goldstein and Tony Fennelli. The three of us devised a plan to overthrow the ruling political party on campus and take over for the next election. We convinced enough fraternities to defect and come to our side, especially those that did not get any spoils from their old party.

As a campus politician, I never lost an election. I was on the Sophomore Class Council and in the Kite and Key Society (Ben Franklin founded Penn). Also, I was elected to Phi Kappa Beta, the junior honor society, and was president of the junior class, which automatically gave me a seat on the Undergraduate Council.

This story followed me through life. Every year Penn played Navy in football, which was the biggest weekend of the year for juniors and was always at Penn. Traditionally, the president of the Penn junior class invited the president of the Navy junior class to be his guest, to get him a date, and generally entertain him. When the Navy president arrived, I realized he was as funny as anybody I had ever met. He was the son of West Texas dirt farmers, so we got along well, swapping stories of who was the poorest. His name was Ross Perot. Tom Scotes's sister was his date. She went to a neighboring school in the Philadelphia suburbs.

Just before Perot ran for president in 1992, we were on the same stage in Florida giving speeches to a healthcare audience. I went up to him. Mind you, I hadn't seen him since 1952. "You probably don't remember me, but we had fun one weekend."

Instantly, he replied, "Junior Weekend, University of Pennsylvania." When Perot ran for president, he asked me to be head of his healthcare advisory committee, but I had already committed to do the same for George Bush's campaign. I, along with Bill Frist and others, co-chaired the Healthcare Coalition for Bush for President. However, I did tell Perot if he needed to know anything in the healthcare field, I would be happy to discuss it with him. I was chairman and CEO of American Healthcare Systems, the largest hospital organization in the country at that time.

In 1996 my wife and I received The Salvation Army's Tradition of Caring Award, and the chairman of the board was Mrs. Perot. She came to San Diego and presented us the award at a luncheon. As I have mentioned previously, I was always a big supporter of The Salvation Army.

I said to her, "I'm probably the only one who ever fixed your husband up with a date that wasn't you." We laughed together and had a good time swapping stories about Ross. It's truly a small world.

In my senior year I was elected to the Friars Honor Society. Members had made major contributions to the university. I was also elected president of the Interfraternity Council and chairman of the Undergraduate Council. It was our job to mete out the student funds for the various campus activities and to take other actions necessary to govern the student body. I worked very closely with the dean of students, Arnold Henry,

George Peters, vice dean, and Robert Pitt, the assistant dean. The chairman of the Undergraduate Council also became a member of the All-University Student Disciplinary Committee, along with graduate students and faculty.

We were quite busy because of the Rowbottom riots. Lore has it that, back in the 1920s, Penn alum Joseph T. Rowbottom would come home drunk and yell, "Rowbottom," and people would throw things out the windows. "Yea, Rowbottom!" served as the rallying call for mass student disturbances at Penn during much of the twentieth century.

My junior year some students poured gasoline on streetcar tracks. The police captain, Frank Rizzo, later mayor of Philadelphia, was not a nice person. He brought his troopers and actually "bashed a few heads." I think it could have been handled much better. The Disciplinary Committee had the job of sorting out who the ringleaders were, then holding hearings and meting out punishment, which in many cases was suspension from school. We were also involved in a number of other incidents.

Harold Stassen was president of the university in my senior year. A big issue was whether or not Penn, which up until that time had played a national football schedule, should keep a big-time football program or go completely Ivy League. I participated in all those discussions and was pro-Ivy League. The decision was to leave the big-time football to others. I am still convinced it was the right decision. In my opinion, you don't need a big-time athletic program to be a great university.

I was a member of the Christian Association Cabinet, the Spirit Committee, and the Dean's College Advisory Committee. When I graduated, I was given the Spade Award, a sterling silver shovel used to plant the ivy for my class. Each graduating class planted ivy somewhere on campus. I also received the Alumni Award of Merit. Usually one was given to an undergraduate, all others to alumni.

Some of my classmates and good friends went on to become well known themselves. Dick Maser became director of plastic surgery at the Palo Alto Clinic and a professor at Stanford University. Peter Yurchak became a Harvard professor of cardiology. John Potts became head physician of Massachusetts General Hospital, and Peter Jannetta head of neurosurgery at the University of Pittsburgh.

I had fairly good grades in college, but I did almost flunk one course. I had a D in physics. I thought that would put the kibosh on medical school, but apparently because of my extracurricular activities and work responsibilities, I was admitted to Penn Medical School. Since I basically could not afford it, state Sen. Harvey Taylor gave me a tuition scholarship. I earned my dorm room by working as proctor, but in order to pay all the other expenses, like eating, I continued as head of the parking lots for all four years.

I was very, very busy in medical school. Sleep deprivation was the norm and probably accounts for why I can still function fully on only five hours of sleep. Supervising thirteen to fourteen parking lots with sixty to seventy employees and three dorms full of students, plus studying and counseling, did not make for an easy four years.

The Navy commissioned me as an ensign when I graduated from college in 1953 (a program now called the 1995 Program). I had to agree to serve four years in the Navy as a doctor. I was promoted to full lieutenant when I graduated from medical school. I had reached the rank of lieutenant commander when I resigned my commission and was honorably discharged.

Chapter 4

Medical School Stories

I have always been grateful for so many incidents that taught me compassion.

Starting in my junior year, I was also a dorm advisor for a freshman dorm. I received a free room for which I had to be available to freshmen in case they had any problems.

One that I remember from medical school happened when I was a junior. We were assigned patients and mine was a five-year-old boy with leukemia. In those days there were no medicines to treat his disease, so in fact he was dying. He loved Notre Dame and talked about its football players all the time. Notre Dame was coming to play football at Penn. I wanted to take him to the game, but I never realized how much work it would be to get all the permissions. His father was in the Navy and out of the country; his mother was completely indifferent, apparently losing interest when he fell ill. So even obtaining parental permission took care and time. I also talked to Jim Shada, captain of the Penn team, and asked him to write to the Notre Dame captain to see if he would arrange for some of the players to talk to this little boy.

The great player of the time was Paul Hornung. After the

game, which Notre Dame won by the way, Paul walked to the Penn bench where I was sitting, picked up my little friend, and gave him the game ball. Then Paul carried him to the Notre Dame dressing room and placed him on Coach Terry Brennan's knee. All the Notre Dame players then signed the game ball. Of course, that ball was his most cherished possession. Sadly, our little boy died about five weeks later.

Some stories you never forget.

I wrote to the president of Notre Dame, Father Theodore Hesburgh, and thanked him for what the coach and team did for my patient. I received a lovely letter saying this was far more important than football and was the kind of thing in which he was delighted to have his team participate.

When Sandy and I were living in California, we were invited to a Salvation Army lunch honoring Joan Kroc, widow of Ray Kroc, McDonald's founder and owner. Father Hesburgh attended the lunch.

I said to him, "You probably don't remember, but we corresponded forty some years ago about an incident with your football team." I went on to summarize the boy's story.

He said that he remembered the incident vividly and was happy to meet the person on the other end of that situation.

While I was in medical school, I worked as an intern at Polyclinic Hospital in Harrisburg to gain experience and make some money. I was involved in patient care, spent the good part of the summer in the emergency room, worked up new admissions, and saw a lot of trauma and many young lives snuffed out by auto accidents.

My rotating internship was at Great Lakes Naval Hospital outside of Chicago. I have never spent a colder winter in my life although I have lived in Pennsylvania and Connecticut for numerous years. We rotated through all kinds of duties. For example, I spent six weeks in medicine, six in surgery, six in pediatrics, etc. I met some fellow interns, including John

Beaumier, who became an orthopedic surgeon in Fargo, North Dakota, and in time introduced me to my wife.

When we were together on pediatric service, a young boy was brought in with severe encephalitis. The child was literally burning up from high fever that was cooking his brain. Tom Duffy, chief of pediatrics, was my boss. In a Chicago suburb years later, he would become the pediatrician for my nieces and nephew. John, Dr. Duffy, and I told the parents the child would probably be dead by morning.

That night I went to the library to learn what I could and found an obscure article describing a case report of childhood encephalitis. It noted a new drug that was an IV cortisone product–rare then. The drug helped with the survival of the child in that case. The medicine had to be given intravenously every two hours by a doctor.

I discussed this with John. "If we can get the parents and Dr. Duffy to agree, would you take a night shift with me to give the medicine?" He agreed.

We conferred with Dr. Duffy. His thought was that, since there was no other hope for the kid, we should get the parents' permission and go for it.

The parents said, "What is there to lose? Go ahead."

By midday the next day, the boy's temperature dropped rapidly, and he woke from his coma. Two days later he went home with his parents. To the best of my knowledge, he had no residual effects from his high fever.

Again, one of those stories you never forget.

One of the major problems we had in medicine at Great Lakes Hospital was meningitis. We had more than our share of outbreaks and more than our share of rheumatic fever. Today rheumatic fever is rare because streptococcal infections are quickly diagnosed and treated with antibiotics.

One night a sailor was brought in with a diagnosis of schizophrenia. He was sent in to be admitted to our psychiatric ward. When I saw him in the emergency room, something didn't seem right. He was so agitated. I told the corpsman to strap him down and I would do a spinal tap. He did not have a high fever. By looking at the spinal fluid, I knew immediately he had meningitis. I gave him massive doses of penicillin. He made a complete recovery, but if I had committed him to the psychiatric ward he would have died by morning.

There were also many accident victims with broken bones, lacerations, and other injuries you could expect from a group of eighteen- to twenty-two-year-old sailors.

I was considered a rebel because I didn't like the way some of the nurses treated the patients. One nurse in particular whacked the feet of sleeping patients to wake them up. The nurses complained about me constantly.

My boss was George Monroe Davis. He was a great doctor, and he kept me out of trouble. When I worked for Sterling Drug and he was the surgeon general of the United States Naval Medical Corps, he asked me if I would return to the Navy and oversee its drug abuse program. At that time I had become somewhat of an expert on drugs, writing and lecturing frequently on drugs and drug abuse. Foreign governments even invited me to lecture in their countries. I chose not to accept the Navy position.

George finally retired to Florida. He was the best doctor I ever knew in the Navy and a perfect gentleman to boot.

Chapter 5

Meeting Sandy

The best thing that happened to me while at Great Lakes was that I met the woman who would become my wife. I know blind dates usually do not work out, but ours did.

I heard all the time about Big Ten football and how different it was from the Ivy League. I talked to two fellow interns to see if they were interested in going to a game. John Beaumier said he could get us tickets to the Wisconsin-Illinois game, and he would even get us dates. I said I wanted the tallest since I am 6'5" tall.

One Saturday we drove to Madison, Wisconsin, and went to Kappa Alpha Theta, where three lovely young ladies were waiting for us. Sandy was the tallest, so she was my date. I don't remember who won the football game because it was no different from Penn's games before they went strictly Ivy League. Sandy and I hit it off right away, but I did not think of marriage until later in our relationship.

After that I made many trips from Great Lakes to Madison and ended up with several speeding tickets trying to get back to the base by midnight. One late night there was an accident, and I stopped to help. Then I would really be late getting back.

I ended up speeding and of course got caught. I explained to the officer I was late because I had stopped at the accident. He checked and let me go about my business but said he didn't want any more accidents.

One time Sandy tried to impress me by asking me if I would like some hot chocolate. I said yes. She put milk with chocolate in it on the stove and promptly forgot about it. It boiled over and even crackled onto the wall. I have never let her forget it.

I have to say that, when I went to Appleton to meet Sandy's parents, I don't think I made a great impression on her mom. I was too tall, from the East, and an Ivy Leaguer, but really her problem was that she thought I was going to take her daughter away from the Midwest. We later became good friends. Her father was great; he was also tall and always treated me like a member of the family. Sandy—still a kid—obviously didn't agree with her mother because, as I often tell her, she fell in love with my uniform.

We saw each other as often as possible until I received orders sending me to be the regimental surgeon for the Third Regiment of the Third Marine Division on Okinawa. All during the time I was in Okinawa, I corresponded with my wife-to-be, both through letters and by CB radio. A civilian on Okinawa allowed military people to use his radio to talk to people in the States. That is how I talked to Sandy. An operator there called her phone at a prearranged time. There would follow a very public call punctuated by "Over" at the end of each person's speech. We joke today about how much we talked about the weather. We also wrote a lot of letters and exchanged a lot of pictures. We still have many of them.

I left Great Lakes in July 1958 for six weeks of basic training at Camp Pendleton in California. They taught me to shoot an M-1 rifle and a .45-caliber pistol. They toughened me up with fourteen-mile marches and trips through obstacle courses with live ammo flying over my head. The area was infested with rattlesnakes and tarantulas. We were told that when we went through the obstacle courses, if we came across a snake or a tarantula while we were crawling on our bellies, we should freeze. They would stop the live ammo fire and come out to rescue us. They also warned us to empty our boots before we put them on every morning because tarantulas liked to get into warm boots.

I totally admired the discipline of the Marine Corps and was glad that if I had to go into battle I was with such a well-trained group. After finishing basic training, we were sent to Camp Kinser on Okinawa. The following fifteen months were one of the most fascinating periods of my life. I was introduced to Col. Jess Ferrell, who was my commanding officer and was known as one of the hardest noses in the Marine Corps. We actually became good friends. When he retired, he became president of a bank in Florida, where I saw him on several occasions when I visited that area.

Our commanding general for the division was Gen. David Monroe Shoup, who had won the Congressional Medal of Honor at Tarawa during World War II. General Shoup later became commandant of the U.S. Marine Corps.

I was living in a Quonset hut with five other Marine Corps captains, including William Britt, who had won the Navy Cross in Korea and whom I later met at Camp Pendleton when I moved to California to become CEO of American Healthcare Systems. Another was Smedley Butler, with whom I only recently lost contact.

The Marines, and especially these two, loved to play tricks on their doctors and to tease me about being in the Navy. Once about three in the morning, Captain Britt, who had a hi-fi set, blasted at top volume "The Marines' Hymn" to wake me up. In return, weeks later I played "Anchors Aweigh" at the same hour at the same volume.

My life on Okinawa consisted of holding sick bay for the

troops and taking turns in the emergency room. One of the major problems among the troops was venereal disease (VD). There were three battalions, each with a physician and sixty-five corpsmen, and it was my job to devise ways of preventing VD. The first medical paper I ever published was in the journal *Military Medicine* on a case of gonococcal endocarditis. This was a rare disease affecting the patient's heart valves. Usually the individual had been treated for gonorrhea before he developed arthritis or endocarditis. In this case, we had to ship the patient back to the United States, where I believe he was sent to the University of Michigan for heart valve replacement.

A number of different types of VD exist, and we saw them all on Okinawa.

Because of the VD problem, many Marines wound up with balinitis, an inflammation of the head of the penis, in large part because they were uncircumcised. Circumcising adults is not easy and obviously not a pleasant experience for the individual.

I remember vividly one night I had emergency duty and a young lieutenant who had been circumcised about a week earlier went out on the town too vigorously, and as a result was brought into the emergency room. He had ripped all his stitches and was bleeding profusely. It was not an easy job to stop the bleeding in the most vascular area in the male body.

I was named the island safety officer, which basically meant I had to get into a tank when a typhoon struck. The tank was the only thing that could move, enabling me to help people injured in the typhoon. Typhoons were quite destructive, especially when you consider the living conditions for the natives and the troops on the island. I remember being at the Army Hospital in Sukiran when a typhoon struck. Even though the walls of the building were of modern construction, almost all the larger windows were blown out.

We also had numerous helicopter crashes and lost some high-ranking officers. Because of the experience of seeing these crash victims, I have avoided helicopters ever since.

One of the major medical problems on Okinawa was Japanese B encephalitis. At that time, about 80 percent of those who got this disease died because they developed very high temperatures and basically fried their brains. The only solution was to stay under mosquito netting at night. For many reasons, however, troops still contracted encephalitis. We tried to bring their temperature down with ice or cold alcohol, but the efforts were usually not successful. We attempted to notify the parents or next of kin about the problem as soon as we made the diagnosis. The Salvation Army helped by notifying parents so they could come to Okinawa to see their dying sons.

Early one morning my commanding colonel awakened me. We were living in Quonset huts left over from World War II. He told me to get dressed at once, that there was an emergency. We went to Marine headquarters, Camp Hague, where the commanding general's quarters were, and I was ushered into a room with a strong odor of acetone, an indication that someone had diabetes. General Shoup was unconscious on the bed. I quickly assessed the situation and ordered some regular insulin with an IV setup to be brought immediately. After I infused the insulin, General Shoup roused from his coma. Even so, I thought he should be transferred by air to Yokosuka Naval Hospital in Japan. One of the senior officers instructed me not to write diabetes as the diagnosis. My omission helped save his career. If he had been diagnosed with diabetes, he would never have become commandant. He was promoted over many senior officers to commandant. Much later, he died from complications of diabetes according to newspaper reports.

Later I told the story to a retired Marine Corps general who apparently did not like General Shoup. He gently chided me for not reporting his diabetes.

Notwithstanding evidence to the contrary, the Japanese and many others still believed that leprosy was highly contagious, so anybody contracting the disease was isolated from the rest of society. Even in the United States where most doctors knew better, a hospital was maintained exclusively for lepers in Louisiana. The Japanese put their lepers on little islands. I spent some weekends treating the lepers' medical problems on an island near Okinawa and also performing some minor surgery, mostly amputating fingers.

I also spent several weeks refreshing medical skills at the Sukiran Army Hospital on Okinawa and then another six weeks at Yokosuka Naval Hospital in Japan.

The worst job I had on Okinawa was to inspect the local military prison. Some of the prisoners were violent, and some hated any kind of authority, no matter if you were there to help them or not. I am not that familiar with civilian prison life, but I can tell you that the military version is not the good life.

Some things I learned by observation. When the Marines take care of their own, it is not always kind-spirited. One platoon in our regiment had a young Marine who could not do anything without messing up. He created many problems for others in his platoon. His fellow Marines gave him a "steel brush shower," which landed him in my sick bay. After that he never got in trouble again.

Another such incident I saw one day when I drove by a field where a whole platoon of naked Marines was picking crab lice from their bodies. Their lieutenant apparently was fed up with his group's problems with these creatures, which were usually the result of promiscuity. He decided to teach them a lesson.

My driver while I was in Okinawa was a young Marine who was a very good soldier. However, he got into some trouble and had to go to Captain's Mast, the lightest form of punishment in the military. The captain of the regimental headquarters was a "mustang" (an enlisted man who later becomes an officer) from Texas named Tex Winfield. Since he had come up through the enlisted ranks, he was a real hard-nose—or at least he pretended to be. Actually, behind his façade he was someone with a tender heart. Since my driver reported to me, I had to attend Captain's Mast with him. Tex Winfield ripped into him, up one side and down the other, finishing with, "Now, private, what do you have to say for yourself?"

My driver, shaken up, stammered, "Well, sir, if you give me a second to regain my composure…"

I broke out laughing; Captain Winfield broke out laughing; and the charge was dismissed.

Because I have always been interested in the law, I was frequently asked to serve as defense counsel for Marines and Navy personnel who got in trouble. (When I separated from the service, I went to law school and earned an LL.B. degree in 1964 and J.D. degree in 1969.) Many Marine officers—and I still joke about this with Ted Scotes, a retired Marine lieutenant colonel—believed that anyone charged with a crime was guilty until proven innocent, instead of the presumption of innocence until proved guilty as enshrined in the U.S. Constitution. I decided to change this. I was being asked from all over to defend people because I had never lost a case. When General Shoup got wind of this, he appointed me to the special court martial board, which prevented me from being able to defend the troops.

The one thing he forgot was that I was the second-ranking officer on the board, second only to the president of the court. When the president had to return to the United States on emergency leave, I became president of the board. My philosophy was that the cases should be tried and we would not automatically accept guilty pleas.

One memorable case was that of a young man who had sold drugs on the black market and was Susan Hayward's son. She had just won an Oscar for *I Want to Live!* portraying a female prisoner. In those days, if you won an Oscar, you were world famous. This young man had been tried and found guilty by a previous court martial board and sentenced to "six-six-and-a-kick," which is six months of hard labor, six months' loss of pay, and a bad conduct discharge.

The case went up the line but was sent back, and we got it as a retrial. We did not know the previous results, but we also found him guilty and gave him the same penalty. In military justice there are two phases to a trial. The first determines guilt or innocence. If one is guilty, a penalty phase follows, when the accused can provide any mitigating circumstances. I remember his speech to the board even today. He really didn't need the money from selling the drugs. He claimed he did what he did because he was angry with his mother and wanted to embarrass her.

While I was deployed, the North Koreans were making threatening noises, and the U.S. decided to have a show of force. The Third Marine Division traveled by troop ship from Okinawa to Korea, where we made an amphibious landing. On the way to Korea our small flotilla was hit by a typhoon, and we had to ride out the storm at sea. The troop ship was packed with bunk beds six high. The biggest mess I have ever seen was when the Marine in the top bunk vomited on the others. We fed them crackers and water, but there were still an awful lot of seasick people. We made our landing by climbing rope ladders down to smaller vessels that transported us to the beaches.

We later went on training exercises to the Philippines.

My tour of duty was supposed to be twelve months, and I vividly remember going to Kadena Air Force Base to board an airplane home to be married. However, while I was waiting for the plane, a young Marine came up to me and said, "Lieutenant Trout?"

"Yes."

"I have a change of orders for you."

"You must have the wrong person. I am about to get on a plane to go home to get married."

"No, sir, you must report to the First Regiment because of an emergency." He handed me the orders and left.

I was furious.

I went to the First Marine Regimental Camp, where the colonel told me I should get the three battalions combat-ready. I knew when the doctors were ordered to give morphine to the corpsmen and to obtain live ammo for our .45s that it was serious. I assembled the three battalion surgeons, and we made the preparations for whatever was to come. Next thing I knew, we were taken to Kadena Air Force Base, where we boarded the big troop-carrying planes. After we took off, we were told our destination. Apparently something had happened, and President Dwight Eisenhower was ordering the Marines into Laos. The incident was resolved, and our planes returned to Kadena. However, for the next three months we stayed at Kadena in pup tents, waiting. Fortunately, nothing happened, and I received new orders to return home.

No flights were available, and I had to return by troop ship from Manila to San Francisco. The other order was for me to be the ship's doctor. It was a long trip. I imagine the reason there were no flights was that they needed a ship's doctor. I also often wondered if my change of orders was deliberate because of my involvement with General Shoup's medical case.

Chapter 6

Marrying Medicine and Law

My next assignment was to report to Portsmouth Naval Hospital, where I was the physician in the sick officers' ward. This was an interesting assignment because I ran into the worst of the Navy Medical Corps, and also the best. My immediate superior was unfortunately an alcoholic who had forgotten a large part of his medical education. On the other hand, two of the physicians with whom I worked closely were outstanding doctors. Caully Gunnels became professor of nephrology (study and treatment of kidneys) at Duke University after he left the Navy. Forty-five years later I spoke with him about sending over a friend, Henry McIlwaine, who was in dire straits with kidney disease and not being helped in Knoxville. I called Ralph Snyderman, the vice chancellor of health affairs at Duke, to make arrangements for my friend to be admitted. I am pleased to report that, after his stay at Duke, Henry has been well and is still quite active in the horticultural field.

Dr. William Jacoby, who became the youngest admiral in the Navy Medical Corps, was an excellent cardiologist. The last I heard he was the commanding officer at Bethesda

Naval Hospital, the premier hospital in all the services.

One of the most interesting patients I treated during my stay at Portsmouth was Lt. Gen. Lewis "Chesty" Puller. One day I received a call from the admiral's office stating that Chesty would be checking in to the hospital for a lung problem. He was a legend in the Marine Corps from World War II and other campaigns and was revered by all of his troops. He won five Navy Crosses, the highest honor for bravery in combat awarded by the Department of the Navy. His son, Pulitzer Prize-winning author and war hero Lewis Puller Jr., lost both legs in Vietnam. He went on to earn a law degree, marry, and raise a family but died of a self-inflicted gunshot wound in 1994. What a tragic ending for a family that had given so much for the defense of their country.

I had heard so much about Chesty from my Marine Corps buddies that I was in awe of his arrival. I expected a strapping, big-chested Marine Corps general. Instead, when he arrived in civilian clothes, I was amazed to see a man of slight stature. He was a most gracious and humble patient and was as nice a person as anyone would want to meet. I am glad he left the hospital with his problem solved.

Finally, I married Sandy on June 11, 1960. We were both Lutherans–she of the Wisconsin Synod and I of the Missouri Synod. We were married in St. Paul's Lutheran Church in Appleton, Wisconsin.

Two funny things happened prior to our marriage. I was already a practicing physician and had spent time on Okinawa treating a variety of venereal diseases. The Rev. Frederick Brandt, pastor of St. Paul's Lutheran Church, insisted that we attend sessions with him about the birds and the bees. Sandy and I have both chuckled about that many times over the years. When we went to apply for our marriage license, the county clerk insisted on giving us a list of ten secrets for a successful marriage. The last was, "Don't expect too much out of life."

We moved into a second-floor apartment in a private home in Portsmouth, Virginia. One evening we walked into our apartment, and the floor was covered with what we thought were ants. They turned out to be termites. We called the owner who sprayed them with bug spray, shrugged his shoulders, stroked his chin, and said "not to worry" on his way out. We spent many hours cleaning up the dead bugs and worrying about another infestation. It did not occur.

Another time we heard a hurricane was coming, and we were not sure what to do with our new Oldsmobile. I decided to park it across the street on a fenced school ground with no bushes or trees. However, my landlord convinced me to bring it back and park under a huge tree. The hurricane struck that night, and next morning we found the tree had fallen on our car. Fortunately, a large branch held the tree off the roof of the car, which had only minor scratches.

I became thoroughly disgusted working under my alcoholic boss, who nipped at work and was not pleasant to be around. That, combined with my experience at Great Lakes Naval Hospital, made me sure I did not want to be a Navy doctor. I submitted my resignation after eight years of active duty. I was honorably discharged in June 1961.

I had applied for a job as doctor at Camp Mataponi in Maine for the summer. I had been accepted into Dickinson School of Law and thought a camp job would be relaxing before starting a very demanding schedule. At Mataponi I had one of my first serious illnesses. I developed a kidney stone and had to be admitted to the nearby Portsmouth Medical Center. Fortunately, I passed the stone without surgery.

When we had time off from my work as a doctor and Sandy's work as a swim instructor, we explored the sights of Maine, and became so enamored of the state that in the late 1970s we purchased thirteen acres on the water at South Penobscot. Sandy designed a house overlooking the water. We wanted a house that would be low maintenance and at the same time easy to close down and open up. For example, all the water could be drained from the pipes by opening one valve in the basement into a drain. All the bedrooms were paneled with pinewood. We also used old barnwood in the living and dining areas. The only area not low maintenance was an outside deck that wrapped around half of the house. It had to be treated constantly to prevent water damage.

After our stint at Mataponi, which turned out to be as idyllic as we thought it would be, we moved back to Harrisburg into a new house in a new area. The house was built for us while we were still living in Portsmouth. It was a modest three-bedroom brick house with minimal landscaping. Since we both loved roses, we planted more than a hundred rose bushes in the back and sides. They were high maintenance, and we did learn a lot about the care that roses require.

I had also applied for a job at Harrisburg State Hospital, which was a 2,700-bed mental hospital. Around four to five hundred of the patients were physically ill at any one time. I became the chief of medicine there in September 1961. I was amazed to discover the number of diabetic patients on the wards. One observation I made was that some of the sicker mental patients became extremely lucid after we brought their diabetes under control.

I also noticed that many patients had fractured their hips. I obtained all their medical records and learned they all had been heavily sedated prior to their falls and fractures. It apparently had been far more convenient for the doctors and nurses to sedate unruly patients, even though they were aged, than to treat them otherwise. I guess this is to be expected when you are short of qualified personnel, and we were all the time. One of the first orders I gave was to stop all sedation and to start it only at my request. Our rate of hip fractures decreased dramatically.

The hospital employed a large number of foreign physicians to treat the mental patients. It was actually not a wise thing to do because these doctors often did not understand the American culture.

Every week the staff met to evaluate new patients. Even though I was not hired as a psychiatrist, the head of the hospital asked me to be on the committee to evaluate new patients.

I remember distinctly a young man who was admitted as a schizophrenic. His parents were Amish. He rebelled against his parents' customs, wanting to drive cars and do all the other things teens liked to do in those days. His parents, being devout Amish, could not understand. As a result, the young man was sent to the state hospital for evaluation. Because my family had lived in Pennsylvania since 1738, I was acquainted with the Amish beliefs. I told the committee I thought there was nothing wrong with the young man except that he was trying to break free of his parents' strict culture. The foreign doctors still thought he was schizophrenic. Dr. Eaton, chief of the hospital, finally decided the young man was not mentally ill and could be discharged.

Another thing that amazed me was the number of long-term patients in the hospital whose relatives lost interest after the patients were there for several months. In fact, when some of them became gravely ill, it was difficult locating the next of kin.

The hospital at that time was fairly self-sufficient. There was an area for growing all kinds of vegetables which provided a large proportion of the food. Patients tended the fields and did much of the maintenance in the hospital. It was almost like taking care of their own home and well-being.

The hospital is still in existence but is down to fewer than four hundred patients since the well-meaning but shortsighted powers-that-be decided they should be released onto the streets. They are then characterized as homeless.

Because I was licensed to practice medicine, during the

three years I lived in Harrisburg I ran a small private practice in my house but only saw patients on Saturdays and responded to emergency house calls on weekends. I still spent several hours each Saturday and Sunday at the hospital taking care of the sickest patients.

My own father fell ill of influenza and died on March 11, 1962, while I was in my first year of law school. He died at the Polyclinic Hospital in Harrisburg, where my older son, Monroe Jr., was born.

Meantime, I started my studies at Dickinson School of Law in Carlisle, approximately twenty miles from Harrisburg. That was the beginning of three years of eighteen- to twenty-hour workdays. I usually rose at 5 a.m., got to the hospital about 6, made my rounds, and left the hospital around 8, drove to the law school where I attended class from 9 to noon, and then returned to the hospital, where I stayed usually until 8 or 9 p.m. I returned home and spent a couple of hours studying my law books. My wife typed all my legal briefs. I think she learned as much about the law as I did.

In law school I had excellent grades even though I found the law to be boring. I was elected to the *Dickinson Law Review* and later to the Order of the Coif, which is a legal honor society. To be elected to the *Law Review*, I had to publish a scholarly legal paper. I remembered when I was in high school, the physician for the football team got himself into legal trouble because he performed abortions on young women who became pregnant by members of the football team. We did not have all the contraceptive measures back in those days that we do today. It was against the law to perform abortions. As a result of trying to prevent dangerous back-alley abortions with coat hangers, this fine physician was prosecuted. Therefore, I decided to write a paper entitled "Abortion Laws Need Therapy." This paper was published in the *Temple Law Quarterly* and preceded the U.S. Supreme Court decision in the *Roe v. Wade* case in 1973. The article I wrote traced abortion from the points of view of three major religions over the centuries. My conclusion was that abortion should be legalized for rape and incest victims and to protect the health of the mother.

In my second year of law school, I taught a course in legal medicine, one of the first ever in the United States. As a result, I was the first person ever to appear in the yearbook as both a student and a professor. I taught the course from noon to 1 after I had finished the classes I was taking. It added another couple of hours to my workload. I am happy to report that the course I started at Dickinson and taught for many years after I graduated is still being taught by other physician lawyers.

During my law school career, I also chaired a major medical legal symposium for the Third Circuit. When I graduated law school, I was told I was only the seventy-fifth person to have a combined medical-legal education. It was rare then, but it is quite common now with some schools offering combined degrees in medicine and the law. Today there are thousands with that combination. So I was on the cutting edge.

Chapter 7

The Dawn of a Drug Company Career

As I mentioned, I found law school to be boring and decided not to practice law after I graduated. Since I was not able to spend much time with my son during his first two and a half years of life, I decided to do something in which I did not have to work eighteen- to twenty-hour days, seven days a week. I was really burned out from the long hours.

In 1962 Congress passed the Harris-Kefauver amendments to the food and drug laws requiring drug companies to demonstrate the effectiveness of new drugs before they could be approved by the Food and Drug Administration (FDA). Pharmaceutical companies were looking for individuals to interpret that law and represent them in Washington, D.C., before a myriad of federal agencies and Congress. Since I had combined degrees in law and medicine, several companies approached me to work in their federal government liaison offices.

In June 1964, one day after I graduated from law school, I went to work for Pfizer Inc., then known as Charles Pfizer Inc., in New York City. The same month I moved the family to a new house in New Canaan, Connecticut. It was a hard time to sell a house in Harrisburg because of the real estate market. We finally sold the house at a loss to a church that was going to use it as a parsonage.

I welcomed my new job at Pfizer. I commuted from New Canaan to New York every day by train, a sixty-five-minute trip each way. I left on the 6:30 a.m. train and caught the 5:08 p.m. train home. My boss, J. Philip Smith, vice president of Pfizer Inc., and tough but fair, asked me why I always rushed out at 4:50. I told him I had to leave home at 6 a.m. to have everything ready for him when he arrived at work, and if I didn't take the 5:08 train home, I would have no opportunity to see and talk to my son who would be asleep if I got home later.

He said, "I can't think of a better reason," and never mentioned it again.

Shortly after this, our son Timothy William was born on April 11, 1966.

My job at Pfizer was in the government liaison office, so I spent at least two days a week in Washington. As a result, I came to know many politicians and regulators at the FDA, Centers for Disease Control, and National Institutes of Health.

At last I could become an active community member. Sandy and I became very active in the Lutheran Church in New Canaan. It was an LCA church, which means to Lutherans that it was much more liberal than either the Wisconsin or Missouri synods. Because of our contributions to the life of the church, I soon became president of the church council. As a result, I became a delegate to the synod conventions and was asked to chair Lutheran Social Service for New England. This committee basically ran the various nursing homes and homes for the aged for the Lutheran Church in New England. It was a demanding job, and I spent numerous weekends visiting and inspecting facilities in New England. Today that position is filled by a full-time paid staff with many employees. In my day it was a volunteer position. Because of that job and because of my reputation at that time as being an expert on drugs, I was asked to author several drug books on marijuana and other addictive drugs for the national church. These booklets were then published and distributed to all the churches of the LCA throughout the United States.

As president of the church council, I had all the problems that a church faces: property maintenance, payroll, handling complaints, and so on. One of the grave crises I quickly faced was when one of the parishioners complained that his teenage son had been approached by the minister for sexual favors. Shortly afterwards, I received a number of other complaints. I held a special meeting of the church council without the pastor. A divided council decided that I should ask for his resignation. I approached him with the allegations, which he denied. He refused to resign.

The council then asked me to appeal to the bishop of the synod for help, which I did. The bishop was one year away from retirement, didn't want any problems, and refused to do anything. Since we were at an impasse, many members resigned and left the church. It was already a small congregation and this decimated it. I too resigned both as president of the council and a member of the church. This went on for approximately another two years until a new bishop was elected and installed. I visited with him at his request and told him what had happened. He was quite decisive and immediately forced the resignation of the pastor.

The church employed a number of interim pastors, and we tried to get some of the old parishioners to return, but because of bitterness some of them never did come back. Finally before we left New Canaan, the church hired a permanent pastor who appeared to be a good fit. Many years after we left New Canaan, however, he too was forced out because of questionable behavior.

One of the parishioners, whom we got to know very well

and who was a good friend, was a German immigrant working on an estate of a wealthy lawyer as a caretaker. He had been a member of the German army during World War II, but was so appalled by what Hitler had done, he could not wait to get out of Germany after the war. He became a U.S. citizen, but I always thought he felt he had to atone for his service in the German military. His son was visiting Germany and apparently was acting oddly. The son returned to the U.S. but was detained at customs because they thought he had a psychiatric problem.

The only way he could be released from detention was if a physician went to New York and vouched for him. My friend approached me, and I immediately said I would go with him to get his son. We were able to take him home, where he was evaluated by a local psychiatric group that prescribed medicine but said he was perfectly able to function by himself. I am pleased to say he is functioning very well, married with several children, and a productive citizen. His mother and sister have died, but I still talk to his father occasionally.

Chapter 8

Leading the American College of Legal Medicine

At Pfizer I worked under Joe Aterno in the government liaison office. I really enjoyed my two years with Joe primarily because of his great gift of humor. Next I became assistant to the vice president for pharmaceuticals, J. Philip Smith. This was sort of a training job for a management position, and after a year working for him I became director of the liaison office and reversed roles with Mr. Aterno. There was no acrimony, and we worked extremely well together. However, I was becoming restless in the job and asked Mr. Smith what my future was to be. He told me I was doing such an excellent job where I was that I would probably be there for at least another five years.

This did not appeal to me, so in 1968 I accepted an offer to become executive medical director of Winthrop Labs, a division of Sterling Drug, under Dr. Theodore Klumpp. Within six months the vice president of medical affairs retired, and I became vice president and director of medical affairs.

While still at Pfizer, I joined the American College of Legal Medicine (ACLM). It was such a small group that we could sit around one table for meetings. However, because of all the medical-legal problems in the United States, it rapidly expanded under the leadership of Drs. Charles Letorneau, Carl Wasmuth, and Cyril Wecht. In five years I became the president.

As a result of my malpractice writings, the editor of *Medical Economics* asked if I would participate in its malpractice cassette series for physicians and lawyers. The choice of a series moderator was interesting. His name was Norton Mockridge, a well-known humor columnist in papers throughout the U.S. He knew nothing about malpractice but was a very fast learner and did a superb job of organizing a malpractice symposium on tape. We became very good friends, and he even wrote a column on a funny incident that happened to my family and me.

ACLM was having its annual conference in San Francisco. As president I had invited F. Lee Bailey, a renowned Boston attorney, to be the main speaker at the meeting. I received a phone call the day before Bailey was to give his speech, saying he would not be able to attend. He was stuck in some legal proceeding in Florida. I was frantic. I had people from around the world in town and no main speaker. I happened to pick up the San Francisco newspaper and saw that Norton Mockridge was in town. I contacted him and asked if he would do me a major favor and be the substitute speaker. I could sense some reluctance on his part, but I think he really wanted to help me out. I told him he could actually wing it and just tell some of the funny things he had written about over the years. He gave one of the funniest speeches I have ever heard and received a standing ovation.

I knew Norton was receiving large sums of money to speak, and I didn't think our honorarium would be enough. I was completely surprised when he said there would be no fee. This is what true friendship is all about. I could never repay him any more than could I have paid Ilana Vered for playing the piano. Norton later retired and moved to Mexico, and I ultimately lost all contact with him.

Because I was the ACLM president, Gov. Winfield Dunn of Tennessee invited me to moderate a debate on medical malpractice by the presidents of the American Medical Association (AMA) and the American Bar Association. As a thank-you, Governor Dunn made us all Tennessee colonels and aides-de-camp on his staff. We also received a certificate citing our contributions.

For my work with ACLM I received the President's Award in 1976, 1978, 1988, and 1989. In 1983 I founded the American College of Legal Medicine Foundation and became its first chairman, serving until 1986. I was on the board until 1990. In 1999 the ACLM awarded me its gold medal for lifetime achievement.

My early involvement with ACLM proved fortuitous because President Richard Nixon, in recognition of the malpractice crisis, decided to appoint a national commission. I was chosen, along with such distinguished Americans as Carl Hoffman, president of the AMA; William Curran, a Harvard professor; Howard Hazzard and Jim Ludlam, two superb hospital and malpractice attorneys; John Linster, a lawyer and officer of an insurance company in Wisconsin; Carl Wasmuth, a lawyer, doctor, and head of the Cleveland Clinic and also one of my predecessors as ACLM president; George Northrup, president of the American Osteopathy Association; and thirteen other distinguished Americans. Wendell Freeland, a lawyer from Pittsburgh, was chairman, and Eli Bernzweig was executive director. Don Harper Mills and David Rubsuman, both members of ACLM and well-known malpractice lawyers, were consultants. Later as president of American Healthcare Systems, I worked closely with Hazzard and Ludlam.

As a result of serving on the national commission, I was asked by Bill McGill, president of Columbia University and the chairman of the New York State Advisory Panel on Medical Malpractice appointed by the governor around 1975, to be his informal advisor and sounding board for some of the commission's ideas.

Also, I became one of the first board members of the Cleveland Clinic who lived outside of Cleveland. I served on that board from 1970 to 1986 and helped lead the clinic into a self-insurance program that saved it millions of dollars over the next decade.

At about the same time, I became good friends with Ted Meredith, an executive with a medical publishing company in New York. Ted and I were talking on the tennis court about publications, and I asked him if he would be interested in developing a medical-legal journal. He and his boss, Don Gussow, the owner of the company, were extremely interested, and thus we started *The Journal of Legal Medicine*, which today is probably the most prestigious journal in its field.

Being on Nixon's Malpractice Commission put me in great demand to give speeches around the country and in other parts of the world. The largest audience I ever spoke to was the American College of Surgeons, headed by Dr. Rollins Hanlon, who became a good friend and advisor. More than sixteen thousand were in the audience. I was also asked to speak to a medical group in Sydney, Australia. Many of the 190-plus articles or speeches I have written and published were on medical malpractice.

The assistant secretary of health, Dr. Monty DuVal, asked Don Harper Mills and me to be his advisors on medical malpractice, as two of the country's experts in that area. Monty and I forged a friendship that lasted a lifetime. He was one of the most accomplished people I have known and he died in December 2006. He founded the University of Arizona Medical School, was its first president, and was head of more health-care educational groups than I can remember. I believe he was instrumental in having me elected to the Society of Medical Administrators in 1989, which supposedly is composed of the top fifty medical administrators in the country. It is a very exclusive group in view of the fact that a new member cannot be elected until an old one resigns or dies. There can only be fifty members.

Back when I was still at Pfizer in 1968, I became a charter member and one of the three founders of Medical Executives, comprised of chief medical officers from the major corporations in the New York-New Jersey-Connecticut area. In 1974 I became president, served through 1976, and received the distinguished service award from the organization when my term as president was over.

An interesting but time-consuming assignment was as an adjunct associate professor at the Brooklyn College of Pharmacy, a division of Long Island University. I taught a three-hour weekly seminar on new drug development. Grading exams and preparing lectures was a real chore, but I enjoyed the give-and-take with the students, all of whom were obtaining their master's degrees in pharmacy. One of my students was the daughter of the prime minister of Thailand, and when she graduated, she gave me a gold tie clip with the insignia of the Thai Royal Society of Medicine. I still have the clip.

I continued at the same time as a special lecturer at the Dickinson School of Law from 1968 to 1987. I also became a faculty member of the Practicing Law Institute in 1968 and served until 1970. I served as a faculty member at the Institute of Continuing Legal Education in Ann Arbor, Michigan, in 1967 and 1970.

Chapter 9

Research Saves Lives

The story of my years with Sterling Drug Inc., includes one of my two proudest life achievements. The drug research I directed then brought to market many drugs that saved lives or enabled diagnosis of numerous illnesses. In October 1970, I was appointed medical director of all of Sterling USA. I served in that position until 1973, when I became medical director of Sterling Worldwide. In January 1974, I became a vice president of Sterling Drug Inc. In 1978 I became senior vice president and a member of the board of directors.

My responsibilities included drug regulatory affairs, worldwide research, employee health, and medical aspects of marketing for all the divisions. The medical directors of all divisions reported to me. As a director, I became a member of the Management Committee, the chairman of the Drug Safety Committee, chairman of the Medical Research Committee, chairman of the Corporate Giving Committee, and a member of the publications, licensing, acquisitions, and pension committees of the corporation. In 1982 I became chairman of SterlPac, our political action committee.

As chairman of the Corporate Giving Committee, I changed

the policies of giving. Instead of trying to give a small amount to a huge number of organizations, we decided to give a larger amount to a smaller number. We started the program by giving an endowment for visiting professorships in pharmacology to medical schools around the world. For example, we gave one to Columbia University in honor of Mike Molinas, one of the three founders of Medical Executives. We gave another to Cornell in honor of Wally Riker, also chairman of our Research Advisory Committee. I learned that Dr. Louis Goodman and Dr. Alfred Gilman, whose definitive text of pharmacology every medical student uses, had never been honored by anyone. As a result, we endowed a visiting professorship in Dr. Gilman's name at Yale University and one in Dr. Goodman's name at the University of Oregon. Dr. Gilman's son, who teaches in Texas, later won a Nobel Prize in Medicine. Dr. Goodman actually spent his career at the University of Utah but was a graduate of the University of Oregon Medical School. We decided to give it to Oregon because Bill Riker, Wally's brother, was chairman of the Department of Pharmacology there.

Later we endowed a professorship in pharmacology at the University of Michigan in honor of "Mo" Seevers, who was the longtime department chairman there and also my traveling companion to Australia.

Mo would have made a great "most unforgettable character" for the *Reader's Digest* series of that name. He was a member of the President's Commission on Illicit Drug Use, and as a result was asked to lecture all over the world. To perform that task well, he believed he needed to have examples of all the illicit drugs to show his audiences. So he carried a small case of samples. On our flight to Australia, Mo kept the flight attendants quite busy bringing martinis and was a little under the weather when we landed in Sydney. He forgot to tell the customs people about his little case, and when they discovered it on their own, we were both put in detention.

After much discussion and because we were both planning to lecture at different places and meet with high government officials in Canberra, we were allowed to continue on our journey. However, on returning to the United States, we were again stopped at customs and asked if we had drugs or any other items that were illegal to import.

Mo said, "Oh, yes, I have some heroin, marijuana… "

The customs official flipped. He was calmed only when Mo showed him his identification as a member of the President's Illicit Drug Commission. Then we were allowed to go on our way.

We endowed another professorship at Edinburgh University in Scotland in honor of Robert "Binks" Inch. Binks was a Scottish laird and one of the heroes of the battle of Dunkirk, in which he suffered a major leg wound and was captured. The Germans did not treat his leg, so he had to care for himself the best he could. He was left with a lifelong limp and bum leg.

A French partisan group led by his future wife—I believe she was a member of French royalty—rescued Binks from a concentration camp where he was imprisoned. They fell in love and married. They had five children; some became English citizens and some French.

I first met Binks when he was heading European operations for Sterling Drug, and I was asked to escort him around the United States to show him our various plants. His wife was dying of breast cancer. Binks was so devastated when she died and became so depressed that he could no longer function as director of our European operations. To his credit, he accepted a lesser position as director of European government affairs, at which he was quite good because he knew high government officials on a personal basis in every major European country. Soon he and I were lifelong friends.

He later visited us at our vacation house in Maine. I have never known anyone who more embodied the perfect gentleman than Binks. For example, for all his renown in the medical field and his Scottish titles, he helped Sandy in the kitchen. I made one mistake during his visit when I asked him to explain the hierarchy of dukes, lords, earls, and so on. Four hours later he was still explaining it.

Binks also introduced me to a fine gentleman, a New Zealander, named Arthur Porritt, a surgeon to King George and later to Queen Elizabeth. He was a member of the International Olympic Committee from about 1928 until his death. He was one of the runners portrayed in *Chariots of Fire* and actually played the role of the dean in that movie as well as serving as an advisor for the film.

Arthur was named governor general of New Zealand by Queen Elizabeth. When my wife and I visited there in 1986 to celebrate our twenty-fifth wedding anniversary, we saw many monuments dedicated by him during his tenure. Yet even with his high status as a member of the House of Lords, he was one of the most down-to-earth individuals I have ever known.

Arthur called me from London one day and said he had to come to New York the following week but could not find a hotel room anywhere because of a big convention. Could I help? I said I would try, but I could not find anything suitable either. I told him we couldn't find a room, but Sandy and I would be delighted if he would stay with us. He agreed. I told our two boys we were going to have a distinguished visitor and they needed to be on their best behavior. They mildly protested at having to entertain an old geezer. Within five minutes of his arrival at the house, they both were enthralled by his stories of the many Olympics games he had attended. After he left, they asked me why I hadn't told them he was so interesting.

Another distinguished gentleman I met through Binks was Sir Derrick Dunlop, who originated the first "FDA" in England and headed a government commission named after him. He was an extremely intelligent and "common sense" kind of man. If his principles on drug research and approval had been adopted worldwide, this would be a much healthier world in which to live. Sir Derrick wrote a well-known book called *Medicine in Our Times*, published in 1973.

We had many interesting discussions over the years during my twice-yearly visits to the United Kingdom.

Chapter 10

Drug Wars

During my tenure at Sterling Drug, we did extensive research on malaria, which was and is still one of the most ubiquitous diseases known to man. The disease kills a million people every year. At the time, the largest research center in the United States for malaria was at the state prison in Illinois. We and many others conducted research there. Many other types of research were being performed using prisoners in the federal system. A national debate raged over whether a prisoner could ever give true informed consent for any research. Jessica Mitford, the famous British author who wrote *The American Way of Death*, became involved. One of her other books, *Cruel and Unusual Punishment*, raised the issue of prisoner research, and she was giving speeches and signing books in the United States.

At the same time a PBS-TV weekly debate program called *The Advocates* was being shown. It originated at Faneuil Hall in Boston. Michael Dukakis, later the governor of Massachusetts and the 1988 Democratic presidential candidate, was the moderator. He was the son of Greek immigrants, and when I was asked to debate Jessica on the issue of prisoner research, I was able to use my little bit of Greek learned from my college roommate to break the ice with Mr. Dukakis.

For a long time I mulled over whether to take on this world-famous author. At the urging of my boss, Dr. Wescoe, I finally said yes. I believe I was so scared of debating on national TV that I totally over-prepared for it. The debate took place before a large audience in Faneuil Hall. The local audience voted at the end of the program for the winner, and the moderator immediately announced the result on national TV. Everyone watching could vote by mail, and that result was announced the following week. The audience was composed mostly of students from Harvard and other schools around the local area. They had a decidedly liberal bent, so Mr. Dukakis told me I would probably lose the local vote but had a chance to win the national vote.

During the debate, I pressed Jessica for alternatives to help us win the battles against malaria, tuberculosis, arthritis, cancer, heart disease, etc. She had none. As a result, I won the student vote and later received more than 65 percent of the national vote. Jessica was not happy with the vote in Faneuil Hall, but I didn't really care because I thought she was only trying to sell books. At a party for all the participants after the show, she would not talk to me. I guess she thought that I had hurt her credibility or her chances to sell more books. The lesson I learned from this is that you could never be too prepared for anything.

As medical director of Sterling Drug, I fought a major battle to save pHisoHex, a skin cleanser that had been on the market for decades. pHisoHex was lifesaving in preventing staphylococcal disease in newborns, and was also used by adults for cleansing wounds. The active ingredient was hexachlorophene. It was made by Givaudon Corp., headed by Julian Dorsky and Milton Manowitz, who were extremely helpful in providing scientific data to me. In the early 1970s, it was reported that rats when fed or painted with hexachlorophene developed a spongy-form lesion in the brain. Then a neuropathologist reported that some infants who had died from other causes had the same lesions. The FDA's Jean Lockhart, who had received a presidential medal from John F. Kennedy for preventing a thalidomide disaster from occurring in the United States, decided that pHisoHex should be removed from the marketplace. This started a national debate as to the risks and rewards of the drug that was sold at the time without a doctor's prescription.

No one had ever been able to attribute any deaths or long-term effects to the drug. Dr. Vern Plueckhahn of Geelong, Australia, had done studies on thousands of babies and found no side effects of any kind. Dr. Heinz Eichenwald, one of the most respected names in pediatrics, was not convinced of any major problems. Neither were other respected pediatricians.

But some did side with Lockhart. Neil Chayet, a prominent litigator of FDA matters, formed a support group to assist us and was quite helpful. The debate reached the national news. I was interviewed for the *CBS Evening News with Walter Cronkite*. The subject was debated for more than a year by the top pediatricians and neuropathologists around the world. Many articles appeared on the subject, including one I wrote for *The Journal of Pediatrics*.

Because many hospitals gave up the use of pHisoHex in their newborn nurseries, we began hearing of staph epidemics causing deaths from around the world. No other product at that time was as effective in preventing staph as hexachlorophene. I had personally used pHisoHex on my own two sons when they were small, and it certainly had no negative impact on them.

The FDA finally took action and made the drug pHisoHex, which had been an over-the-counter product, prescription-use only. I am convinced to this day that, as a result of the FDA's action, many more babies have died from staphylococcal infections. And as far as I know, it has never been proven that a baby died from the use of pHisoHex.

A number of divisions in Sterling Drug were not essentially medical but sometimes got involved with medical problems. An important instance concerned Lehn and Fink, which marketed Lysol. We were very interested in being able to claim that Lysol killed viruses as well as bacteria. Dr. Jack Gwaltney, professor of medicine at the University of Virginia, was a viral expert. We engaged him to perform a number of studies for us. The first issue was whether viruses survived for long periods on hard surfaces from which they could be transmitted to another person. The then-prevailing opinion was that viruses were transmitted through the air. Dr. Gwaltney was able to prove that viruses not only survived for more than twenty-four hours on hard surfaces such as doorknobs and faucet handles, but that this was a major method of transmission. With his help, we were then able to prove that doorknobs and faucet handles and other common contact points could be sprayed regularly with Lysol to kill the viruses. This was breakthrough research. We not only made the world a little safer, but were able to boost the sales of Lysol.

Another scientific breakthrough occurred when a group of researchers at Purdue University reported on the integration of two drugs from our research program into crystallized form with the common cold virus.

Some of the non-medical divisions of Sterling Drug provided me the opportunity to meet interesting people. One division, d-Con, sold pesticides and rat poisons. The advertising people invited me to go to a resort in the Borscht Belt of New York to watch a television ad being created for the d-Con division featuring Muhammad Ali. It was one of the most successful TV ads ever and showed Ali with his big fist coming at you exclaiming, "d-Con power!". I must say that I thoroughly enjoyed my conversations with him. He had a very quick wit and was an easy conversationalist.

Through its Stridex division, Sterling Drug sponsored a major tennis tournament just before the U.S. Open. I met Chris Evert, Bjorn Borg, Jimmy Connors, and many other international players. In contrast to the easy conversation with Ali, I found it extremely difficult to talk to Bjorn Borg, whose entire life was wrapped up in tennis.

Chapter 11

Global Travels as Lecturer and Spy

Sterling Drug was one of the major vaccine manufacturers in the world in the early 1970s. However, because of poor profit margins and very high liability concerns, the company got out of the vaccine manufacturing business. We were not the only company to do this. At one time, the number of companies in the vaccine business was in the double digits, but because of liability concerns only three remained. As a result, some of the most widely used vaccines were in short supply. At the time I was still a consultant to the Department of Health, Education, and Welfare, the predecessor of Health and Human Services, and heard that some countries were accusing the United States of genocide because we were no longer providing the vaccines they needed. In fact, it was tough for the few manufacturers to make enough supplies for the United States' consumption. I wrote a paper on this problem which was published in the *New York Law Journal* in July 1977.

At about the same time, the government was wrestling with whether to order swine flu vaccinations for the general population or leave the vaccines only for emergency medical personnel. I was opposed to the general population vaccinations, primarily because I thought insufficient evidence existed to support the premise that a major epidemic would occur. Sterling Drug had one of the largest ongoing viral research programs at the time. Of course, I made my views known. However, the government decided to make swine flu vaccine generally available to all. Before this could be done, Congress had to pass a law stating that the government would accept liability for any problems. Unfortunately, many problems arose, primarily with Guillain-Barré syndrome.

Years later, while I served on the board of Baxter International, U.S. health authorities thought there would be another flu pandemic similar to that of 1918 and contacted companies to see if each could provide a minimum of 50 million doses of vaccine. Baxter received the contract, and as I remember, used a new manufacturing process to produce about 150 million doses.

Even today we are talking about a worldwide pandemic of bird flu. Since it is a new strain, we have no dependable vaccine. It will be interesting to see how the U.S. government and other countries will react.

Another product Sterling Drug owned was Bayer Aspirin. Sterling had acquired Bayer from the Alien Property Custodian office of the U.S. government during World War II. Bayer had been confiscated from the German company, Bayer Inc. After the war Bayer wanted this very lucrative franchise back and made many offers over the years, including one for $85 million in the 1970s. However, Bayer Aspirin was not for sale as long as Sterling owned it.

Much of my time was spent testifying before the FDA and Federal Trade Commission (FTC) in what was then called "the aspirin wars." Three manufacturers were vying for a major share of the aches-and-pains market: Bayer; Tylenol of MacNeil Labs, a division of Johnson & Johnson, and Anacin, made by American Home Products Co. They were constantly suing one another for misleading advertising and criticizing one another to the FDA or FTC. The number of man-hours spent on these battles was astronomical. The FTC started its own lawsuit against us and the others. Nothing the FTC did at that time was ever settled rapidly.

In the meantime, Sterling continued to invest millions of dollars in new uses for aspirin. One of the largest research projects I became directly involved with was to prove that aspirin prevented stroke and heart attacks. Large studies indicated that it was effective. Before the FDA would approve the indication, we had to appear before its advisory committee. Dr. William Soller was the medical director of Glenbrook Labs, a division of Sterling Drug. I placed him directly in charge of this presentation. He did a brilliant job of bringing together the world's experts for this FDA committee review, including Dr. Jack Hirsch of McMaster University, Dr. Richard Peto of Oxford University, and Dr. Peter Elwood. Dr. Peto, a world-famous statistician who had concluded that aspirin was quite effective, had even paid his own transportation to the meeting. All had performed independent studies on aspirin without Sterling's financial help. When I arrived for the hearing, Dr. Peto appeared in the most casual clothes anyone could wear, and I was appalled.

I said to Bill Soller, "Who in the hell is this guy anyway?"

A book was later written called *The Aspirin Wars* and included my quotation.

Dr. Peto was outstanding and responded positively to some of the toughest questions I have ever heard at hearings of this kind. Now I, too, am taking my daily aspirin to prevent a second heart attack.

In our research on aspirin, we found, for example, that two aspirin taken daily by diabetics would prevent cataracts, retinopathy, and diabetic neuropathy. It's even good for gout–it lowers uric acid. The bark of the willow tree has natural aspirin. You can chew it.

My wife inspired one of the more amusing pieces of research. She took aspirin to help her sleep, and I always pooh-poohed it. Finally, as a result of her persistence, we did a sleep study at Dartmouth and found that Sandy was absolutely right about aspirin. There is even a good chemical explanation for why it works.

The Atomic Energy Commission showed that taking aspirin prior to being exposed to radiation prevented radiation sickness. Years later a good friend of mine, who was vice chairman of Johnson & Johnson, called me to discuss his prostate cancer radiation treatments. He didn't know if he could complete the treatments because they caused such severe diarrhea and pain. I suggested that he talk to his physician about taking regular doses of aspirin the day before his treatment. I warned him that his doctor would probably say he didn't think it would hurt, but it wouldn't help either. My friend took the aspirin and called me back a few months later to thank me for the suggestion because it did prevent his pain and diarrhea.

In 1980 I was invited by the Chinese government to lecture on the newer uses of aspirin and the research we were doing at the time. I spoke at Fu Wai Hospital in Beijing and at numerous other hospitals. China at that time was not really open to tourists. I asked my boss, Dr. Clark Wescoe, previously chancellor of the University of Kansas, if I should go. He encouraged me to do so.

I was treated royally in Beijing. My host, the head of Fu Wai Hospital, was also the equivalent in the Chinese government of a U.S. senator. I was given the royal tour of the Great Wall, the Forbidden City, and the Ming Tombs.

When my friends return from China today and I ask them what they saw in the Forbidden City, I am surprised to learn that many of the things I thought were spectacular were not on the regular tourist routes.

I quickly learned after giving my first lecture the real purpose behind my visit. At the time, the Soviets were making noises about the Chinese, who apparently were deathly afraid of a nuclear bomb being dropped on them. They learned of our research on radiation sickness. All the questions after the lecture were always on radiation sickness.

One of the more interesting people I met in China was Dr. Ma Haide, a North Carolina Medical School graduate who had come to China as a medical missionary and ended up accompanying Mao Tse Tung on the entire Long March. Dr. Haide became revered by the Chinese government, married a Chinese woman, and stayed in China the rest of his life. His main interest during my visit was to try to eradicate leprosy and venereal disease in China. We had some interesting conversations in light of my experience on Okinawa. We corresponded for long periods after that on various medical issues. After he died, I still received letters from his wife who had become very interested in the AIDS epidemic. As a couple, they were probably the most influential advisors to the Chinese government on health affairs.

I remember having dinner with them and the Chinese minister of health in a private room at the largest Peking Duck restaurant in all of China. It reportedly had more than a thousand rooms serving Peking Duck. It was an interesting dining experience because everyone at the table ate from the same bowl. We also toured several major hospitals, which was informative for me. One incident is still etched in my mind. We were visiting an intensive care unit where staff members had a lot of modern equipment but were not proficient in using it. One patient was hooked up to several monitoring machines. When I noticed a flat EKG on the screen, I mentioned it. Somehow the patient had become disconnected from the monitor and no one had noticed.

When I returned to my hotel one night, I flipped the lights

on in my room, only to see hundreds of huge roaches. I slept from then on with my light on. This was before all the new hotels were built and tourist facilities modernized.

At that time Tiananmen Square in the middle of Beijing was filled with nothing but bicycles. As a matter of fact, the only cars you saw were those of high government officials. I understand that today it has all changed and you see nothing but cars.

Any trip to China is worthwhile if the only attraction you see is the Great Wall. It is a magnificent structure and goes as far as the eye can see. I understand the wall is the only clearly identifiable object on Earth that the astronauts can see from space.

Another pleasant experience was visiting several art galleries. At that time, I was beginning to become very serious about collecting art. With the help of my host, I obtained two very fine paintings by Pao Li and Jiang.

To return to Sterling Drug's research, one of the newest products we developed was called Talwin, the first non-narcotic analgesic to become available for patient use. Because of its chemical background and all the research performed, this product initially was introduced to the marketplace devoid of any Drug Enforcement Administration restrictions. After widespread use, there were reports of misuse, addiction, and skin sloughs.

As a result of some of these reports, attorneys thought this would be the next major lode to fill their coffers. Two cases I remember in particular were in Westchester, New York, and Alabama. In testimony for the latter, the plaintiff's attorney asked if I wasn't one of those "major drug dealers" from New York City. This gave me my first taste of southern justice. The defense objected strenuously and asked for a mistrial because of the prejudicial remarks that could not be erased from the jurors' minds. No mistrial was granted, and the verdict against

With Dr. Alfred Farah (right) at Sterling Research Center in Rensselear.

With top scientists of Sterling Drug Research Group in Alnwick, England.

With mayor of Dijon, France, and Drs. Legros and Margetts. Sterling Drug had a pharma-ceutical research facility in Dijon.

With Robert "Binks" Inch. Sterling Drug endowed a professorship in honor of Binks at Edinburgh University, Scotland.

Lord Arthur Porritt, me, Robert "Binks" Inch, and rector of Edinburgh University, Dr. John Burnett.

Sandy and I at University of California, San Diego (UCSD) Medical Center, "An Evening With..."

The UCSD Civis Universitatis Award. I also received an Honorary Alumnus Award from UCSD.

Sandy and I hold two of the six paintings I did for the new Ben Atchley State Veteran's Home in Knoxville, Tennessee. I painted one in honor of each service: Air Force, Army, Marines, Navy, Coast Guard, and the Defense Department.

With Carol Jacobs and the violin I painted for the Knoxville Symphony League Auction. Pictured below is a closeup of the violin.

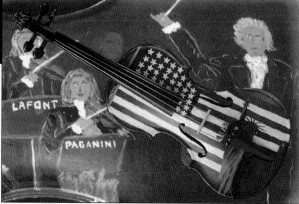

Sterling was subsequently appealed.

The case in Westchester was filed by a well-known plaintiff's attorney whose brother actually worked for Sterling Drug. He sued Sterling for millions of dollars and he spent an enormous amount of his own money on the case. He asked me one question about Talwin while I was on the witness stand which helped decide the verdict.

"Do you know of any substance that is more addictive than Talwin?"

"Yes," I said. "Water. I have to take it every day and am totally dependent on it."

This broke up the jury and the judge and destroyed the attorney's line of reasoning. The jury found for the defense. Later the jurors were asked why they had voted as they did. To a man, they cited the question about addiction and water. I believe the plaintiff's attorney had to declare bankruptcy. Attorneys in such cases work on a contingency basis and get paid only if they win. Our attorneys had my testimony framed and gave it to me as a memento of the case.

Because of the number of complaints we were getting, I hired a young professor of neurology at Mt. Sinai Medical School. His name was Peter Herman. Peter had very long hair, which was not the norm for business executives at that time. Dr. J. Mark Hiebert, the predecessor of Dr. Wescoe and CEO, saw Dr. Herman for the first time in the executive dining room. Dr. Hiebert called me to his office and broached the subject of Dr. Herman, who needed a haircut. He asked me why I had hired him. I told Dr. Hiebert I was more interested in what was on the inside of Dr. Herman's head than what was on the outside. After smiling he dismissed me, and the subject never came up again.

Dr. Herman at the time was married to Ilana Vered, who was a world-famous Israeli pianist. Anyone who saw Arthur Fiedler and the Boston Pops on TV would have seen and heard Ilana play. Later when B'nai B'rith honored me with its International Healthcare Award, Ilana volunteered to play for me *gratis* at the ceremonies. She attracted the largest crowd B'nai B'rith had ever had for one of its fundraising dinners at the Waldorf Astoria in New York. The chairman of that dinner was Charles Lauer, the publisher of *Modern Healthcare*. Chuck became a very good friend. He was one of the icons of the healthcare scene for the last thirty years. Between his chairmanship and Ilana's playing, the evening was a huge success.

Somehow when my wife and I left our home in California to fly to New York, I forgot my tuxedo. I could not readily find a rental tux anywhere in the city, and I panicked. However, I did have my formal shirt and black tie and a dark navy suit. I wore my formal shirt and black bow tie, along with the navy trousers from my suit and a light blue silk sport jacket I had with me. I went to the event somewhat embarrassed. To my surprise, everybody complimented me on my avant-garde tux from California. And that was the end of that.

In 1968 I was approached by a gentleman I had never met who asked me if I would be interested in serving my country. He was a contact following up on phone calls I had received.

He said, "You are just the kind of person that we need to help us."

Because I had a medical background and was traveling extensively throughout the world and meeting many high government officials, I was asked if I would be interested in evaluating the health status of the world leaders with whom I came in contact.

This started my surreptitious career helping the CIA. I was told that I could not tell anybody, including my wife, what I was doing. It was only recently that she learned about my activities. When I was ready to make a trip abroad, I called my CIA contacts to tell them where I was going, and they in turn told me whose health status they wanted to know about in those countries. I tried to meet as many persons of interest as I could and assess their health. If I could not meet them, I discreetly asked other government officials about the health of the ones I didn't get to know. When I returned to the States, I met with my "handler" and reported what I had learned. I had a number of different handlers over the next twenty-five years during my participation in the program.

I had become something of an authority on drug use. About 1970 I was invited by the government of South Africa to participate in a conference called Medicines in Our Time: from Concept to Therapeutic Reality. I was to lecture at their two main medical schools on drug abuse and national and international controls. At the time, South Africa was having a major epidemic of kaht use, a very strong form of marijuana.

Because of my involvement with developing Talwin, I became very familiar with the drug scene in the U.S. and spent some time with Drs. Smith and Gay at the Haight-Ashbury Clinic in San Francisco. I was also in contact with people like Drs. William Martin and Nathan Eddy, two of the foremost authorities on drug misuse in the U.S. Dr. Martin was professor of pharmacology at the University of Kentucky, and Dr. Eddy worked for the federal government. I still have the Nathan Eddy medal awarded to outstanding workers in this field.

Later I served on a New York State Division of Substance Abuse Services Committee on prescription drug misuse and on the advisory board of the National Council on Patient Information and Education. I also was named a consultant to the New York State Health Planning Commission in 1977 and was appointed to the Commission on Prescription Drug Use by Sen. Edward Kennedy, Dr. Ted Cooper, assistant secretary of Health, Education, and Welfare, and Dr. David Hamburg, president of the Institute of Medicine.

One of the first places I lectured in South Africa was the medical school at Pretoria where Dr. Henry Snyman was the dean. My host was Lawrence Wood of Durban, a member of the South African parliament. He was also a pharmacist. As a result, I met the leaders of parliament and also a direct relative of Jan Smuts, one of the leaders of modern South Africa. I also met Dr. Harry Grant-Whyte, professor of anesthesiology at the medical school in Durban. Harry visited with us many times after that, both when we lived in Connecticut and in California. He was a delightful Englishman with more funny stories than anyone I've known. He was also a gracious host and an interesting, genial, and appreciative guest.

As a result of my lecture tour, my host in parliament gave me a saucer from the last governor-general's dinner service set with the Crown of England on it. Apparently when South Africa received its independence, the governor-general gave a piece of his dinner set to each member of the new parliament. The saucer is truly a piece of South African history.

Dr. Snyman, who was a plate collector, tried to convince me to give him the saucer, even suggesting that I might not get it through customs on my exit. I understand why Henry wanted it. I packed it in my hand luggage, which was never inspected, and I have had the saucer ever since.

Another *objet d'art* that I purchased on my trip was an Ashanti gold weight made in the mines by a true artiste.

Henry visited with me in the States thereafter, and I always joked about the saucer he coveted.

Chapter 12

Important Visitors along the Highway

D r. Roger Egeberg, who was involved in helping Anwar Sadat's brother to be treated for liver disease at the National Institutes of Health Hospital, became a friend when we were both invited by the Scandia Insurance Company to speak at the Karolinska Institute in Stockholm. The conference was on malpractice. I spoke on the complications of medical devices, and Roger's presentation was titled "Governmental Approach to Unexpected Complications through Information and Control Systems." The proceedings were published in the book *Unexpected Complications in Medical Care* by Almquist and Wiksell International (Stockholm 1979).

Roger was a big Norwegian, a bear of a man, as tall as I am and twice as round. He had been the personal physician for Gen. Douglas MacArthur during World War II and later became the dean of UCLA's medical school. After his stint as assistant secretary of Health, Education, and Welfare, while in his mid-seventies, he was named a counselor to President Gerald Ford. The Russians seemed to love Roger because of his size and his bluntness, and it is one of the reasons Ford appointed him.

After our return from Stockholm, Roger was invited to Paris to participate in a TV program on MacArthur. However, his host forgot to book him a hotel room. All rooms in Paris were filled. He called me in New York to see if I knew anybody in Paris who could get him a room. I called my friend Binks Inch, who was able to get Roger a room at the Ritz. Roger was put in the President's Suite, the largest in the hotel.

"Monroe, this is the most lavish place I have ever been, but I can't afford it."

"Don't worry, Roger, your rate is the same as the most modest room there."

Later when Binks visited the U.S., we had dinner with Roger in Washington at a very fine restaurant that served wines from the Inch vineyards in France.

Roger was an amazing guy. He had adopted a philosophy of life when he was in his seventies that he should live each day to the fullest for it might be his last. As I said, he lived to be in his nineties. His biography was published after his death.

While at Sterling Drug, several important visitors came to the headquarters. I first met Sen. Bob Dole in Dr. Clark Wescoe's office. They were great friends from Clark's days as chancellor of the University of Kansas. Later Dole met with several of us about health matters. Of course, he was interested in having our political action committee support many of his candidates. I was later involved in helping him raise money for his presidential campaign. I also met with him in Washington and met his chief of staff, Sheila Burke. Later I worked closely with Sheila when Hillary Clinton was trying to rally America around her healthcare plan. We also worked on legislation that affected hospitals.

Another important visitor was Chief Buthelezi from South Africa. Buthelezi visited Sterling to ask that we continue our manufacturing operations in South Africa, even though many people wanted boycotts because of the apartheid situation.

Buthelezi, a very important black chieftain, told us that providing jobs to poor South Africans was extremely important to their economy. Sterling had a large operation and business in South Africa and was torn by the debate over a boycott. As a result of his visit, we decided to stay in South Africa and continue operations there.

In the mid-1970s, I met Dr. Lou Sullivan, the first president of Morehouse School of Medicine and later secretary of Health and Human Services under President George H.W. Bush. At the time, he was professor of hematology at the Boston University Medical School in Massachusetts. I was so impressed with him I invited him to visit when ever he was in New York.

A few years later he phoned saying he was in New York and would like to meet with me. He told me he had just been appointed president of Morehouse College's medical school–which at the time consisted solely of him. He asked if I could help raise some money so he could open an office. As chairman of the corporate giving committee at Sterling, I called the members together and we agreed to give him $50,000. I told him I could get him more money if he stayed overnight.

Since he had no room in the city, I offered him a room at our house. I had basketball tickets for that evening to watch my son play in a high school game. Lou later told all his friends how passionate I could become and how loud I could yell at a basketball game.

In New York the chairs of the various corporate giving committees met frequently at lunch to discuss how to improve corporate giving. I called a few of my friends at companies like Mobil Oil and Bristol-Myers and asked them for help for the new medical school. In one day we raised approximately $400,000 to help Lou get started. The new medical school at first was an adjunct of Morehouse College, so a Board of Visitors was appointed. I was one of them, and later when the

Recognition of my service on the Morehouse School of Medicine Board of Trustees.

school of medicine became independent of the college, I was asked to be the first chairman of the board. I refused because I thought the chairman should be an African American so the students would have a good African-American role model.

Dr. Clint Warner, an Atlanta physician, was chosen as chairman, and I was the vice chairman and first chairman of the development committee. I immediately recruited Bob Froelke, the chairman of the board of Equitable Life Insurance Co. I also recommended him to the board as my successor as chairman of the development committee.

Bob Froelke and I thought it would be great if we could get Barbara Bush to be on the Morehouse Board of Trustees. We persuaded her over lunch at Sterling Drug. She promptly organized fundraising lunches for Morehouse in all the major cities of the country.

I remember attending one board meeting where some of the other members were making somewhat disparaging remarks about the administration's policies.

Barbara apparently heard some of these comments that were probably said so she would report to Washington and get a change of policy. Since she is not known to be shy, she said, "Gentlemen, I was not elected vice president of the United States. If you want to meet with him, please make an appointment in Washington."

As a result of her efforts, Morehouse raised about $17 million, enabling it to build its first facility.

I stayed on the board until 1989. As is often the case for new organizations, we had many challenges. Many times I thought the school would not survive. However, we were able to overcome most of the problems, and today Morehouse is a thriving medical school educating new doctors for primary care.

During my years on the board, my wife and I endowed a scholarship, and we still receive some letters from the recipients.

Andrew Young, the former U.S ambassador to the United

Nations, was also on the board. At the time, he was serving as the mayor of Atlanta. I once asked him how it felt to go from the international stage to being mayor.

He replied, "I can't believe people can become so passionate about a pothole."

The board of directors included African-American leaders from across America and a number of whites from the business world. We were able to recruit Mrs. Pritzker of the Pritzker empire, along with David Winfield, the famous outfielder for the New York Yankees. Because he had played for the San Diego Padres, he knew Joan Kroc, the McDonald's heiress, and convinced her to donate a million dollars to Morehouse.

Sarah Austin-Crosthwaite had served as an executive with many African-American organizations, had been in charge of community relations for General Dynamics, and had served as executive director of the Cleveland Business Roundtable. She was the first secretary of the Morehouse board and chairperson of the nominating committee. Because we were both blunt in our assessment of certain problems, we became not only "colleagues in arms" but lifelong friends. She and her husband have visited with us, and we still talk on the telephone. She met her husband, Harold Crosthwaite, a professor of dentistry at Ohio State, in college. They now live in retirement in Virginia. We still reminisce about some of the funny things and some of the crises which, if they had not been resolved, would probably have ended a noble endeavor.

Some of Sterling Drug's manufacturing plants were unionized. The largest research institute for Sterling was at Rensselaer in New York, where we also had a large manufacturing plant. We had a particularly bitter strike that went on for several months. Everything was at a standstill. Since I visited the research center regularly, the chairman asked me to meet with the union leaders on my next visit. The union head told me I was the first person with any authority who had sat down and talked about the problem with him. We talked for a long time and came to some mutual conclusions. I told him I could probably persuade the chairman to agree, and he thought he could get the union to agree, and so the strike was settled.

I was commuting into New York City from New Canaan, Connecticut. I sometimes think I have spent my life in a commuter train or in an aluminum tube flying somewhere around the world.

The dynamics on the train were interesting. First of all, the cars were non-smoking except for one. Secondly, if you held a conversation with your neighbor on the train, others would frown upon you. To pass the time, I read the *New York Times* or played bridge with fellow passengers. Bidding out loud was tolerated but not rehashes of hands. In the evenings I read my mail and other business communications I had received that day.

The train ride could be quite harrowing. In the early 1970s, I had to go into New York on a Sunday afternoon. When I tried to return home on the train later that afternoon, a huge snowstorm had stopped the trains. The passengers could not spend the night on the train because there was no heat, food, or water, so I walked about a mile on the railroad tracks to Stamford to a large building run by The Salvation Army. This was where I had to spend the night, sleeping on the floor of the gymnasium with only my topcoat for comfort. The place was quite crowded, and the only food available was some cans of soup mixed together and heated up by the one staff member on duty. Obviously, there was not enough for everybody. Some ruffians who had also sought refuge commandeered the kitchen. It was not a good situation.

The next day we were still snowed in. I determined I would not spend another night there, even though The Salvation Army was trying to make it as nice as possible. I walked about a mile to the New England Thruway, where the plows were working to clear the snow. I hitched a ride sitting on the back of a sand truck to Norwalk, about five miles from my home. I walked through knee-deep snow to get home.

Of course, my wife had no idea where I was. When I arrived home, I was totally exhausted. Sandy told me she had never seen me looking so bad. She and the boys were trying to shovel a path in our driveway, but I went to bed and slept a long time.

A similar incident happened in the early 1970s when a major ice storm hit New Canaan. It knocked out all the electrical power. We had no heat or light and no water because we were on a well. The temperatures stayed in the teens for an entire week. We thought we could gut it out by building a fire for cooking and by sleeping next to the fireplace for warmth. After one night we decided we could not continue to do this with the boys, so we farmed them out to friends who had electricity. Sandy and I and the dog stayed in the house. When the electricity came on, we discovered all the pipes had frozen and broken as they expanded. As they thawed, water dripped everywhere. No plumbers could be enticed to help us even though they were charging ten times their normal rate. Our next-door neighbor, John Campbell, who was quite a good mechanic, finally came over and was able to fix all the pipes for us.

Another incident happened on the commuter train on July 13, 1976. I was involved in a head-on train collision, and the front car where I was sitting took the brunt of the crash. The two young ladies sitting in front of me were both killed. One was almost decapitated, and the other was crushed. I was very lucky to escape with only minor lacerations and a broken hand. More than thirty passengers were injured seriously enough to be taken to the hospital. Since my adrenalin was pumping at full tilt, I did not feel any pain and did not think of my own

CHAPTER 12 *Important Visitors along the Highway* 91

injuries but tried to help others in the car. First I attended those who were bleeding. I was later called a "hero" by some papers because I stayed on the car until all the injured were evacuated. I didn't really feel like a hero. I was doing the job I was trained to do in medical school.

July 13, 1976, is a date I don't forget.

My wife and I were involved in another accident that occurred on a trip to Carlisle, Pennsylvania, to attend a Dickinson School of Law board meeting.

President Judge Dale Shughart was the chairman of the board of trustees. He had originally recruited me to the board and became a lifelong mentor, advisor, and good friend. We were driving on a four-lane highway in the passing lane when the car in front of us suddenly stopped to make a left-hand turn, and we plowed into it. Our car was turned sideways. The car in back hit us and knocked us into the opposite lane where we were hit again. It was a complete miracle that none of the people in any of the four cars were seriously injured. As it turned out, the driver of the car we hit was that of a Drug Enforcement Administration (DEA) agent who was going on a drug bust at one of the motels on the opposite side of the road. The car that hit us was occupied by former Governor John Fine of Pennsylvania. He was the one who gave the famous "Pennsylvania will never pass" speech at the 1952 Republican National Convention, when Dwight Eisenhower defeated Sen. Robert Taft for the nomination and went on to become president of the U.S. The car in the opposing lane that hit us was occupied by a prominent lawyer. The three of us were going to attend the same board meeting. We all waited for the state police in a motel where we had coffee together. The driver of the car that caused the accident refused to identify himself at first. But when the state police commander and the president judge of the local courts arrived, the driver reluctantly told us whom he represented and revealed his identity. My car was totaled, but the federal government replaced it and also the cars of the other two victims. What an accident to be in with a DEA agent, a former governor, a physician, and a prominent attorney.

During this time, my boys were growing up. Tim at a young age was interested in reptiles and frequently brought snakes home. This was not to my liking. We went to the local pet store and bought a gecko after being assured by the pet store owner that it would probably die within a year. The gecko would only eat live crickets, and we had to import them from Tennessee. In the summer I took a tennis-ball can and caught grasshoppers around the tennis courts for the gecko. Two years later we returned the gecko to the pet store and told the owner he could sell it to someone else for the last years of its life.

Also during that period of time, we owned several dogs with unfortunate results. Our first, a black Labrador, caught a wild rabbit and must have developed some disease from it. Within days the dog bit Timothy's finger twice and turned on me. We took the dog to the vet, who suggested putting our pet to sleep. We left the dog behind and told the boys the vet had suggested it be put on a farm somewhere out in the country.

One of our beloved collies was sitting at the end of the driveway when the trash truck barreled in, killing the dog. I was furious, especially since the boys could have been there also. We changed trash pickup companies. Another collie we adopted when a friend moved had a dreadful fear of thunder and lightning. Every time a storm occurred, she climbed into one of our beds and tried to get as far under the covers as she could. Unfortunately, this collie ended up having a twisted gut and subsequently died at the vet's.

The boys were both superb athletes and superb students. They were both Connecticut swimming champions, which meant we spent many weekends summer and winter traveling around the state to swim meets. They played all sports until high school, when they decided to concentrate on basketball. They both led their teams to the finals of the state championships, and both became all-state players. As a result, both were heavily recruited by colleges all over the country.

Monroe Jr. chose to go to Harvard, where he graduated *magna cum laude*. He played on the basketball team all four years and was co-captain his senior year. Timothy went to William & Mary, where he started all four years and was captain his senior year. After graduating, both had successful business careers.

I remember one incident returning from an all-star game. Sandy and I had been asked by the coach of another team in our league to take two of his players to the all-star game, which we readily agreed to do. They were both African-American. On the way back, the four of us decided to stop at a restaurant, and we told the boys to go on in and order while we were getting gas for the car. Meanwhile, the two players were being ignored by the restaurant staff, and it was obvious why. When we entered, walked to the table, and sat down, the staff was relieved. The waiter readily came over to take our order. This was in the mid-1980s when people were still that afraid of one another. I felt bad for the boys.

Tim was selected to play twice on a U.S. collegiate team that toured Europe and played the national teams of eight or nine countries. The first time we did not go along to see any of the games, but Tim related to us how well they were treated in every place they went. The championship game was played in Gmunden, Austria, against the Russians. The U.S. team won and was given a parade through the streets of Gmunden. They were also invited to play an exhibition game in Vienna.

When Tim was selected the second time, we decided to go along. I called the manager of the team to see if we could get tickets to all the games if we came to Europe. He apparently knew I was a physician and asked if I'd be willing to be the team physician, which meant we were part of the official family and could see all the games from the best seats as well as participate in all the activities in the various cities. Again the team was well received everywhere, and the kids in each town swarmed around to get autographs.

I remember being in Pécs, Hungary, and walking with Tim in the town park when we were mobbed by a group of teenagers who wanted autographs. When I spotted a statue of Lenin in the park, I thought a shot of Tim and the Hungarians in front of the statue would make a great picture. We told the kids we would give them autographs if they lined up for a picture. At this time, Hungary was still under Soviet rule, but the kids absolutely refused to have their picture taken with the statue of Lenin. They were quite willing to have it taken someplace else in the park.

Another incident occurred when our bus first crossed the Hungarian border. Soviet guards met us and came on board to inspect the hand luggage. They were big, uniformed, and unsmiling—until one of the assistant coaches gave each of the soldiers a U.S. jersey or hat.

The final game was once again against the Russians, and the U.S. team won. After the last game, some of the players gave their jerseys, caps, and other paraphernalia to the members of the other teams. One of the most prized possessions was a pair of sneakers. Tim made a couple of boys happy with his gifts.

Because I had two children in the school system, and because my boss at Sterling Drug urged me and all other employees to get involved in politics, I became a Republican district leader in New Canaan in 1966, and was able to get out to the polls more than 90 percent of the Republican voters in my district. I kept this job for three years. I then ran for the school board and lost by a narrow margin because I advocated reducing its double-digit-inflated budgets. I did not take my defeat well and stayed out of politics for several years.

The budgets continued to inflate at double-digit rates, so I finally decided to become involved again–only this time for the town council, which actually controlled the school budgets. Members of the town council selected me to fill an unexpired term in 1978. I was re-elected overwhelmingly twice again. I was appointed chairman of both the education and finance committees, and in 1985 became vice chairman of the council, serving until we moved to California the next year. The school board was determined to continue the double-digit increases, and I was determined to reduce the budget increases to single-digit. The town was already spending more per student than most other communities in the United States. The school superintendent did everything he could to get me defeated, but I won with more than 65 percent of the vote each time I ran. There is always waste and excess in government, and you need to root it out.

One of the facts I discovered was that the superintendent was paying his secretary more than that of the secretaries of most corporate CEOs in New York. As a result of this knowledge and some other excesses, I was able to get the council to reduce the budget into single-digit inflation, and it stayed there throughout my tenure.

The school system was superb. The budget reductions had no effect on the quality of education in the system because we were only reducing the increases requested rather than the budget per se.

Erna Green, a Democrat, was also on the council, and we had our political differences but greatly respected each other's opinions. Her husband, Leonard, was a local podiatrist who operated on the toes of one of our sons. Erna was also the executive recruiter for a prominent firm in New York, and we collaborated on a number of her searches. We often played bridge together on the weekends, and long after I left New Canaan we kept in touch. Unfortunately, she died too young, but we did see Leonard on one of our recent visits to New Canaan.

Chapter 13

Helping Heal Osteoporosis to Endometriosis

Another crisis that occurred while I was at Sterling Drug happened when the Communicable Disease Center published a report linking Reye's syndrome in children to aspirin. This was a tenuous link, which received worldwide attention and was in all the newspapers and television reports at the time. The pediatric world was shocked, and it was pointed out that distinguishing between the diagnosis of Reye's syndrome and inborn errors of metabolism was very difficult. Also, many sections of the world where large amounts of aspirin were consumed never reported a case of Reye's syndrome.

The Food and Drug Administration held several advisory committee meetings on the subject, but the FDA, Centers for Disease Control (CDC), and National Institutes of Health (NIH) could not agree on cause and effect. The secretary of Health, Education, and Welfare (HEW) issued several statements and proposed rulemaking in the *Federal Register* on the subject. The scientific community was divided because, if a warning about Reye's syndrome was placed on the label, aspirin might not be used for patients who need it such as those with juvenile rheumatoid arthritis. Finally, after months of meetings with all of the scientific groups concerned, the HEW secretary made a decision to put the warning on the labeling. Scientific issues rarely reached the secretary's office. Usually such issues were settled by the CDC, FDA, or NIH. However, since the agencies could not agree, he decided to err on the side of caution and issued his order.

The possible link between Reye's syndrome and aspirin and between pHisoHex and spongy form lesions of the brain presented probably the greatest medical controversies of the 1970s. I was deeply involved in both major issues.

Another major issue at the time involved Sterling peripherally because we were the largest manufacturer of acetaminophen in the world. We did sell it in Europe under the trade name Panadol but not in the U.S., where Johnson & Johnson had the market with its product Tylenol. However, Johnson & Johnson bought a large portion of its supplies of the drug from us. The issue was twofold: Did apap (acetaminophen) in combination with aspirin and other analgesics over a long period of time cause kidney disease, and what was the safe dosage of apap to be used to prevent liver problems? It had been well established that in huge doses apap caused liver failure.

These products took up a great deal of my time because I had to meet frequently with the scientists of Johnson & Johnson and of Hoechst, also a large manufacturer and seller of apap. I even visited with Dr. Wolfgang Laxy at Hoechst headquarters in Germany and was extremely impressed that the town where it was located was truly a company town.

I have been discussing some of the major problems of drugs Sterling marketed at the time I was the medical director. There were also other minor flare-ups that could keep one busy.

However, the major part of my job after 1978 was heading up worldwide research. Sterling Drug at the time had more than three thousand scientific personnel working on pharmaceutical research in three major research facilities. I spent more than $40 million renovating two and building the third on a completely new green site. The largest facility was located in Rensselaer and the other in Dijon, France. Dr. Wescoe selected April 5, 1981, for the dedication of the new green-site facility, a date I remember because it was my fiftieth birthday. The new facility was built in Alnwick, England, after a long search for the site.

We had actually chosen another place, but PETA, the animal rights group, raised so much controversy we decided not to build there. The duke of Northumberland, who had his castle in Alnwick, was looking for a way to provide jobs for the community and also to upgrade the educational system. He thought he could solve both problems by having a major research facility there, so he approached us. He promised we would not encounter such problems with PETA, and he was right. However, PETA's antics even in the United States were such that, when we built the new facility, we had to spend millions of dollars on security.

The duke of Northumberland was quite proud and invited government officials from all over Europe to attend the dedication.

It was truly a memorable event because many people came just to see the fourteenth-century pharmacy that we had purchased and transported to the site to become the new lobby. It had been sitting elsewhere in the town, standing empty for years. Officials had decided to tear it down when we rescued it. It was probably the best extraneous expenditure we made. In addition to its historical charm, the pharmacy endeared our company to the townspeople who realized that we were also interested in preserving their heritage.

To honor the occasion, the duke himself hosted a dinner in the great hall of his castle. Little did I know that it was not only a dinner for all the government officials and participants in the dedication, but also a birthday party for me. When it came time for the dessert to be served, the lights went out and a huge cake with fifty candles was brought into the great hall. Also, the town council presented me a tie with the Alnwick's insignia. I have not worn it often, but I still have it.

The duke was also kind enough to give me a personal tour of the castle, and I was stunned to see many great paintings that I had read and heard about casually hung there. One the duke was particularly pleased with was a painting of Bunker Hill done by one of his distant relatives who had served in the British Army during the Revolutionary War.

During my first six years as head of research, we filed nineteen new drug applications for Food and Drug Administration approval. In addition, we introduced a number of other new compounds to other countries. As a matter of fact, in 1985 Sterling led all other companies in number of NDAs (new drug approvals). That year the FDA approved trilostane for Cushing's syndrome. The compound modulated the secretions of the adrenal gland and inhibited adrenal steroidogenesis, thus preventing the disease.

Another product was iohexol, which was a new radiopaque diagnostic. This product was used to help diagnose many disease states in which a radiopaque substance in the blood vessels would help delineate the problem. Another important product at the time was bitolterol, a bronchodilator that was sold under the name of Tornalate by Breon Laboratory, a division of Sterling Drug.

A major new product that we introduced to ameliorate endometriosis was Danazol. Until its introduction, the only treatment had been surgery. Endometriosis is a disease of women who have extra endometrial tissue in different parts of their bodies, sometimes including their lungs, and this tissue bleeds each month during the menstrual period. The disease can cause severe pain and even threaten the patient's life.

We on the scientific side of Sterling thought this was a major breakthrough medicine. But the marketing people decided there was no market for Danazol. The president of the division that had the marketing responsibility refused to market it. This created a great controversy between the two groups and even some animosity, although the divisional president remained a good friend and was one of my neighbors in New Canaan. The marketers could not find a market because the only treatment available had been surgery, and they could not find the number of surgeries performed in their schemata.

I appealed to Dr. Wescoe, who had a big meeting, listened to all sides, and finally told the divisional president to market it or he would find someone else to do so. I was somewhat apprehensive about this, because put in that position, one could easily try to scuttle the introduction. However, to Bill Murphy's credit, he took Danazol into the marketplace like any other new introduction, and after a few years it became a $100 million drug in sales. At the time, that was a huge amount.

This product was also later discovered by scientists at the National Institutes of Health to block the mechanism of action causing hereditary angio-neurotic edema. This was a rare disease that at the time afflicted about eighteen thousand Americans each year. Most of them died by the age of twenty from one of the anaphylactic reactions that appeared spontaneously. Danazol was and is a real lifesaver, and the patient can live a normal lifespan if he or she continues to take the drug. Danazol was used in other countries for fibrocystic breast disease. Fibrocystic disease of the breast is quite painful to many women, and Danazol relieves the symptoms.

Another product approved was Amipaque which, because it was water soluble, was able to be introduced into a spinal canal, allowing many diseases originating there to be diagnosed for the first time. It was widely used throughout the world.

A very interesting compound, discovered by chance by one of our scientists working at home on another project, was durapatite. It is a bone-replacement material and was studied by dentists to augment the alveolar ridge and also to augment and restore bone in the jaw that had been eroded by periodontal disease.

We also introduced stanozolol, which was approved in many parts of the world, such as Australia, for treatment of osteoporosis. Actually, this was an old drug but a new indication. Unfortunately, this product, sold under the name of Winstrol, is in the news today because some athletes take it to enhance their athletic prowess.

I mentioned Talwin and some of the problems we were having with addiction reports. In 1982 we reformulated it with Naloxone, a compound used to prevent narcotic addiction.

During my time in research, we were beginning to receive reports of penicillin-resistant gonorrhea. Since this is a major disease in all parts of the world, and because of my previous experiences treating the disease on Okinawa, I asked our scientists to develop an antibiotic for penicillin-resistant gonorrhea. They came up with rosoxacin, which was sold under the name Eradasil. It quickly became a big seller in the Philippines and Brazil. Even though rosoxacin was approved and sold in dozens of countries around the world, we could never obtain Food and Drug Administration approval for use in the United States. Unfortunately, as with most antibiotics, it became widely used and was not reserved for only penicillin-resistant gonorrhea. As a result, resistance to it developed.

Because of the previously discussed problems with pHiso-Hex, we also developed a chlorhexidine skin cleanser to be used in nurseries to prevent newborn infections. However, it was not as effective as pHisoHex. Still today we are having outbreaks of staphylococcal skin diseases.

In our cardiovascular unit, we hoped to find a major drug

for heart failure. We spent much time and money developing Amrinone and Milrinone. Amrinone was developed first, and since it was called the "Lazarus drug" it became known throughout the world. The press was relentless in following its every up and down. Some of the best scientists in the world studied the drug, including Dr. Eugene Braunwald of Harvard University and Dr. Ed Sonnenblich of Albert Einstein College of Medicine in New York. They were most encouraging, and the short-term results were very good. The first patient we treated with Amrinone was a physician who had been brought into the hospital to die of heart failure. He was given Amrinone intravenously, and within twenty-four hours was walking around the hospital and was later discharged. He was again able to take up golf, which he had not played for many years.

The Lazarus drug, Amrinone, literally brought patients back from the brink of death. However, as with all drugs, you encounter side effects and must make a risk-versus-reward decision as to whether you want to continue with the research.

Amrinone became a favorite drug to study by those who didn't want to see it in the marketplace. At the time, we were getting calls from the Russian embassy to supply the drug for the Russian premier, from the secretary of state of the Vatican, and for John Hay Whitney, former U.S. ambassador to the United Kingdom, who was in Cornell University's hospital. To make a long story short, Amrinone was approved only in the intravenous form and therefore never received worldwide acceptance.

Since it was obvious we could not get Amrinone approved for oral use, we took the successor drug, Milrinone, into research. This too was approved by the Food and Drug Administration, and Milrinone IV is still being used to save lives of children who need certain major heart operations.

We probably spent $100 million to develop these two drugs.

Another compound studied for herpes genitalis was arildone. Herpes, like gonorrhea, is a global disease, and was a major problem in Brazil. It is also known to cause cervical cancer. In 1982 I was asked to visit Brazil and meet with the minister of health about our studies on this disease in his country. Unfortunately, the time interval for curing the disease was not much shorter than that for a placebo. After extensive testing in the U.S. and other parts of the world, the compound was abandoned.

A very effective compound was epostane. It was the first pregnancy interceptive drug ever to be studied and was quite effective as a morning-after pill. However, because of the raging political battle over abortion and the strong beliefs of some religions, the chairman and CEO of the company—over my objections—ordered the product to be abandoned. It is of interest that almost thirty years later, the first morning-after pill has been introduced into the marketplace with more howls for it than against it.

Our research team discovered another drug still in use today, Urokinase. It is used to dissolve clots in both the heart and the brain if the clots are discovered and treated within a few hours. It is truly a lifesaving drug and an interesting one since it was originally derived from human urine. We used to collect the urine from military bases around the country and transport it in huge tanker trucks to the manufacturing facility. Through some experiments in outer space, the drug was able to be manufactured without human urine. It is still being sold today by Abbott, under the name, I believe, of Abbokinase. This illustrates again that many lifesaving drugs have been derived from exotic soils, plants, corals under the sea, and even what is considered a waste—human urine. Of course, most antibiotics originally came from soil, bacteria, molds, and so on.

We continued to look for other indications for the drugs we had already marketed. Marcaine, first introduced as a long-acting local anesthetic for use by dentists, was approved in addition for spinal anesthesia and is still widely used. As a matter of fact, recently I had to have a tooth removed at a local hospital, and when the oral surgeon told me he was going to use Marcaine, I told him it was my research team's product. He told me he thought it was one of the major innovations in dentistry. As a thank-you, I guess, he never sent me a bill for extracting my tooth.

Another new drug approved was Conagraf, which used durapatite as a root replacement for teeth.

Many other indications were also approved for Amipaque and iohexol.

I must mention some of the brilliant scientists who headed up our research at the different laboratories while I was director of worldwide research. At Rensselaer we had Dr. Alfred Farah, former chairman of the department of pharmacology at Syracuse University, to be followed by Dr. Irving Lepow, formerly chief of internal medicine at the University of Connecticut School of Medicine, and Dr. Lawrence Chakrin, a pharmacologist who joined the company and was rapidly promoted until he headed the research department. Dr. Legros in France and Dr. George Margetts in the United Kingdom were all stellar performers and greatly enhanced the reputation of Sterling's Research Institutes. In addition, Dr. Walter Riker, head of pharmacology at Cornell University, chaired our research advisory board, and on it were Dr. John Laragh, professor of medicine at Cornell, and Dr. Frank Standaert, head of pharmacology at Georgetown University and later dean of the medical school in Dayton, Ohio.

I could not have completed all my tasks without the help of Dr. Ernst Zander. Ernie was the deputy medical director of Winthrop Labs and was expected to be the medical director when I was brought in over him. He was an extremely loyal employee and immediately adapted to his new position. As I went up the ladder, I took Ernie with me. He was extremely capable in implementing policies and plans and became a very good friend to my wife and me.

I certainly must mention my secretary for almost twenty years at Sterling Drug, Lily Borland. She constantly kept me out of trouble. She had the unusual knack of holding letters for several days after I had written them in anger and asking me if I wanted to review and perhaps change them. I invariably did.

I remember one incident in particular when I was on the Health, Education, and Welfare Malpractice Commission. I was invited to speak to the Medical Society of New Jersey. I was not told that the wives of the doctors would be at the meeting, and my presentation was geared to the doctors and somewhat scientific. When I walked into the ballroom and saw the number of ladies in the audience, I realized my mistake but had no recourse than to give the paper I had written. As a result, I started off the meeting by stating that I apologized to the distaff members of the audience because my remarks might bore them. I also said I was very pleased to see so much pulchritude in the audience.

After my presentation, which I thought went very well and was much appreciated, a lady approached me at the dais and immediately started berating me about "the pulchritude in the audience" comment. "I didn't hear you talking about the hand-some men in the audience."

I realized she was a women's libber and decided to get out quickly. However, this did not end the affair. I got a letter from the editor of the *New Jersey Medical Journal* saying that he had received a letter criticizing my presentation, especially "the pulchritude of the audience" comment. I became very agitated and wrote a reply, saying I was sorry if I offended the writer because the word "pulchritude" did not apply to her. I said a few other things in the letter which Lily did not think appropriate, and after several days she returned the letter and asked me if I really wanted to send it. I reread the letter and called the editor to tell him I was not going to reply because it would prolong the argument and I was not interested in doing that.

Chapter 14

Boosting Professional Standards

T he issue of malpractice dominated discussions on health policy throughout the 1970s. Even though I was appointed to the commission by Health, Education, and Welfare Secretary Elliot Richardson, I continued to meet with his successor, Caspar Weinberger, through 1974 and 1975. The assistant secretary during that time changed from Dr. Monty DuVal to Dr. Charles Edwards to Dr. Roger Egeberg. Mr. Weinberger issued the final report of the commission on April 18, 1973. The governor of New York in 1975 appointed his own malpractice commission to make recommendations for New York State. This commission was headed by William McGill, president of Columbia University. After meeting with him at his request, I outlined a list of recommendations I thought might be useful to the commission to achieve. He acknowledged these in a letter to me dated July 18, 1975, and asked me to be his personal informal advisor for the life of the commission.

I put him in touch with Roger Egeberg so that he would have a good idea what the federal government was considering. Roger was gracious enough to come to New York to

THE SECRETARY OF HEALTH, EDUCATION, AND WELFARE
WASHINGTON, D. C. 20201

JUL 2   1971

Monroe E. Trout, M.D., J.D.
Vice President
Winthrop Laboratories Division
90 Park Avenue
New York, New York   10016

Dear Dr. Trout:

I am delighted to invite you to serve on the
Secretary's Commission on Medical Malpractice for
a term beginning immediately and ending June 30,
1972, subject to prescribed appointment procedures.

Enclosed is a statement which describes the structure
and the functions of the Commission.

I hope you will find it possible to accept this invitation and give us the benefit of your valued
counsel. You may indicate your acceptance or decli-
nation by signing and returning the enclosed Acknowl-
edgment of Invitation.

Upon learning of your acceptance, I shall ask the
Assistant Secretary for Health and Scientific Affairs
to supply you with further information relating to
your appointment.

With kindest regards,

Sincerely,

Elliot L. Richardson

Secretary

Enclosures

An invitation from Health, Education, and Welfare Secretary Elliot
Richardson to serve on the Commission on Medical Malpractice.

meet with Bill and the executive director of the New York commission.

This was also a time when professional standards review organizations (PSRO) were coming into being. The federal government was contemplating adding amendments on these organizations to the Social Security Act and was interested in how they would affect the malpractice problem. I met several times with the HEW representative, Dr. William Kirby Jr., on the PSRO issue. Kirby also asked for comments from Jim Ludlam, who was on the Malpractice Commission and was a fine attorney from Musick, Peeler and Garrett in Los Angeles. Jim wrote an excellent brief on the subject which I shared with Dr. Kirby at HEW. In the meantime, Mr. Weinberger convened a group from the insurance industry to review malpractice issues pertaining to that group. John E. Linster, who was senior vice president of Employers of Wausau in Wisconsin, was also a member of the HEW Malpractice Commission. John Linster and I had exchanged a number of letters, and on February 28, 1975, I wrote to him:

> I am tired of attending meetings and listening to a lot of rhetoric. It is time to get something done. Roger Egeberg and I are meeting with the New York State Commission, and we are drafting a proposal. The New York group is still looking at a captive insurance company as a last resort, but unless some inroads are made, they will go as broke as other companies that have operated in the state. It is possible that some hospitalized patients in the State of New York will incur approximately $15 a day for the cost of malpractice insurance for every day spent in the hospital. I believe the commission is meeting with the lawyers of the N.Y. Bar Association March 11 and hopefully will begin a feasible plan.

While all the malpractice issues were being discussed, Sen. Edward Kennedy suggested the United States needed a better system for monitoring the use and effects of prescription drugs after they were marketed. In 1976 the Joint Commission on Prescription Drug Use was established with eighteen commissioners selected by Sen. Kennedy, Dr. Theodore Cooper, assistant secretary of HEW, and Dr. David J. Hamburg, president of the Institute of Medicine (part of the National Academy of Sciences).

The commission was mired in controversy almost from the beginning. First, there was some disagreement on the appointment of the executive secretary and his staff. The chairman of the commission was Dr. Kenneth Melmon from Stanford, and Dr. Marcus W. Reidenberg from Cornell was the vice chairman. They were both pharmacologists. The second controversy was over whether the commission members should be paid. This issue created a major firestorm in 1979 when the chairman was accused in an anonymous letter of charging too much for expenses while working for the commission. This was finally resolved, but it detracted from the work that needed to be done. (I never accepted a penny either for expenses or salary at that time or any other.)

A major issue for the commission was post-marketing surveillance. After acrimonious debate, the commission agreed that events greater than 1:1,000 adverse effects from a drug could be a basis for further investigation. Marcia Greenberger, a lawyer and consumer activist, wanted the commission to adopt a 1:10,000 ratio. This would mean that every drug studied for approval would be given to at least ten thousand patients before it could be sent to the Food and Drug Administration for new drug approval. Many of the anti-cancer drugs would have never reached the marketplace since it would have been almost impossible to round up ten thousand research subjects.

Another major issue was whether the government should establish a rival organization to the FDA with physical facilities and full-time staff. This was rejected as being too expensive and duplicative.

The commission wrestled with the problem of what drugs should be surveyed and developed a list with new chemical entities at the top. Some commission members even wanted over-the-counter drugs to be under surveillance.

The cost-benefit ratio was never addressed satisfactorily by the commission. Some commissioners wanted lifetime follow-up on all new drugs. The cost would be prohibitive and would bar availability of old drugs for new uses. Because the malpractice issues were still operative, the commission recommended a limited shield law protecting the confidentiality of medical records. Many members, including me, thought an absolute shield law similar to that protecting information for the Social Security system should be enacted.

One of the biggest deterrents to the reporting of adverse reactions at the time of this writing, in my opinion, is the fact that the Food and Drug Administration will not and cannot keep its information confidential. I will categorically state that no post-marketing surveillance will ever be successful in the U.S. until the issue of confidentiality is faced squarely.

Dr. Angela Bowen of Washington State wrote a letter stating she was being sued as a result of information given under the table by a Health, Education, and Welfare attorney. This attorney had "released" information regarding the adverse effects of a drug that Dr. Bowen had prescribed. Also, a hospital in Cleveland was sued as a result of information made public by the Food and Drug Administration with regard to adverse reactions. Other lawsuits were filed against Upjohn Co. immediately after an attorney filed a subpoena for adverse reaction data. It is easy to see how irresponsibly releasing information could deter companies from volunteering to report adverse reaction data.

Another issue left vague by the committee was that of relative safety and efficacy and what should happen to products shown to be less safe than others—even though they may be necessary for some patients. Some of us thought the commission should not address this issue at all. However, the commission thought that relative safety and efficacy flowed naturally from any post-marketing surveillance system and that compounds shown to be less safe should be removed from the marketplace.

Many others contributed proposals and research for the report. Several volumes of material on systems around the world on post-marketing surveillance are excellent reference sources. The description of various methods of surveillance and what could be done with such methods are superb. The myth that post-marketing surveillance would shorten the drug approval lag was debunked.

One of the commission's most important services to society was stating that more and better information on the use and misuse of drugs needed to be made public.

The commission sent its report to Sen. Kennedy, HEW, and the Institute of Medicine on January 3, 1980. The report consists of two volumes and makes good reading.

As a result of serving on the commission, I was asked to testify on the Drug Regulation Reform Act of 1978. I appeared before a subcommittee of the House on June 19, 1978, to give my testimony. Rep. Paul Rogers was the chairman of that committee. I later worked with Paul on forming the National Library of Medicine's Friends Committee and also worked with him after his retirement from Congress on many health-care issues.

Chapter 15

Giving Service: Board Memberships

Meanwhile, I also began to serve on many charitable boards. I was appointed to the New Canaan Interchurch Service Commission. I served from 1965 to 1969 and was a member of the executive committee. This commission was a joint effort of all the churches in New Canaan to provide services to those in need. I also served on the board of the Lake Club, a swim and racquet club in New Canaan. I served from 1973 to 1976 and was the vice president for the last two years. In July 1976, I was asked by Dr. Harry Kleiman to serve on the board of the Athletes Kidney Foundation. Dr. Kleiman was professor of urology at a New York medical school and had conducted research for Sterling on antibiotics. He was the first to discover that all athletes after a strenuous game or workout had blood in their urine. As a result, he formed the Athletes Kidney Foundation to explore the implications.

We became good friends, and he and his wife, Michelline, visited with us on Sundays in New Canaan. He asked us one week if he could bring a guest to dinner. We said, "Absolutely." The guest turned out to be Harry Hershfield, the well-known

A treasured drawing by noted cartoonist Harry Hershfield.

originator of the *Ish Kabibble* series. Harry was a delightful gentleman, and he drew pictures for us during his visit. Most of them have been lost, but one is framed and hanging in our art gallery. Harry's works are now in many museums throughout the world.

Dr. Kleiman was also the physician for the New York State Boxing Commission, and he asked me on one occasion if I would like to see a boxing match at Madison Square Garden. I readily agreed, not knowing he had something else in mind. He later asked if I would assist him in taking care of the fighters after the matches since they frequently needed stitches or other medical services. I helped Harry provide these. It was a fascinating period of my life. I was asked to help treat many of the famous names in boxing.

Harry and Michelline were lifelong friends. He died a number of years ago. Michelline died a couple of years later after moving to Florida. Their daughter has been on the editorial staff of the *New York Times*.

Also in 1976 I was asked to be a member of the professional advisory board for Commercial Credit Corp., which in 1978 was purchased by Control Data Corp. I was asked to continue on the board at Control Data, located in Minneapolis. I did so until 1982. It was obvious to us on the advisory board that the founder and chairman of Control Data—who had done a brilliant job of building the company—was not accepting any advice in his older years and had proceeded to make some bad business decisions. When it was obvious that all advice was being ignored, I resigned from the board, as did Monty DuVal and a number of others. Control Data went bankrupt a short time later, resulting in thousands of employees losing their jobs. I have never forgotten what I learned from that. Years later, when I served on the board of Science Applications International Corporation, I used that experience to help save the jobs there.

In 1971 I was asked to be a member of the board of trustees of the Cleveland Clinic, as I mentioned previously. I convinced the clinic to self-insure, thus saving it millions of dollars over the next decade. The board was a very distinguished one. Once it had to decide a dispute between a famous heart surgeon and the king of Saudi Arabia, who had surgery at the clinic and was charged what he considered an exorbitant amount of money. The board agreed with the king, and as a result, the surgeon resigned. I finally had to leave the board in 1987 because of a conflict of interest in my new job at American Healthcare Systems.

I was also asked in 1977 to serve on the board of Albany Medical School, which later became the Albany Medical Center when it was combined with the hospital in 1983. At that time, I became a trustee and served as a member of the finance and professional affairs committee. Dr. Friedlander, the dean of the medical school, was appointed to a higher position in Union University, and I was asked to be on the search committee to find a new president of the center, which was just coming into its own in the top ranks of medical schools. We recruited Dr. Richard Gaintner, who was from Johns Hopkins. Dick turned out to be an absolutely superb president. He had a brilliant career in medicine and retired to Florida, where he died a few years ago of pancreatic cancer. I had left as trustee in 1986, but I saw him yearly at the Society of Medical Administrators meetings and considered him one of my lifetime friends.

In 1980 Ilana Vered, the world-famous Israeli pianist and wife of one of my staff physicians, asked me to serve on the advisory board of Artists Against Hunger. This made me aware of a major effort by many different groups to help solve world hunger problems.

The same year I was asked by the White House to serve on the executive committee of the White House Mini-Conference on Aging, to be held in New York. It was an interesting experience and led to later meetings I held with Sen. John Heinz of Pennsylvania, the Senate chairman of the Committee on Aging.

One of the more interesting experiences of my career occurred after Sterling Drug agreed to finance a system for the hearing impaired at the Circle in the Square Theater in New York. Paul Libin, managing director, and Ted Mann, artistic director, asked me to join the board of directors. Also serving on the board at the time were George C. Scott, Colleen Dewhurst, and Dustin Hoffman. Colleen Dewhurst was married to George C. Scott, but they later divorced. The theater staged many productions by Eugene O'Neill and August Strindberg. On one occasion they decided to have a fundraising gala with excerpts from O'Neill and Strindberg plays spoken by famous actors and actresses. Since Strindberg is Swedish, we invited the king and queen of Sweden. To our delight, they accepted the invitation. I remember one very compelling performance that evening by James Earl Jones. Before the performance, the board held a dinner for the king and queen. It was my first occasion to meet royalty. I later saw them again in Stockholm when my wife and I attended the Nobel Prize ceremonies. Later I also joined James Earl Jones as an elected member of the Horatio Alger Association.

Also while in New York, I served on the board of directors of Magnetic Resonance Corp. and Medical Magnetics Corp. for four years.

In 1986 Rep. Paul Rogers of Florida asked me to become a founding member of the board of directors of the Friends of the National Library of Medicine. There I met Tenley Albright, the 1956 Olympic ice-skating gold medalist and a member of the President's Council on Physical Fitness. Tenley was also a professor of orthopedics at Harvard. I had previously worked with her husband, Jerry Blakely, in raising money for George

Bush and Ronald Reagan. Jerry built the Ritz Hotel at Laguna Niguel in California.

The National Library of Medicine is probably the largest repository of medical literature anywhere in the world. It is basically the last resort for any American physician wanting to research some medical problem.

My longest service was for twenty-one years on the board of trustees of the Dickinson School of Law, beginning in June 1973 and including eighteen years as a member of the executive committee. I became an emeritus trustee in 1994 and finally resigned in 1998 after Dickinson merged with Pennsylvania State University and was no longer an independent law school.

Dale Shughart was the longtime chairman of the board of trustees and was also the presiding judge of Cumberland County, Pennsylvania. He and his wife, Mary Ann, almost "adopted" me into their family. We worked on many projects together to improve the School of Law.

During the time I served on the board, I also acted as an adjunct professor and held a seminar on legal medicine at least once a year for the entire twenty-one years.

By 1978 I was a senior vice president of Sterling Drug and a member of the board of directors. I became a member of the management committee and was also elected to the executive committee of the board in January 1983. All of these jobs could not have been accomplished without the aid of my secretary, Lily Borland, and my direct reports who managed other groups of the corporation for which I was ultimately responsible.

In addition, each year I was asked as a member of the board to accept responsibility for our businesses on a different continent of the world. I traveled all through Africa, Asia, Europe, and South America to review the business plans of the various countries' affiliates that were part of our worldwide organization. This also put me in contact with many government officials and famous individuals in different countries. For example, when I visited Dijon, France, I attended a reception given by the mayor because we had a large number of employees there. This was true for other countries as well. When I visited the Philippines, our medical director was the uncle of Imelda Marcos, wife of the president. As a result, I was able to meet her and to see the inside of the president's palace.

One of the scariest episodes was in Africa. I remember landing in Gabon and seeing soldiers surrounding the airplane. Soldiers boarded to escort us inside the arrivals building. I'd never experienced this before. Fortunately, nothing untoward happened.

On one of my visits to South Africa, I brought the family over to meet me in Nairobi, Kenya, for a safari. We had a great time. One night when we were in our tents out in the middle of the Serengeti, a noise outside awakened us. Curious, we peeked out the slit in the tent to see a lion not ten feet away.

We saw many animals in the wild. We happened to be in the Serengeti during the great migration of wildebeests; literally a half-million of them stretched as far as the eye could see.

On our way back to Nairobi we stopped at the Ngorongoro Crater. When it was time for lunch, we were surprised that all the guides moved under a car or under shelter. We were not aware that "dive-bombing birds" would swoop down and take your sandwich right out of your hand. We learned by experience.

While we were on our way home, Idi Amin of Uganda was acting up and expelling all the Indians from his country. Our commercial plane was diverted to Kampala, Uganda, to pick up some of the Indians expelled by the dictator. It was an extremely frightening situation. The pilot told us to hide all our jewelry in our shoes or elsewhere before the soldiers came on board. They were quite menacing but did not ask us to do anything. We sat as quietly as we could during the ordeal, but

I was quite anxious because we had our two young boys with us. The Indians boarded carrying everything they owned that they could carry. I was afraid the plane would never get off the ground. It did, but on the way back we ran low on fuel and had to stop in Athens before proceeding to Belgium, where we all disembarked.

Another scary moment was during my trip to Argentina when our branch office in that country reported to me. Argentina had recently completed the Falklands War with England. When I left the plane, our country manager met me with a car and a guard who carried a submachine gun. I was informed that I should not open the window because when the car stopped for a red light, a robber might cut off my finger just to get my ring. Later during the visit we shopped at a large department store, where one of the Argentinians obviously mistook me for a Brit and started shouting at the top of her voice. We had to leave fast to prevent a major scene from occurring.

We also had armed guards the whole time I was in Colombia because of the kidnappings happening in South America at the time. One of our neighbors from New Canaan who worked for an oil company was kidnapped during that period of time and held for ransom. Nobody ever said that having overseas responsibility was the safest job in the world.

At the time, we were doling out large sums of money from SterlPac, and I was getting calls from all over the U.S. to donate to different candidates. One of my frequent callers was Strom Thurmond, who was president of the Senate. Strom and I became very good telephone mates.

He would call and say, "Now, Monroe, we have this very fine candidate out in Timbuktu who is going to help us with our Republican majority if you can find some money to help him win the election."

Once he called to ask if we could supply a particular drug

for his chief of staff who had a chronic bowel problem. The Food and Drug Administration had asked us to remove the product from the marketplace for lack of efficacy, and since sales were negligible we had agreed. However, the product obviously did help some people. Because the product had been removed from the market, we could not supply it to Strom's employee without FDA approval. I told Senator Thurmond that if he could get the approval we would make a special run just for his chief of staff. I really didn't think he would ever get approval, but he did. We then made the drug once a year for his aide. This obviously cost a lot of money because we had to clean the production lines before and after making each batch–but it was good PR.

Others to whom we gave political action committee money were Reps. Don Sundquist and John Duncan and Sen. Howard Baker from Tennessee. Sen. Orrin Hatch also received our aid. He became a friend and supporter. Later we hired his chief of staff, Dr. David Sundwall, to work for us at American Healthcare Systems.

During this time I became involved in the election campaign of a friend of my good friend Bernie Goldstein. His name was Mike Roth, and he was running for attorney general of the state of New York. Mike had his own law firm in New York and was married to a delightful European. Unfortunately, he lost the election. Many of the senators and congressmen I got to know became important in a later episode in my life.

In 1985 when the position of secretary of Health and Human Services became open, a list of forty-some names was published in the newspapers for the position. My name was on that list, and I began receiving phone calls from all over the country offering me support and encouragement. I was first interviewed by a low-ranking official in the White House. Over many weeks I was called to the White House for different levels of interviews. As the process wore on, many members of Congress asked me to meet with them to discuss my views on healthcare. I remember vividly one meeting with Newt Gingrich of Georgia and Vin Weber of Minnesota, who were both congressmen at the time and hence had no vote in the confirmation but obviously had influence in the White House. Newt later became speaker of the House and an expert on healthcare. I also had several meetings with Orrin Hatch, with my own senators at the time, and many other well-known politicians who wanted to know my views. With my background of teaching both in medical and law schools, of serving on Nixon's Malpractice Commission and Sen. Kennedy's Drug Surveillance Commission, and also having worked with the National Institutes of Health, Centers for Disease Control, Food and Drug Administration, and Institute of Medicine, I was quite familiar with the workings of Health and Human Services (HHS). In addition, Drs. Roger Egeberg and Monty DuVal really gave me a good immersion on what goes on and what is important inside HHS.

In the meantime, the press was badgering me to make statements and also to indicate what I thought my chances were. I avoided them, but it did not stop them from speculating on what was happening. The atmosphere became extremely tense as the candidates were whittled down to the final five. I was making trips to Washington to meet with all sorts of people during those hectic weeks, and it was really wearing me down. I was also hit hard by some of the sensationalist reporting in the newspapers. One newspaper reported that I was almost indicted on some criminal wrongdoing by the FDA. At first I did not respond because it was totally untrue, and I was not even involved in the incident reported. I did not want to give any credence by responding, but finally it got out of hand. I called the editor and gave him all the facts. He apologized but said if I had responded earlier all of this would not have happened. I reminded him that all of this would not have happened if he had not published a falsehood.

Even a letter of apology didn't convince my younger son. He did not want me to be secretary of Health and Human Services.

"Dad, I don't want to read about you in the papers every day with people saying nasty things that aren't true." What a sad commentary on our political situation.

Finally Donald Regan, the president's chief of staff, interviewed the five finalists. I vividly remember walking into his office in the White House. I had read many stories about him and his ego and that he believed all the agency secretaries basically worked for him. His desk where he was sitting was on the left, and on the right was a large sitting area with a couple of low chairs, a low sofa, and one very high chair.

He was fiddling with something at his desk and said, "Go have a seat."

I quickly sized up the situation and realized I should sit in one of the lowest chairs in the area. I was right because when he came over to talk to me he sat in the high chair.

Actually we got along famously because he was quite proud of his service in the Marine Corps. He also came from a poor family. When we talked about our respective backgrounds, we had a lot in common. The interview was supposed to last twenty minutes but lasted more than an hour. When it was over, I said to him that the process had been very wearing on me and my entire family, and I was wondering where it would go next.

As I remember, this was a Thursday afternoon. He said he planned to recommend two people, of whom I was one, to the president. The president would make the choice. As it happened, the other person was Dr. Otis Bowen, who was not only a physician but also the Republican governor of Indiana.

I did not get the job. Mr. Regan said I would be called at 8 o'clock Monday morning, and the nominee would be asked to be at a press conference with the president at noon. Sure enough, I did receive the phone call–only to be told that Dr. Bowen had been selected to be the secretary of HHS, and it would be announced at noon.

On November 8, 1985, I wrote to Mr. Regan and told him Mr. Tuttle had called me and informed me of the president's decision. I wanted him to know I supported that selection and would be happy to work with the administration in any way I could. I also mentioned I would write to Dr. Bowen to congratulate him and give him my best wishes for his success. Finally, I told him I had enjoyed chatting with him about our mutual personal situations.

I also received hundreds of letters from people all over the U.S. saying they had supported my candidacy and were sorry I did not get the job. Sen. Hatch was one of my major support-ers, and I know he had written and called the president on my behalf. During the process I also had some meetings with Vice President Bush, and Barbara asked me to keep her informed of what was happening, which I did.

I became aware that several others had supported my candidacy, including Rep. John Rowland of Connecticut; Rep. Margaret Roukema, Sen. Arlen Specter, and former Sen. Richard Schweicker of Pennsylvania; Rep. Louis Stokes of Ohio; Rep. Gerald Solomon of New York; Sens. Mack Mattingly and Sam Nunn of Georgia; Sen. Jake Garn of Utah; and Reps. Vin Weber of Minnesota and Tom Blyly of Virginia. I was also supported by many judges and heads of organiza-tions throughout the United States.

Some of the others who supported me for the position were the presidents of Morehouse School of Medicine, Tuskegee Institute, Meharry Medical School, Drew School of Medicine, National Urban League, National Medical Association, and Black Social Workers. I had the support of the American Medical Association, Federation of American Hospitals, Proprietary

Association, the food industry, and the insurance industry. The presidents of Dickinson School of Law, Cleveland Clinic, and Albany Medical School and the chairmen of the boards of major corporations, including Equitable Life Insurance, Bristol-Myers, Hershey Foods, and First Boston all sent letters of support.

Dr. Bowen was an extremely gracious individual, and knowing that I was the other candidate, he invited me to Washington to discuss the healthcare situation in the United States with him. I accepted his invitation, and we spent a full day talking about many of the problems in healthcare.

One of the big problems at the time was the AIDS epidemic. He said he was going to start a major program to develop an AIDS vaccine because he believed that was the only way to achieve a quick solution to the problem. It was one of the major points with which I disagreed. I was very aware of the virus family that caused AIDS and also aware that the virus could change its character very quickly. I told him I didn't think a vaccine program would be successful. Twenty-two years later we still do not have an AIDS vaccine.

However, Dr. Bowen kept in touch and sought my advice on several occasions. In 1988 he even sent my nomination to the White House to be on the new AIDS Commission. I received a copy of his letter to the president, along with a letter from Gary Bauer acknowledging my nomination. However, I was not selected for that commission.

Later Dr. Sam Thier, head of the Institute of Medicine, asked if I would help deliver the institute's position paper on AIDS to President George Bush. I agreed to do so, and wrote to Barbara Bush saying it was extremely important that the president read this paper. I received a handwritten reply from her saying she had read the paper with great interest and that her husband also had read it. After that, the White House began paying more attention to the AIDS problem

AmHS ®
American Healthcare Systems

The National Network of Premier Health Systems   San Diego • Washington, DC

Monroe E. Trout, M.D.
Chairman of the Board,
President and CEO

December 14, 1988

VIA FEDERAL EXPRESS

Mrs. George Bush
The Vice President's House
34th at Massachusetts Avenue
Washington, D.C.   20501

Dear Barbara:

I would not bother you at this very busy time of your life unless it was a matter of great importance. Sam Thier, President of the Institute of Medicine, asked me if I would help to get a paper read by George. Since the subject is one which will claim the lives of over 200,000 young Americans in the next four years and cost the government over $10 billion a year, I agreed with Sam that it was a matter which the next President of the United States should focus on. I hope that George will find a few minutes to read the attached from Sam Thier and Frank Press. I have read the paper, myself, and agree with the general gist of it. You might even want to read it, yourself, even though it is not the most pleasant of subjects.

Sandy and I wish you and your family a very happy holiday and a very healthful 1989.

Sincerely,

Monroe E. Trout

MET/amw

Enclosure

1205 Prospect • Suite 520 • San Diego, California 92037 • 619 456-2811

Letter to Barbara Bush about a paper on the AIDS epidemic.

BARBARA BUSH

December 19, 1988

Dear Monroe,

Thank you for your nice letter.
You were so kind to be in touch, and
I am happy to share Sam Thier's paper
with George.

We send our best wishes to you
and Sandy for a wonderful holiday
season,

Warmly,

Barbara

Thanks. Pal! I am
reading away. It isn't
the greatest happiest
subject, but very important.

Barbara Bush's note in reply.

INSTITUTE OF MEDICINE

NATIONAL ACADEMY OF SCIENCES

2101 CONSTITUTION AVENUE   WASHINGTON, D.C. 20418

SAMUEL O. THIER
PRESIDENT

December 23, 1988

PERSONAL AND CONFIDENTIAL

Monroe E. Trout, M.D.
Chairman of the Board
President and Chief Executive Officer
American Healthcare Systems
1205 Prospect
Suite 520
San Diego, California 92037

Dear Monroe:

Many thanks for your prompt and effective help in transmitting our AIDS white paper to the President-Elect. Frank Press and I are very appreciative. We thought you might also like to see the white papers we provided on Science and Technology Advice in the White House and on Federal Science and Technology Budget Priorities. The former paper was sent by Ed Vetter to Governor Sununu and the latter will be presented to Richard Darman the first week in January at a meeting arranged by Senator Domenici.

I'm also enclosing a list of potental candidates for the posititon of White House Science Advisor. Frank Press has provided these names to Peter O'Donnell. As you suggested the AIDS white paper and supporting documents have been sent to Lou Sullivan.

Again, thank you for all of your help.

With best wishes for the holidays,

Sincerely,

Samuel O. Thier, M.D.

Enclosures

Letter from Sam Thier about his AIDS white paper.

and appropriating research money through the National Institutes of Health.

On one of my trips to Washington during the interview process, I sat next to John Gavin, who was the U.S. ambassador to Mexico. He had been a famous actor and was a good friend of Ronald Reagan. He asked me the nature of my business in Washington, and I told him I was being considered to be secretary of Health and Human Services. We immediately hit it off, and I received a nice letter from him sent from the Mexican Embassy.

In 1988 after George Bush was elected president, I again was mentioned as a possible Health and Human Services secretary. This time, since the Bushes knew me well, I decided not to repeat the ordeal I had gone through in 1985. Dr. Sullivan, head of Morehouse School of Medicine, was named secretary of HHS. In the 1992 election, Bush asked me to co-chair his National Healthcare Coalition along with Sen. Bill Frist and to be one of his healthcare spokesmen. I agreed to do so and made several speeches on his behalf and appeared on radio and TV to discuss his views on healthcare. I also helped raise money for the campaign.

This was one of the most interesting episodes of my life, but probably the most exhausting. I would not wish it on anyone.

Chapter 16

Second Career:
San Diego

The time was fast approaching for Dr. Wescoe to retire. He had been CEO of Sterling Drug for more than a decade. As a result of his plan to depart, there was some tense competition to succeed him among the three senior officers: Jim Luther, the general counsel and, of the three of us, the longest-serving employee of Sterling Drug; Jack Pietruski, marketing vice president brought in from the outside; and me.

Jim considered me competition from the first day I arrived at Sterling, I think in large part because I had a law degree. Early on, we agreed I would not interfere in his legal department if he did not interfere in medical research or other medical affairs. Nonetheless, our relationship was not a good one, and every issue became a competition. Since most of the major problems facing Sterling during my tenure were in the medical field, this gave me widespread exposure in the press and on TV. Dr. Wescoe had obviously made up his mind as to his successor. He did ask all of us to write a white paper outlining our thoughts on the future of the company.

After this, he recommended that Jack Pietruski, the newest employee of the three of us, be named his successor. I was very disappointed because I thought that overall I knew more about the company than the other two.

Then I thought Pietruski surely would appoint either Jim or me as president. But instead he went to the outside and hired an individual who had an alcohol problem. After several clashes with the new president, I decided to leave. I could retire at fifty-five, the earliest time allowed under our pension plan. The insult of hiring such a person as the new president was too much to bear. He didn't last long because others became aware of his problem, but I had already retired by then.

Since we owned homes in New Canaan, Connecticut, and South Penobscot, Maine, and a condo in Gulf Shores, Alabama, we had many options for a pleasant, fulfilling retirement.

However, when I was approached to become CEO of a major hospital group in La Jolla, California, my wife urged me to accept by convincing me that I was too young to retire. "For better or worse but not for lunch," as they say. My good friend Monty DuVal had suggested me for the job and had called me and asked me to accept. The position was chairman and CEO of American Healthcare Systems (AmHS), an organization owned by hospitals of various religious denominations. I met with the search committee and was fascinated by some of the things they were doing and their plans for the future. Furthermore, I developed a very good relationship with the chairman of the search committee, who was head of a large hospital system in Los Angeles. Sam Tibbitts was very gruff, but I got on well with him. Healthcare was at a crisis, and I thought that even though I was not selected to be secretary of Health and Human Services, I could have more influence on healthcare policy in that job. So I accepted and agreed to report after taking a long vacation in New Zealand to celebrate our twenty-fifth wedding anniversary.

We had an absolutely great three weeks in New Zealand driving around both islands. Of all the places I have been, it is probably the most beautiful and has the most unusual terrain in the world.

I remember getting lost and stopping at a sheep farm, a common sight in New Zealand. The New Zealanders were extremely friendly and invited us into their home. Even though it was only 9:30 in the morning, they invited us to stay for lunch because they were so eager to hear what was going on in the outside world.

Later we picked up a student hitchhiking to Milford Sound. After we drove through a tunnel and down the mountain, we reached this beautiful, natural fiord. The young man thanked us for the ride, and we checked into the only hotel. While we were having dinner, we looked out at the glorious view of water and mountains and saw our hitchhiker setting up his tent on the shores of Milford Sound. He had the better view. He was on the same boat we were on the next day and asked if he could be a passenger to our next stop. We agreed.

On another excursion to explore some bat caves, we met two physicians from New Zealand. They were extremely friendly. They asked us if we would give them a ride to the airport, where their private plane was parked. On the way they offered to show us New Zealand by air. Being young and reckless, we said yes. The next day we had the most beautiful tour anyone could ever have of the two islands. However, there were some hairy moments when the plane flew low over one of the glaciers and into some of the valleys to get a closer look at the scenery.

It turned out to be probably the best vacation we had ever had.

Upon returning, we had two houses and one condo to sell. Also, we had to pack up to move to Rancho Santa Fe in California.

Of course, we sold our house in New Canaan. But we decided to keep the condo in Alabama, thinking we would use it because we liked the white, sandy beaches and wild dunes.

In San Diego, we found the beaches to be quite comparable, so we never returned to Alabama. We decided to rent the condo, which was a problem from day one. Several months after we purchased the condo, a hurricane hit and took off the roof. We had to replace furniture, carpeting, and more. We also learned that renting was not a good idea either. I can't believe all the things that happened. Once the rental agency told us we had to replace the bathtub because somebody put a hole in it. Knickknacks and other small items regularly disappeared. So we decided to sell our condo.

Even though we had built our house in Maine and loved it, we decided to sell it also. We had a caretaker but also had a great deal of money in the place and thought it was too far from California to maintain. We called in a group of real estate agents, and after they gave their valuations, we tacked on a handsome premium to the highest estimate. The agents were aghast. All but one refused to try to sell it. The one who did put an ad in the *New York Times*, and the house sold within a week.

We had found a house in Fairbanks Ranch, basically a new area of Rancho Santa Fe. The cost of houses was higher in the San Diego area than in Connecticut. The neighbors were not very friendly, and no one welcomed us to the neighborhood. Since I was the new CEO of what was to become the second-largest business in San Diego, we were quickly admitted to the Fairbanks Ranch Country Club. We made many friends through the club, volunteer activities, and my business associations.

When I first entered the offices of American Healthcare Systems in October 1986, my assigned secretary asked if I had come to close the company. I was astonished. I told her I hadn't moved across the country to shut a company down. After several meetings with the chief operating officer and chief financial officer, it became obvious to me that the company was on the verge of bankruptcy. We were not self-sustaining and had to rely on dues paid by the individual hospitals. The hospitals were beginning to balk because they saw no advantages coming from the company.

The first item of business was to change the culture of the company. Two unbusinesslike practices I noticed immediately were the casual clothing everyone wore and the nonchalant lateness to scheduled meetings. I mandated that all males must wear a coat and tie and all females must dress demurely. The next day one secretary wore her "Daisy Mae" outfit, and I sent her home to change. When meetings were called, I locked the doors to the rooms at the appointed time and latecomers could not get in. This quickly changed the culture to a more businesslike atmosphere and the productivity increased.

We took a hard look at everything the company was doing, and soon realized the big bleeder was a health maintenance organization (HMO) being operated at a tremendous loss. I went to the board and recommended we close the HMO. This did not sit well with the board members because of the amount of money they had already spent keeping it afloat. However, it turned out to be a lifesaving move for the company.

A major purpose of the company was to purchase goods and services for all the hospitals in the consortium. However, the hospitals only randomly complied with the purchasing contracts, which created problems with the suppliers. I decided to change the system. I thought that individual companies would be willing to pay a percentage fee if we could guarantee our hospitals would buy under their contracts. We also needed to reduce the number of contracts to a manageable level.

I took my idea around to the major hospital suppliers and pharmaceutical companies that accounted for the bulk of purchasing by the hospital. The CEO of one of the companies I had previously worked for basically kicked me out of his office. Another said, "Why should I do business with you when we

Congressional Record

United States
of America

PROCEEDINGS AND DEBATES OF THE 103^d CONGRESS, SECOND SESSION

| Vol. 140 | WASHINGTON, MONDAY, OCTOBER 3, 1994 | No. 141 |

House of Representatives

October 3, 1994   CONGRESSIONAL RECORD— *Extensions of Remarks*   E 2031

TRIBUTE TO MONROE E. TROUT,
M.D., J.D.

HON. GEORGE W. GEKAS

OF PENNSYLVANIA

IN THE HOUSE OF REPRESENTATIVES

Monday, October 3, 1994

Mr. GEKAS. Mr. Speaker, I would like the Congress to pay special tribute today to Monroe E. Trout, M.D., J.D., an outstanding American. Although he is retiring as chairman of the board, president and chief executive officer of American Healthcare Systems [AmHS], I hope that our recognition of his career will encourage his continued participation in the nation's health affairs and will inspire young people to pursue similar interests.

I rise to this occasion not only because I am well familiar with Dr. Trout's success as an adult, but also because he and I spent our childhood in the same city of Harrisburg and in the same neighborhood of that wonderful city. We grew up together, played together, and together developed our commitment to values and achievement that have led Monroe to the status of the renowned.

Dr. Trout's history reads like an American odyssey. One of 13 children, he worked his way through school with the goal of becoming a private practitioner of medicine. An exceptional student, he received scholarships, and in 1957 graduated from the University of Pennsylvania Medical School. His career has spanned more than four decades, beginning with a medical residency at Portsmouth Naval Hospital and appointment as a regimental surgeon in the U.S. Navy. Subsequently, Dr. Trout served as chief of the EKG and medical department at Harrisburg State Hospital and as a lecturer in legal medicine at the Dickinson School of Law, where he later earned his law degree.

As a physician and an attorney, Dr. Trout has made notable contributions to the American health care system. He has been praised by the medical and business communities, the health care industry, and educational institutions on the local, regional, national, and international levels. In 1964, Dr. Trout left the private practice of medicine to work in the pharmaceutical industry, where he held leadership positions. He believed that through participation in major pharmaceutical research efforts he could contribute to the well-being of many more individuals.

In recent years, Dr. Trout has extended his scope of activity through his leadership of AmHS, one the Nation's largest multihospital system alliances which has as its central goal the increased effectiveness of hospital systems. AmHS develops outstanding services and products at the lowest cost, consistent with high quality. The result has been a contribution to affordable health care for an ever-increasing number of consumers.

As chief executive officer of AmHS, Dr. Trout has played a prominent role in health care reform, working with hospital systems and their officials in developing patients first, a comprehensive proposal to restructure the American health care delivery system. Patients first was the basis for the American Consumers' Health Care Reform Act which I introduced in 1993. Many of the ideas in patients first were also incorporated in other major health care reform bills.

Consistent with his interest in improving the Nation's health care system, Dr. Trout has spearheaded the creation of an annual award—the AmHS Cares Award—which honors innovative programs nationality that improve access to health care for the medically underserved.

An advocate of bipartisan approaches to health care reform, Dr. Trout has met with many Members of Congress, both Republicans and Democrats, to urge market-based community reform that would benefit a majority of Americans. He believes that forces in the health care marketplace can provide the best answers to control over health care costs. He served on the Health Issues Task Force in the 1988 Bush Presidential campaign and on the National Healthcare Coalition for Bush for President in 1992, as well as many other advisory bodies, in both the private and public sectors.

Philanthropy is high on Dr. Trout's agenda. He sits on numerous boards and committees, including the Youth Access to Alcohol Policy Panel. He has served as cochair of the San Diego County Commission on Health Care Reforms and is on the board of the Leon Williams Foundation, a San Diego organization formed to help youths to live constructively and contribute to the American dream of a society based on equality and justice.

Dr. Trout believes strongly in supporting the education of health care providers who will serve generations to come. Through contacts in the biomedical community, he has been instrumental in providing scholarships to worthy students. He has personally funded scholarships at two universities and endowed a chair in pharmacology at the University of California, San Diego. In addition, he is chairman of the board of trustees of the University of California Foundation, San Diego, and serves on the University's California business-higher education forum board and its Connect Steering Committee.

Mr. Speaker, on the occasion of his retirement from AmHS, Monroe Trout is deserving of special public recognition of his many accomplishments and service to American medicine and to our Nation's health care system. Today, I take great pleasure in saluting his outstanding contributions.

Recognition, upon my retirement, of my career at American Healthcare
Systems.

have 80 percent of the market in your hospitals?" The company most receptive to the idea was Baxter International.

As a matter of fact, CEO Vern Loucks not only thought it was a great idea, but agreed to advance a half-million dollars to start the program. He did emphasize, however, it would be absolutely necessary for our hospitals to comply with the contracts. Not only were we asking the companies to reduce their prices for bulk purchases, but also to pay American Healthcare Systems 3 percent of all purchases as a fee for ensuring compliance with the contract. If the hospitals didn't comply, we would not get the fees.

We knew some of the products would be at full price, but overall there would be a marked reduction in pricing. We established a reward-and-punishment system for the hospitals depending on their compliance. In the first year, we were able to turn American Healthcare Systems totally around and make it self-sufficient.

The first couple of years were difficult, but ours became one of the most successful programs ever initiated in the hospital arena in the U.S. The company that threw me out quickly wanted to return to the table, and the company that said it had 80 percent of our business saw its share dwindle considerably. The new CEO visited me in California. His name was Bill Longfield, and we have been super friends ever since. Later I served on a board with him at the West Company, and also brought him on to the Cytyc board when I was chair.

Since American Healthcare Systems had become self-sufficient with money in the bank, we were able to eliminate all the dues being paid by the individual hospitals, which made their CEOs extremely happy. We also had capital to start other programs. Some of these programs were in the insurance arena. Bill Nydam was instrumental in starting five insurance companies, all of which were extremely successful. We hired Jim Jordan, an expert insurance executive, to run them.

Invocation for Dr. Trout... Let us, for a few moments, place ourselves in the presence of God, our creator.

God, we know you have made each one of us unique and in your image.— Tonight, we honor one of your special creations, Monroe Trout. Tonight, each of us brings our own personal memories of what it has meant to be a professional colleague and friend of this fine man.

I come Lord, remembering Monroe in many fond ways. I appreciate his clear vision and his strong, ethical leadership— his gifts of administration and sound financial management. We are especially grateful Lord, for his ability to attract and retain an outstanding Executive Team — a team that is ably carrying on the work of the organization during this time of transition. I have experienced and admire his wonderful ability to bring the warmth of his person to this responsible position. His management team is generous in their expressions of respect for him. He was there as needed — as boss and as friend.

Father, I know his leadership is not limited to AMHS. Communities of the city of San Diego have been the recipient of his enthusiastic involvement in civic and voluntary efforts. His many awards speak to his talent and generosity. And it is my privilege to know, that many persons — single parents and others— have experienced His compassion and support.

So tonight Lord, we ask you to abundantly bless your special creation, Monroe Trout. We are grateful to have shared and benefited from the personal and professional gifts he brought to AMHS, and we look forward to a wonderful evening that is an expression of appreciation and love for Monroe. May all we are now ready to enjoy — the food, the drink, and the conversation we share — may all these good gifts please you God and bring pleasure to Monroe, Sandy, and to each of us.

Amen

A prayer written by AmHS board member, Sister Monica Heeran, for my retirement dinner.

Jim hired Fritz Heirick and Frank Heckman to manage the risk aspects of each company. In the meantime Jack Bernard, vice president of marketing, did a superb job in increasing our shareholder base of hospitals, and Lynn Detlor, president of Purchasing Partners Inc., deftly managed to continuously reduce the costs from our suppliers.

We also used our cash to start two venture capital funds run by outside experts Rick Blume and Kinny Johnson. In addition, we started an internal new business development group headed by Bruce Kaechel and ably assisted by Mike Miyagi. This group found small companies with innovative products that improved patient care and reduced costs. We invested in many of them to encourage innovation, and it paid off in huge financial gains for AmHS. We also spun off the joint-venture HMO with Provident Insurance Company in Tennessee and Transamerica in Los Angeles. Over nine years we built a company worth over $4.5 billion (as valued by independent appraisers) and had over $200 million in cash in the bank. The company was a private, for-profit company owned by forty non-profit hospital systems. The major religious groups in the country owned these hospital systems. The only place you could get a Catholic nun to agree with a real Southern Baptist was on my board of directors. Sister Monica Heeran always reminded me, "No money, no mission." She was very happy with our performance and wrote a beautiful prayer for my retirement dinner.

Later Bill Nydam, my chief financial officer, became the chief operating officer. When I retired, Bill was the acting CEO and my choice for permanent CEO, but the board decided to hire an outsider. Bill had more ideas to grow the business than Carter had liver pills. He was extremely innovative and was full of energy to get the job done. We would not have been successful without him and the team he gathered to fulfill our mission.

In early 1988, as so often happens when management changes, Sterling Drug became a target for a hostile takeover. Jack Pietruski could not withstand the hostile offer from Hoffmann-La Roche. Kodak, a "white knight," bought Sterling Drug. However, Sterling was not a good fit since it was outside Kodak's realm of expertise. Pietruski left Sterling soon thereafter and began his own consulting firm. Who knows what would have happened if either Jim Luther or I had become the CEO?

Since American Healthcare Systems was buying a lot of X-ray film from Kodak, the CEO of Kodak invited me to visit with him in Rochester, New York. One of the topics of conversation was Sterling's research program, which I once headed. I already knew all the good research people had left Sterling because Kodak had put in charge someone with little awareness of pharmaceutical research. As a matter of fact, he disrupted the entire research program by deciding to abandon the research facilities in Rensselaer and start with a new facility built outside Philadelphia. This was a terrible mistake. Kodak could not make a success of the business and had to split it up and sell it.

Fortunately for me, I had not sold any of the shares of Sterling I had bought on the open market, received as bonuses or purchased from stock option programs. Kodak bought the company for $89.50 per share. With this money and my savings, I invested in thirteen start-up companies in the medical field, some of which became quite successful. Some of the companies I personally invested in were Somatogen, Criticare, Cytyc, BioTransplant, Cytran, and CompuCyte. Criticare and BioTransplant are public companies. Somatogen was later purchased by Baxter. CompuCyte is still a private company operating in the Boston area, and Cytran failed.

When I finally retired, AmHS was returning to each hospital system in the consortium over $1 million a year in dividends.

In 1987 I became very concerned about the future of health-care in the U.S. and started writing papers on this subject. It was so important to me in my capacity as CEO of AmHS that I appointed a national commission to examine the subject of affordable healthcare for all. I served on this commission, which published a report entitled "Patients First." This was delivered to Congress, and several bills based on our report were introduced, including one by Rep. Jim Cooper of Tennessee and one by Rep. George Gekas of Pennsylvania. The report was also given to Vice President George Bush as possible material for his campaign in 1988. The report was well received by the "Blue Dog Democrats" in the House of Representatives. As a result of the national publicity this report received, I was asked to meet with different members of Congress, appear on radio talk shows, and speak to groups throughout the country. The Prudential-Bache Group asked me to speak at a major conference it was holding.

While heading up American Healthcare Systems, I became deeply involved with the University of California, San Diego (UCSD). Shortly after I arrived, the chancellor of the university, Richard Atkinson, invited me to have lunch. He asked me to become a member of Chancellors Associates, a group of citizens monetarily supporting the university and advising the chancellor on "town-gown" problems. The associates met several times a year at the chancellor's residence for a program, camaraderie, and good food and drink.

I was also actively involved with a program called CONNECT, developed by Bill Otterson, who was hired by a consortium of the university, the business community—especially the biotech industry—and the city government to foster new businesses in San Diego. It was hoped that new businesses would come from discoveries by professors at the university. For example, before CONNECT existed, Science Applications International Corp.

(SAIC) was started by Bob Beyster in his garage. In addition, Qualcom was started by Irwin Jacobs, an engineering professor. These companies are multibillion-dollar operations today. We wanted other companies nurtured by CONNECT to reach that status. Many of the biotech companies were begun with the help of CONNECT. The whole purpose was to place start-up companies in touch with angels for venture capital funds. Also, CONNECT fostered programs at the university on subjects that were important to the biotech and other industries. It was a very effective program created by one individual, a retired businessman who worked extremely hard to make it a go.

While I was at American Healthcare Systems, I was also asked to serve on the board of the St. Vincent de Paul Center for the Homeless. This center was founded by Father Joe Carroll, who was a charismatic and revered priest in the area. The center in the same year received an award from the Vatican and from the archbishop of Canterbury naming it the finest shelter for the homeless in the world. Father Joe asked me to serve on the board soon after I arrived in San Diego. I was reluctant to take on any additional work and at first turned him down.

However, he was quite persistent, until finally I said, "But Father Joe, you don't understand. I'm not even Catholic."

And his retort to me was, "And neither are the homeless."

With that we bonded, and I became a member of the executive committee of his board at the St. Vincent de Paul Center for the Homeless. I also was on the National Commission for the Homeless chaired by Susan Baker, wife of Secretary of State James Baker.

In the meantime I also served on the University of California, San Diego Medical Center Board, which was having a major problem financing its poison control center and emergency room. I was able to go out and convince enough people to provide funds for the poison control center as an insurance policy for their children or grandchildren who might get into trouble in the future. There was no other control center in all of San Diego. The medical school auxiliary group decided to hold fundraisers for the emergency room and came up with the idea of a gala dinner where they would honor an individual. It was entitled "An Evening with..." I was the first individual to be so honored. The fundraiser was successful enough to keep the emergency room in operation. It is still going strong.

As a result of my work with CONNECT, Dick Atkinson asked me to be a member of the board of the UCSD Foundation, helping raise money for the university. Then I was asked to be president of the foundation. Before I agreed to do so, I told Dick that my emphasis in fundraising would be in the endowed professorship area and seeking new money from alumni. Since the school was only about thirty years old, he didn't think there would be enough wealthy alumni to make a difference. He was also somewhat concerned about endowed professorships since I wanted to increase the number from forty-one to at least fifty during my two-year tenure as president. They had only secured forty-one endowed chairs in the entire existence of the school. He reluctantly agreed.

I used the angle of "living in perpetuity" to raise money for more endowed chairs. I convinced a number of people to endow chairs by telling them that buildings may be torn down and renamed. If they really wanted their names to live forever, they should endow a chair. I mentioned that Ben Franklin had endowed the first chair at the University of Pennsylvania, and it was still part of the school. This struck a chord, and we quickly surpassed my goal of fifty endowed chairs. I also realized that, if I was going to emphasize endowed chairs, I would have to endow one myself. Sandy and I decided to endow our own chair at UCSD in pharmacology, a field that had given me the expertise to be successful.

When I left San Diego in 1999, the university had more than seventy-five endowed chairs, including another in surgery endowed by me. Dr. A.R. Moosa, a fine surgeon and head of the department of surgery, asked if I could find money to endow a chair in surgery since none existed at that time. They wanted to keep a brilliant young researcher at UCSD. Since it was urgent to do so, I decided to endow the chair. Baxter, knowing that I was retiring from American Healthcare Systems, contributed to the chair in my honor. When my term as president was up, I was to be succeeded by Bob Beyster, the chairman and founder of SAIC. Because of business reasons, he was not able to take the presidency, and I was asked to continue serving until he could take over. I did so for another year.

While in California I also served on the board of overseers of the University of Pennsylvania Nursing School and as an associate member of the board of trustees of the University of Pennsylvania. In addition, I was on the panel of visitors of the School of Health Administration and Policy of Arizona State University. On a completely different subject, I served on the selection committee in 1993 for the most innovative new product by a San Diego company.

I was on the advisory board of *Modern Healthcare*, a weekly newsmagazine in the healthcare field. I was also vice chairman of the Children's Hospital of San Diego Dinner Committee in 1994. I chaired the committee to merge the UCSD Medical Center and the Scripps Hospitals. Unfortunately, this was a tremendous amount of work with no positive results. We had the same outcome in trying to merge the San Diego Children's Hospital with the UCSD Medical Center. However, in 2007 that merger finally did take place. In 1988 I was asked to become a member of the board of directors of the National Committee for Quality Healthcare in Washington, D.C. I served for three years.

I also served a four-year term on the governing council of the American Hospital Association's Section on Multi-Hospital Systems.

Chapter 17

Following in Horatio Alger's Footsteps

I n 1995 the Horatio Alger Association of Distinguished Americans elected me as a member. This prestigious organization honors the achievements of individuals in our society who have succeeded in spite of adversity. It also supports young people in pursuit of their dreams through higher education.

The "Horatio Alger Heroes" of today have achieved prominence in various fields thanks to hard work and dedication. They don't rest on their laurels but give financial support, time, and energy to launch the heroes of tomorrow on their own path to greatness.

The association, founded by Norman Vincent Peale in 1947, brings the generations together by bestowing the Horatio Alger Award each year and by providing more than $12 million annually in college scholarships.

Other members of the Horatio Alger Association have included Dwight Eisenhower and his brother Milton, Henry Kissinger, Justice Clarence Thomas, Sen. Charles Hagel of Nebraska, Don Shula of the Miami Dolphins, Jim Clayton, Ed McMahon, Tom Selleck, Lou Dobbs, Stan Musial, Roger

Staubach, and Dr. Peter Jannetta, chairman of the Department of Neurosurgery at the University of Pittsburgh and the originator of the Jannetta procedure for Tic Doloreaux. At one time, Knoxville, Tennessee, had three association members: Jim Clayton, Dave Thomas, founder of Wendy's restaurants, and me. This is truly remarkable for one medium-sized city since there are only about 250 living members of the association.

All have risen from adversity to success, and all have given back to their communities by marrying philanthropy with achievement.

While I'm honored to be in such good company, I find the greatest reward is helping to support Horatio Alger Scholars. These students across the United States and its territories have faced challenges and realize a college education is the avenue to a better future. A committee of Horatio Alger Association members selects the scholarship winners.

My induction was held in Washington, D.C., where I received a medal from Justice Clarence Thomas in the chambers of the Supreme Court. Peter Jannetta, a classmate of mine both in college and medical school at the University of Pennsylvania, presented me with a bust of Horatio Alger at the ceremonies held in the Warner Theater. The emcee was the comedian John Ritter. Ray Charles played the piano intermittently during the ceremonies. The entire production was staged by Don Johnson, the actor and producer. Later, at a banquet at the Ritz-Carlton where all of us were introduced, the Marine Corps Band played patriotic songs and Van Cliburn played the piano. It was truly a spectacular week.

I don't think I was out of school before I knew that many seemingly accidental acquaintances and strangers had a great impact on my life. Years later Dr. Dorothy Brown, a Horatio Alger Award winner, gave me a name for these people. She called them "strangers on the highway of life." Dr. Brown is now a retired professor of surgery at Meharry Medical College.

She was an African-American orphan raised in a white orphanage until she was thirteen years old. As a teenager she was reunited with her biological mother, only to suffer repeated beatings. She never knew her father. A year later she was pulled out of school and sent to Albany to work as a domestic. Against unbelievable odds, she worked her way through college and then medical school. Dr. Brown was driven by an unbreakable spirit and a dream and as she says, "With the help of many beautiful strangers I met on God's highway, my dream came true."

I was later asked to go on the board of directors of the association but declined for health reasons. During my first five years in the association, I was able to donate ten scholarships.

Politics and medicine have to mix. While at American Healthcare Systems, I made frequent visits to Washington to meet with different congressmen on healthcare subjects. Once I met with Dan Rostankowski, congressman from Illinois and chairman of one of the House's most powerful committees. We were discussing veterans' benefits, and I suggested to him that veterans would be far better off if they were allowed to be treated at their local hospitals where their families could visit and they could get better care. This was at a time when dead bodies were found on the campuses of some Veterans Affairs hospitals, and other episodes of poor care were being publicized. I also told Rep. Rostankowski I thought the government could save money by sending patients to private hospitals. He looked at me as though I were crazy and said if he were to do what I suggested he would have every veteran chasing him down the street. Little did he know at that time it would be little old ladies chasing him down the street for his ill-fated bill on healthcare for the elderly. He later lost his seat and went to prison for using government funds for his own purposes. Even today the V.A. medical system has not been fixed. A new

A poster ridiculing Hillary Clinton's healthcare plan.

presidential commission is looking into the atrocious care being given to our returning Iraqi war soldiers.

I also worked with Sen. John Heinz III and his staff on healthcare for the elderly. He was a bright and effective senator, and it is too bad that his life was cut short by an airplane accident.

While I was CEO at AmHS, the Clintons moved into the White House. One of the first orders of business was Hillary's healthcare plan. We offered to help, but she preferred Democrats on her team. She produced an abomination. I testified several times before Congress on the pitfalls of her plan.

I met on Capitol Hill with Rep. Newt Gingrich and Sen. Trent Lott and then several times later with Newt in New York and Washington. At the time Hillary was producing her healthcare plan, one of the more memorable meetings was held in September 1993 with Newt, then the House minority whip, and senior members of the company TASC. Nelson Broms, the former chairman of the Equitable Companies, was also in attendance. I was extremely impressed with Gingrich's incisiveness and knowledge of the healthcare arena. After he left Congress, he became deeply involved in healthcare policy.

I wrote a chapter for a book entitled *U.S. Health Care in Transition* by H. Holt and M. Leibovici, giving a critique of Hillary's entire bill. As a result, I was presented a poster highlighting the foibles of her bill.

I was frequently asked to give speeches critiquing her program all across the United States. Her healthcare plan went down to ignominious defeat in the Congress.

George Bush Sr. did not become involved in any debate about healthcare and had a minimal program of his own. We did present to him our commission's plan called "Patients First," and snippets of it were later used in the campaign. George Gekas, congressman from Pennsylvania and later head of the judiciary committee, introduced a healthcare plan with large parts taken from "Patients First." Unfortunately this bill, Rep. Jim Cooper's bill, and several others never saw the light of day. Perhaps some parts of the plan will be resurrected in the future when the healthcare crisis becomes severe enough and there isn't enough money to pay the bills.

After I retired from American Healthcare Systems, I was approached to become the chairman and CEO of Cytran, one of the companies in which I had made an investment in the early 1990s. The company floundered under the founder's leadership, in large part because there was no focus on what to do with all the products Cytran had obtained from Russia. In addition, one of the Russian scientists who allegedly discovered one of the products was suing Cytran for more money. This was not an unusual situation back in the early days after Russia ended its Communist rule. At any rate, Cytran was almost broke. Because I wanted to protect my investment, I agreed to become CEO. I was commuting back and forth from San Diego to Seattle, which became quite grueling after a while. Nevertheless, I was able to secure additional funding from individuals with whom I was familiar in Texas and Norway. However, I could not get the Seattle group of investors who originally invested most of the money to offer more for the venture. I also was not interested in having on my record a company that went bankrupt while I was CEO. After seven months of bringing in additional funds to complete the studies necessary for Food and Drug Administration approval, I decided to resign. While I was there, a major investor in New York who had AIDS put a lot of money into studying one of the products that appeared to have some impact on the frequently fatal tumors that AIDS patients develop. The studies were conducted at Cornell and Stanford universities by well-respected investigators. The early signs were that the drug was working. However, when the studies were completed much later, the efficacy was just not there. In the meantime, the investor from New York had died. When I resigned, the board placed the founder and CEO who had let the company get to the point of bankruptcy back at the helm. Within the year, the company went bankrupt and the assets sold. I have no idea what happened to all the products in the joint venture between the Russian scientists and the entrepreneurs. I do remember vacationing in Russia and meeting with ministry of health officials and Dr. Mikhail Tikhomirov of the Shemyakin Institute of Bioorganic Chemistry, where the products were originally developed.

One of the highlights of our trip was seeing the Bolshoi Ballet. I also purchased various paintings by well-known Russian artists. When it came time to depart, the customs officer, whom I believe was in cahoots with our guide, wanted twice the amount I had paid for the paintings for customs fees. I told him I did not have that much money. We finally settled for a 50 percent customs duty on the paintings that theoretically should have had none. Later I wrote to my acquaintances in the health ministry to tell them of my experience but never received an answer. My belief was that it was a shakedown by a corrupt customs official.

Chapter 18

Prized Nobel Seats

I should mention another trip abroad that was one of the most interesting experiences of my lifetime. In 1994 Sandy and I were invited to attend the Nobel Prize ceremony in Stockholm, Sweden. Tickets to these events are extremely rare. They are called "tickets of the year" in Europe. We fortunately had tickets to everything, including lectures given by each of the Nobel winners. The lecture halls held only about one hundred-fifty people. The ceremony was held in the Concert Hall of Stockholm with the king and queen of Sweden on one side of the stage and the Nobel participants on the other side. When an individual winner's name was called, he or she was to stand while the major-domo at the center of the stage read the citation. Then the winner was to approach the king and queen to receive his honors.

The physics winner for that year was quite elderly. Once acknowledged, he forgot to walk across the stage to the king and queen and stood for what seemed like forever. The audience of seventeen hundred sat aghast. The king and queen do not approach commoners. After a deadly silence, the king wagged his finger urging the winner to come across the stage to get his prize. The audience broke out in laughter and applause.

There was excellent entertainment. Everything was run very precisely. If anybody tried to enter the Concert Hall after the king and queen had taken their seats, he or she was turned away, and the doors were literally barred. This was true of all the other events, which started precisely on time. After the ceremony, 1,200 of the 1,700 people were transported to the Stockholm Town Hall, where the king and queen held their major audiences. In the Town Hall was a reception room where they greeted all their guests. The hall was arranged with a long dinner table in the center and other tables perpendicular to the main one. We were sitting at one of those perpendicular tables only about twenty feet from the king and queen. All the guests except the diplomatic corps and the Nobel Prize winners were seated ahead of time. Then the king and queen led a long procession from the second floor down a great staircase and took their seats at the center of the table. They were followed by the ambassadors from all the foreign countries represented in Sweden, many of them in their native dress, and by royalty from throughout Europe. Finally the Nobel winners entered. I have never seen as many sparkling tiaras, beautiful gowns, and exotic costumes as I did that evening.

We all toasted the king and queen, and we could take home the glasses, which had gold leaf on them, as souvenirs. The dinner service is used once a year for this particular ceremony. We also learned a lot about the Nobel prizes. For example, prizes in economics are not true Nobel prizes and are designated as the Economics Prize in Honor of Alfred Nobel. The Bank of Sweden established them in the late 1940s to honor Nobel. The winners are seated separately on the stage from the true Nobel winners.

It was one of the most fascinating weeks I have ever spent. Lectures by the winners were truly thought provoking. The year we were there one of the economic sciences prizes went to John Nash, who later was the subject of the famous movie *A Beautiful Mind*.

Other memorable events during this period of my life were the 1988 Winter Olympics held in Calgary, Canada. We watched Bonnie Blair win her gold medal in speed skating and the exciting men's speed-skating races. The antihero of those Olympics was "Eddie the Eagle," a Brit who was entered in the ski-jumping contest. He could hardly jump and literally dropped off the end of the ski ramp. He received more publicity than the Flying Finn, who broke the world record in ski jumping and won the gold. Some interesting new skiing events were also held at these Olympics. We particularly enjoyed the mogul racing.

We also attended the 1992 Summer Olympics in Barcelona. The living quarters were on board an ocean liner docked at the port. It was an exciting time in Spain, but security was extremely tight. We saw many of the tennis matches. We also saw the boxing match where Oscar De La Hoya won the gold medal. One of the most interesting events was European handball, played indoors on a field similar to a soccer field. Players were able to throw the ball and, although they didn't have much protective gear, could be tackled. The final match was between Russia and Sweden. Russia finally won. I have never seen so many huge men on one field for one event in my life.

The "Dream Team" was so exciting in the semifinal game of basketball. So many great talents were assembled on one court.

We also visited most of the attractions in Barcelona. After the Olympics, we toured Spain by ourselves, with the highlight being the Prado in Madrid. We were warned repeatedly that Gypsies might try to rob us by spraying mustard or ketchup on our clothes then pretending to help us while they emptied our pockets. We had to shoo away many such folk.

One of our more interesting experiences was dining. In Spain you cannot find a restaurant open before 9 p.m. We were used to eating much earlier. When we were in Madrid, we found a restaurant made famous by Ernest Hemingway which opened at 8:30. We were always the first customers during our stay in Madrid. I bought a painting by Florence in Costa del Sol, one of the major tourist beach areas.

Chapter 19

The Cytyc Success Story

W hen Cytyc first received approval to market its thin-prep pap test and then went public, all the venture capital board members sold their shares and left. I was asked to become chairman of the board and recruit new members who would add some prestige and acumen. I convinced Bill Little, chairman of the West Company, Bill Longfield, chairman of Bard Inc., Dr. Joe Martin, Harvard Medical School dean, and Walt Boomer, who was on the board of Baxter and a retired assistant commandant of the Marine Corps, to join the board. This made a formidable board along with a few holdovers from the previous board.

Probably the best thing Cytyc ever did was to recruit Pat Sullivan as president and CEO. I was asked to stay on as chairman of the board and mentor for a period of time to help grow the company. I stayed from 1999 to 2002, at which time I decided Pat Sullivan could easily take on the job of chairman and CEO. I had numerous major medical problems, and it was the ideal time for me to retire. We generated net cash of more than $91 million in the third year I was there. We also had $72 million in cash in the bank at the end of 2001. When I retired, the board honored me by making me chairman emeritus. Cytyc became a major presence in women's health, generating hundreds of millions of dollars in sales. The stock split three times during my brief stay as chairman and split again after I left. Cytyc was traded on NASDAQ and has won many awards for being one of the best-run companies in the business. It is usually Cytyc stock that I use to make charitable contributions.

The company made two major acquisitions that added to its tremendous growth. Cytyc has truly been one of the major success stories, with a capitalization of more than $3.5 billion.

On May 21, 2007, Hologic Inc., announced the acquisition of Cytyc at a valuation of $6.2 billion. When I joined the board, Cytyc was worth very little. Under the terms of the deal, Cytyc's shareholders received $46.46 per share–a 33 percent premium over its close. The combined company has a $10 billion market cap. Pat Sullivan became chairman of the new board. Thus ended a company that was tremendously successful. I was proud to be the chairman of the board emeritus and to have played a role in its success.

In 1991 I was asked to go on the West Company's board of directors. Located in Lionsville, Pennsylvania, the company provides most of the syringes and other packaging used by the pharmaceutical industry. Now it is providing unique dosage forms of various drugs to make them easier for patient use.

When I was asked to join the board, I didn't know that the current president was about to lose his job. As a result, the chairman of the board, who was the son of the founder, asked if I would mind waiting until the new president and CEO was hired. Bill Little, a New Zealander, was that person. Bill brought stability and innovation to the company. He hired a scientist named Dr. Don Morel to head the new product development department. Don was a superb choice, and later when Bill retired, he was made the chairman and CEO of the company. Other notable members of the board were Tenley

Albright, whom I knew previously from the board of Friends of the National Library of Medicine. She is truly a remarkable lady with a broad depth of knowledge in many areas. In addition, we brought on John Conway, the new CEO of Crown Holdings. Bill Longfield, chairman of Bard Inc., was also on the West Company board and succeeded me when I retired at seventy as the lead director of the company.

Unfortunately, Bill West, the son of the founder and chairman of the board, a true gentleman, and excellent businessman, died of Parkinsonism. He had a severe case and went downhill quite rapidly.

Other board members at that time were Jack Neafsay, executive vice president of Sun Oil who helped convince me to move to Knoxville, where he had lived at one time when he headed up his company's coal mines. He and his wife apparently loved Knoxville. Jeff Worden, who had previously held a high position on Wall Street but retired to devote his life to charitable work, was a strong financial advisor and, in many respects, the social conscience of the board. Dr. Morel has been able to take West Pharmaceutical Company (renamed from the West Co.) to new heights, with the stock increasing in price.

Chapter 20

Fiduciary Responsibility to Shareholders and Employees

I became friendly with Bob Beyster, the founder and chairman of Science Applications International Corp (SAIC). He was quite interested in expanding the healthcare business and asked me in 1994 if I would be interested in joining his board as a director. I agreed because I found SAIC a fascinating company. It was actually a very large company made up of small mom-and-pop shops that could pursue their own businesses and in some instances were not very well integrated in SAIC. Unfortunately, the senior manager of healthcare was quite familiar with the government business but not with the civilian sector. He made a number of acquisitions, including one large one I advised him not to make. I warned that a great deal of money would be lost, and he would probably lose his job. However, he persisted and convinced Dr. Beyster to make the acquisition. The company lost more than $60 million, and he fell in disfavor and left.

Once that was behind it, the company grew nicely, but it was sitting on a lot of cash that needed to be invested. SAIC made a large investment by purchasing Bell Laboratories in New Jersey, which for a while was a cash cow. However, the business suffered under poor management and was subsequently sold for a large profit. The best acquisition SAIC made was the internet company that provided domain names and at the time had a monopoly. The company stock soared and split several times and was later sold to VeriSign at a huge profit. However, it was necessary for SAIC to invest all the cash that was accumulating to continue its growth rate.

Dr. Beyster was beginning to show his age and came under the influence of a young man who knew little or nothing about the business. This man was invoking Dr. Beyster's name in dealing with senior officers of the company. He persuaded Dr. Beyster to make some poor investments.

I was interested at the time in the investments made by the wholly owned venture capital fund in which profits from all the sales of companies were placed for investment purposes. This fund was run by a separate board of directors but was still owned by SAIC. After I analyzed it in great detail, it was obvious the failures could be traced in large part to the young man who was at the time Dr. Beyster's principal advisor. This did not sit well with the board or even senior management. As one of the senior outside directors, I was urged to lead an effort to bring in a new CEO or at least institute a well-planned succession program.

During my tenure on the board, Dr. Beyster did name quite a few presidents. None of them lasted very long once it became obvious they were itching to replace him as CEO. The last nominee, before Ken Dahlberg was brought in as CEO by the board over Dr. Beyster's objections, lasted only about a month in the position.

Even though I had resisted efforts by other board members to replace Bob as CEO, I remembered my experiences at Control Data and the fact that thousands of individuals had lost their jobs. I did not want the same thing to happen to SAIC. I talked with some of the other senior outside directors, and we decided to force the issue. I requested a meeting with Dr. Beyster to discuss this with him. He brought to the meeting the senior director on the board, Bobby Inman. I told Dr. Beyster how the board's outside directors felt and it was necessary to bring in a new CEO and asked him to retire gracefully. All of the board believed sincerely that Bob had done a terrific job in building the company and wanted to honor him in his retirement. However, this suggestion was not taken in the spirit in which it was offered.

Bobby Inman asked me to meet with him. In a meeting behind closed doors, he became quite irate and told me if I pursued this effort with the rest of the board he would sue me personally and basically threatened and tried to intimidate me. This did not go over well with me. I told him he would have to have a lot of money if he wanted to sue me.

Thus began a long period of discussion with the other board members. If succession were to take place, we would need the vote of at least one inside board member since Inman, an outside director, was siding with the no-succession group. Two of the inside board members agreed to vote with the outside directors, which gave the group a majority. The board confronted Dr. Beyster and asked him to retire voluntarily or the board would set up a search committee to find a new CEO. When it became obvious to Dr. Beyster that we had the majority of the votes of the board, he agreed through his attorneys to retire with honor. The board reiterated it did not want to hurt Dr. Beyster in any way and voted to set up a fund to establish an entrepreneurial institute in his honor at the University of California, San Diego.

Tom Young was named head of a search committee to find a new CEO. After it selected Ken Dahlberg, Bobby Inman called him and said he did not have support of the full board and would have a difficult time running the show. This was totally unauthorized by the board, which was angered by such a call from an individual member. As a consequence, the board decided to strip Inman of his committee assignments and chairmanship of the executive committee if he did not resign. SAIC was paying for an office and secretary for Inman in his hometown of Austin, Texas, which the board eliminated after he resigned.

In spite of Inman's phone call, Ken Dahlberg agreed to take the position even though he knew that many of the inside directors supported an inside person for CEO. I believe most of the employees were happy with the decision. Many became multimillionaires as a result of the company going public. The company has grown nicely under Ken, and his reorganization proved to be what it needed. It was a year of great stress for me because the board asked me to be the lead director after Inman resigned.

The only downside was that I lost Bob's friendship. I still have tremendous admiration for him. Sandy and I both liked Bob and his wife, Betty, very much.

I strongly believe that individual directors of corporations have a fiduciary duty to their shareholders and employees and not to the CEO running the show. With the CEO they must have a certain amount of detachment and independence to properly do their jobs. That proved true in this situation, even though I still feel quite badly about the loss of Bob's friendship. I wish him well in whatever he does.

One of the more devastating mistakes made prior to his retirement was the acceptance of the security operation for the 2004 Summer Olympics held in Greece. Most of the board advised against it, but Beyster decided to pursue it. The company won the contract but lost more than $100 million in the process and is still in arbitration with the Greek government to recover some of the money.

I was quite aware of what was going on in Greece because my college roommate was living in Athens at the time and had many friends in and out of government. He told me the contract was going poorly, and on several occasions I advised Dwayne Andrews of this fact. Dwayne ran the Washington office and was directly in charge of the "Greek Project." He was also Beyster's nominee to succeed him as CEO when the board selected Dahlberg. Unfortunately, I don't think Dwayne took my warnings seriously since he was constantly assured by others that things were going well when in fact they were not. Several emissaries were sent to Greece, and Dwayne made one quick trip himself. The major issues were still not addressed. I was contacted several times by one of SAIC's agents in Athens. Even one of the principals with the SAIC-hired firm contacted me. I met with him in my home since I was the lead director of SAIC at the time and talked with him on the phone several times. He called me; I did not call him. I reported all of these incidents to the SAIC legal department. However, the Olympics did go off without any major glitches in the security system, so something obviously worked.

Long after I retired from the board due to age, the board hired a San Francisco law firm to do an internal investigation of the entire Greek contract. Neither SAIC nor the hired law firm contacted me about my views on the problem. It was apparently suggested that I was in cahoots with the Greeks because of my college roommate.

Any suggestion that I was involved with the Greeks is absolutely absurd. Why would I want to jeopardize my stock holdings in SAIC? Also, why would I want to aid a country to which I have no allegiance and whose government officials I have never met? I confronted the SAIC legal department about the report and was assured the accusations were not in the report. However, other knowledgeable people in the company have told me that such a rumor was circulating. I suspect some insiders who either lost their jobs or were bypassed as a result of Beyster's retirement blamed me for their difficulties, thinking this might be a good way of ruining my reputation at SAIC. I don't know a single one who refused to take the dividend when the company went public.

When we moved to Knoxville in 1999, I relished the fact that SAIC had a very large presence in Oak Ridge headed up by Larry Peck. Peck was not one of Beyster's favorite managers. He reported directly to Andrews, who was not enamored of him either. I believe I was able to change Beyster's mind about Peck since Peck made his numbers every year and brought in much new business to the company. It was a great surprise both to Larry and me when, just before retiring, Beyster gave him the Founder's Award.

I used the teleconferencing center in Oak Ridge to participate in executive committee and board meetings when I was not well enough to travel and attend them in person. I am pleased that Larry was named executive vice president of the company, reporting directly to Dahlberg.

Any time I can help an old friend, I am glad to have the opportunity. As I mentioned before, Vern Loucks of Baxter had made a major investment in American Healthcare Systems when I first appeared on the scene. I had nothing to offer him at the time; it was a leap of faith for him to make that investment. Later on while I was still at AmHS, I learned that Vern was in difficulty with some of his shareholders because he was doing business with Arab countries. His board was not pleased about the publicity surrounding this controversy, and all who went to the annual meeting anticipated major troubles.

Dick Miller, the Baxter representative who called on American Healthcare Systems, told me about this problem. He was greatly concerned, and I called his boss, Terry Mulligan, to discuss the situation. Terry, too, was concerned. I had much respect for Terry's judgment and asked him if he thought it would help if I came to the meeting and spoke up for Vern. He encouraged me to do so, and even offered to send the Baxter plane to take me to the meeting. I declined that offer and paid my own way to Chicago so I could attend the meeting.

It was a raucous affair, with many of the stockholders calling for Vern's resignation. After listening to the tirades, I decided to speak. When I got up, I understand that Mr. Charles Knight, CEO of Emerson Electric and board member at Baxter, turned to the person next to him and said, "Now who is this and what is he going to say?" He was also the father of Lester Knight, executive vice president of Baxter and a first-class businessman. I was sorry that Lester retired later to start his own company, along with a couple of other well-regarded Baxter executives in Chicago.

I started my speech by telling the audience that I was the CEO of Baxter's largest customer. At that time our purchases were about 12 percent of Baxter's annual sales. Since the sales to Arab nations were construed as being anti-Israel, I reminded the audience that I had twice chaired the annual B'nai B'rith dinner in New York and had received the organization's international healthcare award. I believe this was the turning point of the meeting, in which Vern, many Baxter executives, and others in the crowded meeting room concurred. I reminded the audience Baxter was recognized in the business for quality products that saved lives all over the world. I also told them, as Baxter's largest customer, we supported the management. The meeting then progressed to a much calmer closure.

Chapter 21

Board Wars

When I retired from AmHS, Vern Loucks was one of the first to ask me to join his board of directors. Since I had great admiration for Baxter as a company, I readily agreed. I served on the Baxter board from 1995 until I retired because of age in 2003. During my tenure, Vern reached retirement age and set up an orderly and systematic succession process. He had done a great job for Baxter and was extremely well liked by everyone who came in contact with him. He was active on the board of Yale University, of which he was a graduate. The stock of Baxter under his tutelage reached the 60s. When he retired, he recommended the then-chief financial officer as the new CEO.

Harry Kraemer was not my first choice because, in my opinion, Mike Mussallem had more managerial experience. My belief turned out to be prophetic. Baxter spun off the Edwards Lifesciences Division with Mike as the new CEO. As I remember, the stock was in the teens, and in 2003 it had gone over 55. Under Kraemer's regime at Baxter, its stock dropped to the low 20s.

After Harry became chairman, he proposed to the board

that members be paid strictly in stock options for their services. This made no sense to me because the stock was low and going lower. I cast the only dissenting vote when the idea came up for approval.

A couple of years later when all the options awarded to the directors were totally underwater, I proposed that a new system be instituted in which one-third of payment would be in cash, one-third in restricted stock, and one-third in stock options. Having worked for several years without any pay or prospects of pay, the board approved the new plan over Harry's objection.

The first inkling I had of problems at Baxter was when several good, long-term directors decided to leave the board for unstated reasons. They were replaced by Harry's hand-picked choices. Problems with the Food and Drug Administration, Securities and Exchange Commission, and product quality multiplied. Several board members were receiving letters from employees and open letters from major shareholders. The FDA began several major investigations and made threatening demands. One analyst from Morgan Stanley was highly critical of the financial situation. Harry's answer was to call the analyst's boss and threaten to sue Morgan Stanley, a threat promptly squashed by the Baxter board.

During the last year I served on the board, my fellow members elected me the lead director. I think Tom Stallkamp, ex-president of Chrysler who lost his job when Daimler-Benz purchased Chrysler, also wanted to be the lead director.

In addition, the top talent at Baxter was rapidly diminishing with the resignation of at least six senior employees. Harry's Shared Investment Plan program (SIP) offered to the employees a bank loan program to buy stock. They had the loan for five years, during which time the stock should have gone up but continued to decline. There was a severe financial impact for many senior employees.

After continuing disasters, the board was quite eager for Harry to nominate a president and chief operating officer and also to appoint a chief scientific officer. For whatever reason, he chose not to follow this advice. In the meantime, seven members resigned from the board. After each regular board meeting, the board members met without Harry. As lead director, I then relayed the collective thoughts of the board to him. I do not think he believed what I was telling him actually came from the board. Harry gave me the impression that he thought the board worked for him.

The board grew more and more frustrated with the performance of the stock and asked me to have an all-day sit-down with Harry to review his job performance. Because of some surgery, I was not able to travel. Harry used the company plane to fly to my home in Knoxville. We spent the entire day talking about the problems. Harry reacted by saying he wanted another board member to resign.

I reported to the board that I didn't think I was making any headway. They asked me to meet with him again. I did so in his office. When I confronted him about pay raises he was recommending for certain employees who were, in my opinion, less competent than others not recommended, he asked me to resign from the board. I told him I had been on the board long before he became CEO and expected to serve out the term for which I was elected by shareholders.

The board became exasperated and decided to appoint an outside mentor for Harry. The outside mentor visited me in Knoxville and wanted to know what she should be doing to restore the confidence of the board. I told her she had a very difficult task because Harry did not take suggestions very well.

In the meantime, the chief financial officer, along with the general counsel and corporate secretary, approached me with major problems. Anonymous letters regarding other problems were received in the secretary's office.

In executive session I reviewed all these conversations and problems with the board. I also suggested to the board that it was time to seek a new CEO and listed twenty-four major reasons for making a change, not the least of which was a decrease in our credit ratings. The board, led by Tom Stallkamp, decided to take no action. I probably led the healthiest and most in-depth review of the company's problems that the board had participated in for some time. John Forsythe, the last director selected under my predecessor's leadership, was a close ally of Stallkamp. He came on the board with little board experience but "knew it all." I clashed with him many times. Later he accepted a position as chairman of the board of regents that governed the Iowa hospital with which his company did business. Gov. Tom Vilsack, who later ran for president, did not see a conflict of interest, but the medical press did. Much later the attorney general of Iowa cited a conflict of interest and forced Forsythe's resignation. I later sent all the documents to the chair of Baxter's governance committee.

At the end of our prolonged discussion, I suggested to the board that it name a committee to investigate some of the major problems. I appointed Dr. Joe Martin, dean of the Harvard Medical School, as head. All the board members respected Joe for his considered judgments and easy manner in approaching problems. He and his committee at the following board meeting presented a devastating report that placed Harry in a very bad light regarding his business judgments. The committee was unanimous in its recommendation to replace Harry. A consensus of the board was that we should do so. However, a board does not want to take such a momentous action without the overwhelming majority supporting it. Since we were meeting again the next morning, we decided not to make the final judgment. Stallkamp and some of Harry's newer recruits to the board led the dissenting side.

Very early the next morning Walt Boomer, a former assistant commandant of the Marine Corps whom I had recruited for the Cytyc board, visited me in my hotel room. He said Stallkamp and his supporters would vote for replacing Harry as CEO if I resigned as lead director in favor of Tom Stallkamp. I thought this was a small price to pay to get a job done that was sorely needed to protect the employees and shareholders of the company.

Again this episode points out to me that good directors must recognize that their fiduciary responsibilities are to the shareholders and employees–not to an individual CEO who may be jeopardizing the company's welfare. After the board met the following morning, the vote was taken to ask Harry to step down and to accept my resignation as lead director. Tom Stallkamp was elected lead director. Harry was asked to resign and he complied with the request.

One of the biggest mistakes I made at the time was to agree to let Harry remain as CEO until the annual meeting in May although it was January when he was asked to step down. During his interim tenure, several excellent employees decided to leave Baxter because he was, in my opinion, vindictive. The board's next action was to approve a severance package for Harry and to appoint a committee to find a new CEO. I nominated Walt Boomer to head the committee. I thought the severance package was excessive, and I voted against it. However, in light of what is happening today in the corporate world with regard to severance packages, Harry's was minuscule.

The search committee did its job well and finally recommended Robert Parkinson, former COO of Abbott Labs, to be the new CEO and chairman. Bob has done his job superbly. Vern Loucks told me later that nominating Harry was the biggest mistake of his life. If the board had not taken the action to find a new CEO, I probably would have resigned and reported my reasons for resignation to the Securities and Exchange

Commission because I believed the company was heading for total disaster.

When I read Baxter's 2007 annual report, I noted with great interest that all of the board members were receiving approximately $200,000 or more annually for their service. This is a 33-percent increase since I left the board. I hope they earn it.

Jumping forward to an exciting development, in 2003 I received a call from Dr. Gopinathan, whom I did not know. He was professor of neurology at New York University School of Medicine. He told me he and another professor of medicine at NYU, Dr. Michael Makover, and a retired NASA space scientist, Dr. Arthur Tilford, had developed a glove that you put on your right hand, hold over your chest, and with no power but a small Bluetooth box, do a 12-lead EKG and send it either by satellite or phone anywhere in the world. This device was Dr. Gopinathan's idea. Once when he was away from shore on a boat, the friend he was with had a heart attack. That sparked the doctor's desire to develop a device to be used in an emergency and transmit anywhere in the world. The glove was developed using space materials. Sticky electrodes, now used with standard EKGs, were eliminated along with the wiring.

Dr. Gopinathan told me he had found me on the internet and wanted me to be the company's business advisor. I told him I was retired and did not want to become involved. He asked if he could send me some material on the glove, and I said yes. I told my wife and she said I should do it. I was in ill health at the time and was not interested in taking on anything else.

When the materials arrived, I saw that the three men had also developed a glove for athletes to measure blood pressure, pulse rate, and oxygen saturation and do a 3-lead EKG. In addition, another more sophisticated glove with all of those functions and more was developed. After reading about this and believing that such a device would revolutionize medicine,

I decided to accede to their request, my wife's wishes, and my own curiosity and entrepreneurial spirit. I told Dr. Gopinathan I would be a business advisor for a certain percentage of the company. I think I was really hoping that my request would turn him off and I would not be burdened with another job. However, on behalf of the founders he readily accepted my proposal, and I became actively involved in consulting with the company. After about a year, I was asked to become chairman of the board, which I accepted.

Dr. Gopinathan is one of the hardest working, most persistent individuals I have ever known. By his own determination, he was able to assemble the necessary funding for research on the 3-lead EKG and receive FDA approval of the 12-lead glove. Unfortunately, we did not have enough funding for marketing without outside help. The big EKG companies regarded us as a threat since our glove would be cheaper. After a few years I had to resign due to illness. As of this writing, Dr. Gopinathan was still seeking someone to provide funds or establish a second company to market the glove. He had some very promising leads. I am hoping that these innovative, forward-thinking items in the medical device category will reach the market.

This completes my saga of corporate for-profit experiences. During my lifetime, I have served as CEO or chairman of eleven companies and on the boards of twenty for-profit corporations. I have served as the lead director of three Fortune 500 companies. I have only provided a glimpse of what corporate life could be under very trying circumstances. The great majority of the boards were less stressful and more pleasant experiences.

The fascinating part about serving on any board is how much you learn from different businesses, different leadership, different problems, different approaches to those problems, and the interactions of different individuals or groups. It is certainly a microcosm of what makes the world work. The other beneficial experience is learning from some outstanding directors with important positions in government, academia, the corporate world, labor, foundations, and the charitable world. In addition, the thirty-plus charitable boards I have served on have given me a different perspective and in some cases proved just as frustrating as the for-profit ones.

Chapter 22

Friends on the Highway of Life

Moving has blessed us with many new friends, but leaving the old ones is wrenching.

When we moved to New Canaan, we left behind many good friends in Harrisburg, such as Dr. Mary Dufner, the chief of pathology at Harrisburg State Hospital, Dale Shughart, the presiding judge of Cumberland County, Jack Maple, an attorney who was in my college class at the University of Pennsylvania and a fraternity brother, and especially the entire Scotes family. Ted Scotes started working for Merrill Lynch in New York, so when we moved to New Canaan we were still able to see him frequently. He is such a good friend that I persuaded him to help paint my house on weekends.

In New Canaan we made many new friends. We played bridge and tennis with Tucki and Harry Hitch. Nancy and Ted Meredith were also good friends. Ted and I started the *Journal of Legal Medicine* together. Janet and John Campbell and Shirley and Fred Leswing were great neighbors. Erna and Leonard Green were not only good bridge buddies, but Erna was on the town council with me. Karl Grassman was one of the most devout Christians I have ever known. Karl had been an officer in the German army during World War II and came to the U.S. to work for one of the scions of the IBM founder. Many other people in New Canaan had an impact on our lives, including Don Usher, the coach of the high school basketball team.

We also saw a lot of Pat and Bernie Goldstein, a college friend who lived in Rye, New York, close to New Canaan. The Goldsteins' younger son is now a professor at Virginia Tech, where the horrible shootings occurred in 2007. Fortunately, he was off campus at the time.

We moved from Connecticut to California in 1986, from one coast to the other. While parts of the Southern California culture were different than Connecticut's, there are nice people all over. We made lifelong friends. One of our closest is Guggi Quaintance, whose husband, Paul, was a fellow painter and quite a good one. More importantly, he was my closest friend. Sadly, Paul died prematurely from multiple cancers.

One of our best vacation trips was with Lindblad Expeditions along the coast of Norway to the Arctic Circle. Guggi came along with great trepidation, but she still talks about it as one of the best trips she ever took. Ditto for us. The natural beauty would later provide me the material for many paintings.

The other friends we left behind in California when we moved to Tennessee in 1999 were Ben and Helen Chadwell, Bob and Martha McCarter, Bill and Shirle McConnor, Jane and Jim Stockwell, Angie and Chuck Smith, Rod and Mary Rodriguez, Al and Rosemary Scalpone, Marilyn and Arthur Shooter, and Rayburn and Mary Vaughn Smeiser.

While still in California, I was asked by David Hale, chairman and CEO of Gensia, to serve on his board. Since they were in the drug business, I was knowledgeable about the field. It was a good company but almost completely destroyed by Bill Lerach, a fraternity brother of mine who received the

Outstanding Alumnus Award, along with Sen. Timothy Johnson of South Dakota and Sen. Thomas Carper of Delaware, at the same time I did. Bill Lerach is one of the tort kings and at the time was filing class-action lawsuits against a great number of companies. When he filed one against Gensia, I urged the board to fight him all the way because I considered what was happening to many corporations at the time as legal blackmail. However, the board chose to settle for an eight-digit amount, which greatly weakened the company. When the board decided to sell out to an Italian company, I resigned. Lerach was later convicted of conspiracy to defraud, fined, and sent to prison.

As mentioned, I have served on numerous charitable boards. Because of my involvement with CONNECT and many start-up companies, I was named the 1994 Entrepreneur of the Year for San Diego.

I was asked to chair the Youth Access to Alcohol Policy Panel for San Diego County. This was one of the most important positions I have accepted over the years. Led by executive director Ray DeCiccio, the panel was created to make recommendations regarding underage drinking. There was an excessive number of deaths in San Diego County of young people who were able to secure alcohol and then drive motor vehicles. The panel met frequently because of the urgency of the situation. The commission included judges, politicians, prominent citizens, members representing different health-care groups, and many others. We were amenable to meeting frequently and suggesting changes to the authorities. It was one of the most enjoyable committees I have ever worked with because all recognized the stakes and were willing to work to design a creditable plan. We made our report public and gave it to the county commissioners.

Dick Atkinson asked me to serve on the board of the California Business-Higher Education Forum. This group, composed of foundation executives, university presidents, and CEOs from California, met at least twice a year to submit recommendations to the governor to improve education and the business climate in California. One of the individuals on the forum was Dr. Locatelli, the president of Santa Clara University. I have a painting by Andrea Locatelli, whose patrons were King Philip V of Spain and Prince Orsini of Florence, Italy. When I asked Dr. Locatelli if he was aware of an artist in his family, he immediately said, "Andrea." It truly is a small world.

I believe the forum had a major effect on education and the business climate in California. The chairman was J. W. Peltason, who was also president of the California university system. Dick Atkinson, chancellor of the University of California, San Diego, who later became president of the California system, was also a member.

In 1999 to be closer to our grandchildren, who were then living in Bermuda, and because California was becoming so crowded, we decided to move to Knoxville, Tennessee, after a yearlong search. We moved in May into a rental house in Northshore Hills while we were building our house. The people were the friendliest we had encountered during any of our moves. We were not in the house more than an hour when Phil and Pat Moran came to greet us, and Pat brought my wife a plant. Bill Andrews designed our new house–Villa Forelle–and it was built by Billy King and Stuart Grady. Barbara Aston-Wash featured it in *Homes and Living*.

In addition, we were welcomed into Cherokee Country Club and quickly joined the tennis group. Wallace McClure took us under his wing and drove us around Knoxville showing us where everything was located. Wallace and his wife, Patsy, have been great friends and extremely helpful in making us feel that Knoxville is truly our hometown. On the tennis courts I have met a number of really fine Knoxvillians who have interests in different areas. Dave and Helen Traver have been great supporters of the Knoxville Symphony, as have Jim and Ann Johnson. Wallace and Patsy McClure contribute to both the symphony and the opera. Phyllis and Alex Robinson are real opera fans and great bridge players. Frank and Caroline Barnett played either tennis or bridge, and Cathy Youmans and Marsha Mitchell were frequently our bridge partners in big tournaments. Mary Costa, one of the twentieth century's great opera divas, lives in Knoxville, and we have become good friends. Her enthusiasm about everything is infectious. We, along with the Scoteses, have had some fun evenings together. It is a small world. One of my good friends in California, Jim Bowersox, was a friend of one of Mary's friends. Jim is a Delta Tau Delta and was the house advisor when we were in San Diego. We used to have him and the entire Delt house over for steaks. George and Joanne Rothery are supporters of the Tennessee Artists Association, and Jim and Kay Clayton are supporters of everything. John and Mary Stuart Neely have been great patrons of the Clarence Brown Theatre; Phyllis and Charlie Severance are supporters of the opera; and Henry and Sandra McIlwaine are great supporters of Ijams Nature Center. Frankie Gunnels' brother, Bill Regas, also played tennis with us, and every New Year's Eve brings us a delicious red velvet cake.

Tom Gunnels was an inspirational speaker and wrote a book called *Keep Your Lights On*. He started another book on quotations by famous people and asked me if I would collaborate with him and contribute some quotations of my own. Some could be controversial and could be attributed to others when I knew the original source. Some could be indirect quotes if I didn't know them verbatim. I agreed to do this and gave Tom my list. Before he could complete the book, he died tragically of a malignant brain tumor. (The list I gave him appears in the appendix of *Winter Galley*.)

They have all been extremely kind to us and welcomed us to Knoxville with open arms.

Chapter 23

The Art of
Community Service

W
e soon were approached to serve on the boards of
the cultural institutions in Knoxville. I opted for
the boards of the symphony, opera, East Tennessee Historical
Society, and Baptist Health System Foundation. Sandy joined
the Knoxville Museum of Art board, the Community School
of the Arts board, and the board of advisors for the School
of Music at the University of Tennessee. She also served as
president of the Knoxville Museum of Art guild and was on
the executive committee of the opera guild. These have been
interesting experiences for both of us. I resigned from all these
boards when my health began to fail.

In 2000 the director of the opera said he had an idea to
start a Knoxville Opera Rossini Festival similar to the Spoleto
Festival in Charleston, South Carolina. He asked if I would
serve on the soon-to-be-organized festival board to aid in raising funds. He mentioned quite a number of names, including a
New York Metropolitan Opera diva who would be chairman of
the board. I said I would. When the opera director mentioned
he wanted to start the festival the following year, he asked if I
would finance it. I told him I would help, but he had a Rossini

Festival board that should also help–not only to give but to get. The board has never met and has remained only on a piece of stationery. I often have wondered if it really existed. Getting the festival started would take a six-figure investment. My wife and I decided to make this our gift to the city of Knoxville because we strongly believe we should give back to the place where we live. Don Townsend, the Knoxville Opera production manager and chorus master, became chairman of the 2002 festival. Had it not been for his hard work and creativity, the event would not have happened. The festival was far more successful the first year than we ever expected, with more than six thousand people attending.

In 2003 festival chairmen Ted and Thale Scotes created a committee structure to produce the event and spent many hours developing a festival that attracted more than twenty-five thousand people. Succeeding chairmen Peter Acly and Tom Catani and co-chair Lori Huff spent many hours orga-nizing the festival, which certainly has given the opera name recognition. For the next four years I continued to fund it. In 2005 and 2006, more than sixty thousand people attended the festival. One local paper called it the most successful festival Knoxville ever held. On various stages there were dancers, opera singers, orchestral and band ensembles, jazz bands, and children's choruses. The event also featured booths with artisans selling their handcrafts and food provided by local restaurants.

In April 2005 a delegation from the executive committee visited me and said the opera was going to have to declare bankruptcy because of a large debt. I asked if they had any plan to prevent bankruptcy, and I must say that Jackie Wilson and her associates had done their homework. However, since I had already helped the opera out of financial problems more than once, I was reluctant to buy into the new plan. After discussing it with Sandy, who wanted to try to preserve the opera, I reluctantly agreed to help–provided that my contribution was matched by the board in either its own donations or in new monies obtained from others. A new director, Brian Salesky, was brought in. He is not only brilliant artistically, but knows how to run a tight ship financially. I am pleased to say that today the opera is in the black.

When I was asked to be vice president of finance of the Knoxville Symphony Society board, there was a large deficit. Since I was new on the block and had nothing to do with incurring the debt, I proposed it be divided up among the seventy board members who were responsible for it. Even though my proposal was not greeted with unanimous applause, it was finally endorsed by a majority vote. The society was able to end the year without debt. However, in the process a number of board members resigned, and others have not spoken to me since. I also had introduced to them a concept I had learned early on of operating under the three Gs: give, get, or get out.

During my entire business career, my wife and I have felt very strongly about giving back to the community in which we lived. One of the two accomplishments I am proudest of is the number of lifesaving drugs my research team introduced to the practice of medicine. Many of them are still saving lives or making patients more comfortable. The other accomplishment is that I have helped raise a lot of money for charity in my lifetime. As a matter of fact, I have often said, if there is anything on my epitaph, it should be these two achievements.

Besides serving on the boards of and giving to charitable institutions, we have endowed scholarships at the Morehouse School of Medicine in Atlanta, Bloomfield College in Bloomfield, New Jersey, University of the Cumberlands in Williamsburg, Kentucky, and Dickinson School of Law in Carlisle, Pennsylvania. In addition, we endowed an annual legal medicine prize at Dickinson. We have also endowed the Sandra and Monroe Trout Chair in Pharmacology and the

Monroe Trout Chair in Surgery, both at the University of California, San Diego.

In 1991 I had the idea of starting a Cares Award sponsored by American Healthcare Systems and contributed to by many of its leading hospital suppliers. Bill Longfield of Bard Inc., and Vern Loucks of Baxter International Inc., contributed the initial monies to the fund. The award is given annually to the best indigent medical care program that can be duplicated in the U.S. The first-place winner receives $70,000 and the next five receive lesser amounts. The year I retired, the award was named the Monroe E. Trout-AmHS Cares Award. The award is now called the Monroe E. Trout Premier Cares Award. It has become prestigious for any individual, group, or institution to win. The award is presented at a grand dinner at the Biltmore in Phoenix, Arizona. In 2008 healthcare groups submitted 235 entries.

I have judged the competition every year and am continuously impressed by the quality programs that healthcare workers create. In January 2008, I attended the sixteenth annual awards ceremony.

In 2004 my wife and I were named Knoxville's Philanthropists of the Year, and on March 13, 2007, Mayor Ragsdale proclaimed Monroe E. Trout Day in Knox County for the contributions we had made to the community.

In 2006 I wanted to give my wife something special for a significant birthday. I established the Louise and William Lemke Family endowment fund to provide scholarships for needy students at the Fox Valley Lutheran High School in her hometown of Appleton, Wisconsin. We traveled to the high school to make the first presentations of six scholarships. We received two standing ovations from the students, who comprised most of the audience. It was a very emotional, moving experience. The following year we endowed the Florence and David Trout Family Educator of the Year Award at the same high school.

Through the Baptist Healthcare Foundation, we established an endowment fund whose income is used to treat indigent children with heart disease. The funds were transferred to the University of Tennessee Medical Center for the same purpose. I asked that this be done when Baptist was considering selling its hospital to a for-profit group that planned to use the monies in the foundation to pay down debt. It took the attorney general of Tennessee to stop this. I met with his deputy in my home to discuss this travesty.

Also in 2006 we were asked to sponsor a major conference organized by the Baker Center at the University of Tennessee to honor the sixtieth anniversary of Winston Churchill's "Iron Curtain" speech. Henry Kissinger, Winston Churchill II, Brent Scowcroft, Alan Packwood, head of the Churchill Archives Centre at Cambridge University, and Sir John and Lady Julia Boyd were some of the speakers.

At the gala dinner we were seated with Dr. Kissinger and Mary Costa. When he was late to the table, Mary said, "It is about time you got here. I was about ready to eat your roll." This broke up the former secretary of state, who stayed so late that he nearly missed his plane. As a result of our initial sponsorship, we received a bronzed right hand of Churchill by Oscar Nemon, the great British sculptor. We also purchased the "Churchill trip" to England, where we were treated royally by the Packwoods, the Churchills, and the Boyds. As a Churchill "nut" (I believe he was the greatest person of the twentieth century), I have collected several pieces of memorabilia, including an etching of Churchill by his daughter Sarah. After we returned, I sent one of my oil paintings to Sir Winston Churchill II, Sir John and Julia Boyd, and a third to the Churchill Archives Centre at Cambridge University.

Chapter 24

Doctor as Patient

During these very rewarding, creative years, I was also struggling with pain. No one likes to talk about illness, especially me, since I have had twenty-two major surgeries during my lifetime. I tell about my illnesses only to explain how much more difficult it was for me to do the many jobs I have had and to perform the many tasks asked of me than if I had been healthy. Hopefully it will inspire others with illnesses to realize that they can lead fulfilling lives.

On a trip to Tokyo in 1981, I experienced what I thought was a terrible toothache. There was nothing I could do about it in Japan. Immediately upon returning to the United States, I saw my dentist, who told me there was nothing wrong with my teeth but that I really needed to see a neurologist. The pain was excruciating, probably a hundred times worse than the kidney pain I had twenty years earlier. The neurologist gave me the bad news that I had Tic Doloreaux. At first I was put on different medications, which helped somewhat. However, whenever I went out into the cold from a warm home or office, I felt as if someone had stuck a red-hot poker through my jaw, up to my eye and through my brain. The pain could come at any time and sometimes lasted only a few seconds, but other times it lasted much longer. My only relief was when I fell asleep at night.

In 1984 I could not stand the pain any longer and went to see Dr. Gamach at Cornell University, who tried to perform an electrolysis of the ganglia supplying the facial nerves. The procedure has worked for many people but not for me. Because they could not put me to sleep during the procedure, I suffered unendurable pain. Nonetheless, the pain again became so severe that a year later I had the procedure repeated. Again it was ineffective. No treatment was successful. This excruciating pain followed me to the mid-1990s, slowing me down in everything I did before I finally found relief.

In the early 1990s, I called my good friend Pete Jannetta, head of neurosurgery at the University of Pittsburgh. Several years prior to this, Pete had developed a surgical procedure to help patients with Tic Doloreaux. He discovered that the condition was caused by an artery or vein pressing on the nerve roots in the brain. At first he was reviled by his colleagues, but after achieving a success rate of more than 90 percent his procedure was generally accepted and is now in all the standard textbooks. Pete performed the surgery on me, and found my case was caused by a bunch of veins. The procedure was not effective. The veins grew back. About two years later, Pete repeated the procedure, and again it was ineffective.

Once again I sought relief from Tic Doloreaux. In 1995 I went to see Dr. John Alksne in San Diego, chief of neurosurgery and dean of the medical school at UCSD. At the time, I was chairman of the board of the UCSD Foundation and got to know him very well. He suggested a procedure that was fairly successful in curtailing the pain and that he had performed for many years. It was a balloon compression of the ganglia supplying the facial nerve. He warned me ahead of time that I would lose all sensation on one side of my face. If

the procedure were done correctly, I would not have any loss
of motor function. At that point I was willing to suffer the lack
of sensation rather than have the constant pain. I must admit
that many times I contemplated suicide when I would scream
out from the most horrendous pain anybody could ever have.

The results of the first procedure Dr. Alksne performed
lasted only about a year. Then my pain returned. I went back
into the hospital, and he repeated the procedure. I am happy
to say that, as of 2008, even though I have numbness on the
right side of my face, I have had no pain for the last twelve
years. However, the loss of sensation can be embarrassing. For
example, I do not know if I have food particles on the numb
side of my face. I find it difficult to chew on the right side.
However, all of these inconveniences are better than suffering
the pain. I happily endure them.

A few years later, the San Diego paper attacked Dr. Alksne
and accused him of being a major malpractice offender because
he used an experimental glue in treating his neurosurgical
patients. He was under severe attack, and many thought he
would have to resign his position as dean and chief of neurosurgery. I spoke with the UCSD chancellor, Dr. Richard
Atkinson, who asked what I could do to help. Since I knew
many of the people at the Food and Drug Administration
from my long years of working with them, I called one of the
high-ups in the administration and told him of the newspaper
articles on Dr. Alksne. He said much of what was reported
was inaccurate or untrue and that the glue had been approved
for neurosurgical uses. After learning these facts from him, I
wrote an article and a letter to the editor reporting this. I also
called the reporter whom I had met on several other occasions
to tell him that he was reporting inaccurate information. I
believe that, as a result of my research and my letters, Dr.
Alksne's job as dean and chief of neurosurgery was saved. I'm
sure he would acknowledge this today.

In 1999 I had a cataract operation on my right eye. A cataract had already been removed from my left eye. This was in January, and we were planning to move to Knoxville in May. After the operation I kept returning to the chief of ophthalmology and telling him that I could not see. He at first angrily sent me back to the optometry department to tell them my glasses needed correcting. They said there was nothing wrong with my glasses. Still I could not see. After being examined by several other professors, I was made to feel like I was crazy. I knew I could not see, but they all told me there was nothing wrong with my eye.

When I got to Knoxville and was turned down for a driver's license because of blindness in my right eye, I called Dale Collins, head of Baptist Hospital, who immediately got me an appointment with Dr. William Sullivan. Dr. Sullivan diagnosed my problem immediately. The artificial lens placed in my eye after the cataract removal had fallen back against my retina, and the doctors at the University of California, San Diego didn't want to admit it. Later I obtained my medical records and found that, in suctioning my eye, the nurse had ruptured my posterior capsule which holds in the lens. That is why it had fallen back against my retina. Dr. Sullivan referred me to Dr. James Miller and to Dr. Frank Murchison. After Dr. Miller removed the lens and Dr. Murchison inserted a new one, I was again able to see.

In February 1999, after enduring several painful biopsies because of a high PSA, I was diagnosed as having cancer of the prostate. I chose to have a radical prostatectomy by the chief of urology at UCSD. During the surgical procedure I apparently lost a lot of blood–I suspect because an artery was nicked and not readily found. Nonetheless, the urologist allowed me to lie in my hospital bed with a hematocrit of 22, which is less than half what it should be. When the chief of surgery, Dr. A.R. Moosa, who was a good friend of mine, said that I needed to be transfused, he was basically told to mind his own business by the urologist because I was not his patient. The following day I collapsed, went into heart failure, and had atrial fibrillation. When the cardiologist saw me on an emergency basis, he ordered an immediate transfusion. This started a long series of problems for me.

I believed it was necessary to report my experience in the interest of helping to ensure quality care not only for myself, but for others as well. Dr. Robert Dynes had succeeded Dr. Atkinson as chancellor of the university, and I told him what had occurred.

Because I was chairman of the board of the foundation at the time, his comment was, "This should not happen to you."

"Dammit, Bob. It shouldn't happen to anybody," I replied.

Nonetheless, nothing was done. I reported the incident to the Joint Commission, which certifies hospitals in the U.S. I was well known to them because of my prominence in the healthcare field. They performed a complete inspection of the facility but found nothing wrong.

Since I had been a trustee and chairman of the board of both the medical center and the foundation, I could not bring myself to sue the doctors involved. Plus, it would go against my grain to do so. However, because of my persistent atrial fibrillation resulting from not being transfused in 1999, I had to have a pacemaker installed in March 2001. When I had an attack of atrial fibrillation, I passed out, sometimes on the street. In addition, I had to have five subsequent operations to fix the urinary problems caused by my radical prostate surgery. Again I was promised a result that did not occur. After consulting a new urologist, Dr. Paul Hatcher, I went to Duke University and had a total reconstruction, which was successful. I am indebted to Paul for recommending Dr. George Webster at Duke to me.

In January 2006, on Martin Luther King Jr.'s birthday, I

had a major heart attack at 7:45 in the morning. I had carried the trash out and come back into the house. When Sandy said it was time to eat, I said, "No, it's time to go to the hospital. I am having a heart attack. Call Dr. Bishop."

Fortunately, there was almost no traffic. Dr. Harry Bishop told us to come directly to the emergency room where he would meet us. I have to say I was off the operating table at 9:50 after having a ream job done to my coronary arteries and a stent put in one of them. Because of the prompt and excellent care I received, I have had no permanent heart damage. Dr. Robert "Buck" Thompson, Dr. John Acker, Dr. John Lacey, Dr. Henry Nelson, and Dr. Paul Hatcher provided excellent care. I am indebted to Dr. Bishop for saving my life.

As a result of all my surgical procedures and my failing health while in Knoxville, I felt compelled to resign from all of my charitable boards and some of my corporate boards because I could not carry my weight. During my long career, I would not serve on a board unless I could make a major contribution and attend at least 90 percent of the meetings.

Chapter 25

Political Leanings

Politics has been an interest of mine since I was a school-boy. In the 1960s I worked on the William Scranton and Ray Shafer gubernatorial campaigns in Pennsylvania. Through that association I became friends with Ray Shafer. After serving a term as lieutenant governor, he was elected governor of Pennsylvania. Later I worked with him on several projects after he left the political arena and moved to Washington, D.C. In 1960 and 1962, I worked on Rep. John Kunkel's campaign in the Seventeenth Congressional District of Pennsylvania.

In the early 1980s I became a member of Vice President George Bush's finance committee and also a member of the presidential trust of the Republican National Committee. In 1987 I was asked to become a member of Vice President Bush's health issues policy committee and met with Tony Lopez, Debra Steelman, and Michael Hines. I wrote position papers on health issues and policy for the Bush campaign as well as op-ed pieces. I aided in the formation of a national group of health leaders for Bush and served in the Doctors for Bush Campaign. I spoke to local Republican groups about health policy. I also served on the executive committee of the Fundraiser for Bush in San Diego under the direction of Gordon Luce.

I contributed for more than twenty-five years to Republican candidates throughout the U.S. As a result, when Rep. Bill Lowery of San Diego asked me to be a member of his advisory council, I consented. I was instrumental in convincing LeRoy Zimmerman, the attorney general of Pennsylvania and a good friend of mine, to support Bush early in the primary campaign. I served under Robert Mosbacher and Bruce Gelb as a member of the national finance committee of the Fund for America's Future from 1985 until its closure. I was a delegate to the 1986 gubernatorial convention in Connecticut and supported Dr. Gerald Labriola as the Republican candidate. He won the nomination but lost the election. I also worked on and contributed to the aborted Senate campaign of Prescott Bush, George W. Bush's brother, in Connecticut.

Chapter 26

Hobbies and Travels

Over the years I have engaged in several different hobbies. I started playing tennis without ever having any lessons during my college years, and continued to play all my life. I played in several Pro-Am tournaments while in San Diego and won one tournament along with my pro partner at Fairbanks Ranch Country Club. The following year I was the defending champ and had as my partner Larry Stefanki, who was not only a superb tennis player, but has gone on to become a superb coach and recently has coached some of the top ten tennis players in the world.

I also played in the Pro-Am tournament at PGA East sponsored by Kraft Foods. The proceeds benefited world hunger programs. Some of the world's greatest female tennis players, including Billie Jean King, Chris Evert Lloyd, and Virginia Wade, offered tips for better tennis at clinics. I played tennis with Billie Jean, Chris, and Virginia as my partners. What a thrill it was. I must say they were all great ladies and very down-to-earth.

We have attended the Winter Olympics in Calgary, Canada, and the Summer Olympics in Barcelona, Spain. Since the boys played both high school and college basketball, we have watched many basketball games, including an NCAA final.

Timothy played against David Robinson, who went on to become one of the great stars of the San Antonio Spurs. David's parents were concerned that their son be a very positive role model for other young basketball players. It is obvious from David's career and interest in charitable work that he learned well from his parents.

On a trip to Puerto Rico, Sandy and I stayed in the same hotel as Walter Payton, one of the NFL's great running backs from the Chicago Bears, and throughout the week got to know him. We were saddened by his early death. He was another excellent role model for young athletes.

Shortly after our arrival in San Diego, I read in the newspaper that many high school basketball teams would not be able to play their games because of a lack of referees. Since we had enjoyed watching our boys play, I volunteered to referee. First I had to attend four-hour sessions at San Diego State University every week for several months. I did receive college credit and then certification as a referee for taking the course. My first game was a high school girls' game. My fellow referee called four fouls on a feisty guard, and I unfortunately called the fifth. She sat down on the court and cried. She would not walk to the bench. Finally I told her coach she would have to move or the game would be forfeited. Her parents came down from the stands and escorted her off the floor. Episodes like this were never mentioned in class.

As the season progressed, we were assigned more difficult games and ones played at a faster pace. At the end of the season, I was assigned a "run and gun" game. The pace was so fast that I could not keep up, and by the end of the game I was exhausted. At the post-game confab with my fellow referee, he told me I was a little slow. My exhaustion and his comment convinced me that I should retire from refereeing. I was glad for the experience and for the opportunity to help out.

One of my early hobbies was collecting stamps and coins. On a lecture trip to Montana, I stayed at a motel that each day gave five old silver dollars to a guest whose name was picked out of the hat. I was lucky and won the five silver dollars. In 1965 I started collecting commemorative coins minted by various nations of the world. In addition, I was able to secure one of the coins that was taken to the moon by an early astronaut and then sold when he returned.

My interest in stamp collecting came to an abrupt end when a dealer from New Jersey gave our older son a bad check for part of his collection. Fortunately through friends, we were able to locate and prosecute the dealer.

One of my early passions was collecting art. Over the last forty-five years I have acquired more than one hundred-seventy paintings, etchings, drawings, and mixed-media pieces. Since the walls are filled, I have not done any major collecting for the last couple of years. I enjoy the stories that go along with each painting, etching, and drawing.

I always wanted to paint but thought I had no talent. Others agreed with that assessment. Nonetheless, in 1995 I began to take lessons from some very good painters in the San Diego area, including Carl Fortbrook, Carl Provder, who was a student of Wolfe Kahn, and Ken Goldman, who was well known on the West Coast and has paintings in major museums there. He has written books on techniques of painting. I have given oil paintings to friends and have donated others to charities both in and out-of-town. At auctions, they have sold for as much as $1,000, all of which goes to the charity. My paintings are hanging in the lobby of Baptist Hospital West, in the chapel area of Baptist Hospital of East Tennessee, in the Baker Center at the University of Tennessee, the University of Tennessee president's house, and the Episcopal School and Green Elementary School in Knoxville. Six of my paintings honoring all six branches of service are in the Ben Atchley State Veteran's Home in Knoxville.

I have been juried into more than twenty exhibits, including the Athenaeum in La Jolla and the Rancho Santa Fe Art Guild Gallery, the Tennessee Artist Association Annual Exhibit in 2003, 2004, 2005, and 2006; the Pellissippi State Technical Community College Art Fest in 2005; the Charlotte, North Carolina, Art Fest in 2007; and a couple of times into the Knoxville Museum of Art Artscapes auction.

I was pleased to be one of twelve artists invited by the Knoxville Symphony League to paint a violin to be auctioned at a fundraiser. On one side of the violin is the American flag with the Statue of Liberty superimposed to honor all our service men and women and to remind us all we live in the land of the free and the home of the brave. On the reverse side is Paganini, one of the greatest violinists who ever lived, in his duel with Lafont. Paganini played so well he was believed to be possessed by the devil. On the side of the violin is the "Dies Irae" melody. On the other side is a future Paganini, who has taken time off from his baseball game to practice his scales on the violin.

I was asked to paint a sculpted fiberglass bear (associated with the nearby Smoky Mountains) honoring the Knoxville Opera. It was displayed at the Tennessee Theatre and at the Knoxville Opera Rossini Festival. "Rossini's Orsini" depicted eight Rossini operas for viewers to identify and was adorned with an American flag and dogwood blossoms. Scissors, razor, and music staff denoted *The Barber of Seville*. An apple, arrow, and music staff portrayed *William Tell*. An Italian flag stood for either *The Italian Girl in Algiers* or *The Turk in Italy*. The fleur-de-lis was the symbol for *The Journey to Rheims*. The bird represented *The Thieving Magpie*. A crown and glass slipper were, of course, *Cinderella*. The two masks suggested *Il Signor Bruschino*, and the Moor represented *Otello*.

Because of our interest in art, we sponsored the exhibition of Rembrandt's etchings at the Knoxville Museum of Art. I was told that this was the first time an individual had sponsored an exhibit at the museum.

We also have visited major museums across the world, including the Prado; the Metropolitan Museum of Art; the National Museum; the Tate; the British Museum; museums in Florence, Italy, including the Orsini Palace collection; the Cairo Museum; the Rembrandt Museum; the Picasso Museum; the Louvre; the Vienna Museum; and many other smaller ones. These have been exhilarating experiences.

I have always enjoyed playing a social hand of bridge but never played competitively. However, Sandy had approximately 200 life master points and wanted to become a life master in bridge. In 2006 I started learning different bridge conventions with the help of Mike Waters, Geoffrey Greene, and Marlene Wass. I entered bridge tournaments with Sandy so she could earn the required 300 points to become a life master. She also needed a certain number of gold points, which are awarded at regional and national tournaments. I am happy to say that in Gatlinburg, Tennessee, in April 2007, at the world's largest bridge tournament, she earned the remaining gold points she needed to become a life master. During that period of time, I amassed 115 master points myself, but since I have no great desire to be a life master, I will not play in so many competitions in the future.

Chapter 27

Turbulence on the Sea of Life

W hile I have been blessed with many wonderful opportunities in my life, obviously there have been struggles. To invoke the *Winter Galley* metaphor, my childhood was turbulent, what with growing up poor, having an alcoholic father, and weathering the Great Depression.

But, by far, the greatest storms occurred during my busy career as an adult. They involved tragedies in my immediate family.

My brother Bill and his wife, Elsie, were in their place of business, a bar in uptown Harrisburg, with a customer on November 9, 1977, when two gunmen entered and ordered them to get down on their hands and knees and empty their pockets.

Even though all three victims complied, one of the assailants shot my brother in the back of the head, execution style. Then the men pistol-whipped my sister-in-law and the customer.

Elsie survived, but never left her house thereafter because she was afraid. She became a recluse as a result of this crime.

The murderers were caught and tried but received light

sentences because they were under the influence of alcohol and supposedly not fully aware of what they were doing.

Dauphin County Court Judge William Caldwell called the incident "one of the most heinous and brutal crimes that has been inflicted on our citizens and community in recent years."

Bill's death had an enormous impact on me. But one thing it didn't do was make me prejudiced. You see, the two murderers were African Americans. When they killed my brother in Harrisburg, I was raising contributions to support a new African-American medical school in Atlanta.

I had grown up in a poor, mixed-race neighborhood, studying, playing, and working with African Americans. I had escaped poverty through education and hard work, but many in my neighborhood had not. I thought education and a chance at a better life might help to prevent a tragedy like this from happening to someone else. So I continued to contribute to and raise money for Morehouse School of Medicine in Atlanta. I also made a conscious decision to not stereotype individuals, but to judge them on their own strengths. I wanted to help bridge the broad racial divide of the 1970s and not allow the race of my brother's killers to affect my choices in life.

It's hard and perhaps unfair to apply today's standards to the past, because society has evolved since then. But the 1970s were just a decade after the Civil Rights Act, born in the presidency of John F. Kennedy. That period was a time of great change in this country.

Because of Bill's death, I became a supporter of the death penalty. Later when I was on the board of Baxter, an amnesty group wrote us requesting that we not sell one of the drugs used in the execution of criminals.

I responded to amnesty group members with a personal letter saying I couldn't support their request, and that I wondered what they were doing for the victims instead of the perpetrators. I related the story about my brother and his wife.

I never received a response.

A few years later, on July 21, 1980, my sister Helen died as a result of malpractice at a well-known medical institution in Pennsylvania. Her husband sued the hospital and the doctor, and the case was settled out of court.

In July 1985, my mother, who had been our family's backbone of support during my youth, died of a brain hemorrhage suffered when she fell down the last three steps of the stairs in our home while visiting us in Connecticut. This occurred more than twenty years after my father's death. My mother must have had a dizzy spell. We had been waiting for her so we could all go to church together.

Just before Christmas the following year, my younger brother Arthur, still in his forties, suffered a stroke. I flew to Harrisburg to see him. It was obvious he was paralyzed totally from the neck down and could not speak. Under those circumstances, I had to advise the family not to try any extraordinary therapies to keep him alive. He died in a hospital in Camp Hill.

On Aug. 9, 1992, my brother Herman died of complications from diabetes after having part of both legs amputated. He would not follow his doctors' advice, which I believe contributed to his early death.

My sister Elizabeth died on March 13, 1999. She had had major heart surgery on five different occasions. Betty, as we called her, had rheumatic fever as a child and underwent multiple valve replacements. She was the big sister who took care of me when I was young. When we were both adults, I tried to help her as much as I could. She moved to Harrisburg into a one-room apartment to be closer to brothers and sisters still living there. We were sad that, even so, Betty was alone when she passed away.

We have suffered loss on my wife's side of the family too. Her sister, Janet, died a couple of years ago of cancer of the eye, which is curable today.

May all their memories be a blessing.

My other brothers and sisters are still living but suffering various ailments of old age. Hazel, Pauline, Chet, and Charlie still reside in the Harrisburg area. Harold lives in Virginia, Ted in South Carolina, and Bob in Texas. And I am in Tennessee.

Sandy's brother Bill and his wife, Anne, are living in Appleton, Wisconsin. They have three children: Karen, Allyson, and William. Karen and her husband, Tom Medema, have five children. Allyson and her husband, Eric Breiland, have one boy named Jack. We have been close to my wife's family and exchanged visits, especially when the children were growing up.

I could not talk about loved ones without mentioning some who are really extended family. Certainly this would include all the Scoteses. Tom and Ted are like brothers. Their remarkable mother, Vasiliki Scotes, published her first book in 2008 at the age of one hundred. It is a collection of folk songs, poems, and stories from her childhood in a remote mountain village in Epirus, Greece.

Bernie and Pat Goldstein from college days certainly are like extended family to us. Ed McGinley is another friend from those days. Guggi and Paul Quaintance have been like brother and sister to Sandy and me. Harry and Tucki Hitch, bridge buddies and tennis players from New Canaan days, are still very close friends. We visit back and forth with them. Bill Nydam, who was my chief financial officer and then chief operating officer at AmHS, is also a member of the extended family. I also include in this list Cindy Sullenberger, who has worked for us almost from the day our house was built here in Knoxville. Last but not least is Nelson Chaffin, who now lives in Hawaii after having served as president and CEO of VIBA in California. Nelson, better known as Fluffie, makes me happy every time I speak to him.

As Tom Scotes says in the preface, we are fortunate if we have good family and good friends. I count myself among those so privileged and am grateful for everyone who has stood by in all kinds of weather. I hope I have done the same for them.

Chapter 28

Publications and Honors

My career gave me a window into twentieth-century history. It's interesting what a great role medicine plays in society. I published and/or delivered more than one hundred-ninety papers on topics as diverse as AIDS and aspirin, hexachlorophene and pentazocine.

Although my motive in publishing was to educate experts and the general public and deepen the pool of research literature, appointments resulted.

For instance, I served as a consultant to the U.S. State Department, New York State Health Planning Commission, International Health Issues Council of the Conference Board, and National Council on Patient Information.

A paper I wrote in 1962, "Care of the Aged," received honorable mention from the National Geriatrics Society. I believe this led to my appointment to the White House executive committee's Mini-Conference on Aging in New York.

In 1979, after serving on the Joint Commission on Prescription Drug Use, I published a paper on post-marketing drug surveillance. The topic has been controversial for decades. At last the U.S. Senate has passed a bill mandating the Food and Drug Administration to perform post-marketing surveillance on all drugs.

Another paper I wrote about AIDS led to my appointment to the National Leadership Coalition on AIDS from 1992 through 1994.

My passion for helping doctors prevent malpractice fueled many papers on that issue. They, along with my tenure on the HEW Malpractice Commission, brought about more service opportunities on the boards of four medical schools and the University of Pennsylvania School of Nursing.

A paper I delivered to a combined meeting of the FDA, Pharmaceutical Manufacturers Association, and Justice Department on the role of physicians in industry regarding problems of prescription drug abuse was probably instrumental in Sen. Edward Kennedy's naming me to the Commission on Prescription Drug Use. I also served on the New York State Commission on Prescription Drug Use and the Advisory Board on Patient Information and Education.

As a member of these commissions, I was one of the authors of the final reports that received widespread publicity and consideration by different legislative bodies.

After my paper "Free Clinic Responsibilities" was published, I served on the board of the St. Vincent de Paul Center for the Homeless in San Diego.

Thanks to a paper I wrote on the ethics of medical research, I was invited to participate in the World Health Organization's Conference on Trends and Prospects in Health Care in Geneva, Switzerland, in December 1977.

I delivered a paper at an FDA symposium at Bloomfield College in New Jersey. The college president, Jack Noonan, kindly invited me to be that year's commencement speaker and surprised me with an honorary degree.

I wrote four published law review articles. Needless to say, I didn't shy away from controversial topics. For *Temple Law*

Quarterly, I discussed "Abortion Laws Need Therapy." In the *Dickinson Law Review*, I explored "Blood Transfusions," looking at liability possibilities as well as implications of refusals by Jehovah's Witnesses to have transfusions. In the *Cleveland-Marshall Law Review*, my article "Medical Witnesses–A Review" outlined the responsibilities of physicians testifying in court. In the *New York Law Review*, I wrote on "Immunizations." All of these articles were innovative at the time or were the results of my personal experience.

Other writings included editorials for *The Journal of Legal Medicine* on the international convention on psychotropic substances, immunization warnings, informed consent, cancer phobia, and other topics.

There were also reviews on books like J.E. Horsley's *Testifying in Court*. I had met Jack earlier as a member of the Malpractice Commission. He was a well-known defense lawyer with Craig & Craig in Mattoon, Illinois. We became great pen-pals for many years, especially on malpractice and the law. We stopped writing after he became seriously ill.

I served on the editorial boards of a number of publications, beginning with *Forensic Science*. I was a consulting editor to *Hospital Formulary* from 1969 to 1979, editorial board member of *Legal Aspects of Medical Practice* in 1978 and 1979, board member of the *Journal of Regulatory Toxicology and Pharmacology* from 1981 to 1987, and editorial board member of *Medical Malpractice Prevention* from 1985 to 1990. In 1988 I was asked to be a reviewer for the *Annals of Internal Medicine*.

Lectures and speeches also kept me busy and allowed me to present the latest in medical research to colleagues and the general public.

At one time or another I lectured at the City University of New York, University of California, San Diego, Drew University, Albany Medical College, New York Medical School,

Columbia University Medical School, Cornell University Medical School, University of Michigan, Morehouse School of Medicine, Dickinson School of Law, University of Minnesota School of Pharmacy, Wayne State Medical School, University of Pittsburgh, Duquesne University, Upsala College, and the University of North Carolina.

I also gave the Distinguished Lecture at the Ninth Annual Horton Roundtree Health Law Forum at East Carolina School of Medicine. My topic was "The Impact of Alternative Healthcare Delivery Systems on Physicians and Hospitals."

Healthcare reform has intrigued the nation. I have given speeches on the topic at major hospital systems around the United States, the Goldman Sachs Second Annual Healthcare Conference, American Conference of Healthcare Executives, Society of Medical Administrators, Robert Wood Johnson Foundation, Biomedical Business International, Joint Commission on the Accreditation of Healthcare Organizations, California Society of Plastic Surgeons, Institute of the Americas, and clubs like Kiwanis.

My career also generated unusual ancillary assignments. For instance, in San Diego I was asked to arbitrate a very interesting case by a young man who was suing over a defective pin placed in his leg. Both sides presented compelling arguments. A dramatic presentation of a video by the defense attorneys revealed that the young man was responsible for his own injuries, participating in all sorts of physical activities he should not have been. We found for the company.

I am humbled by how many organizations and publications have honored me. They include the following: *Community Leaders of America*; *Two Thousand Men of Achievement*; *Notable Americans of the Bicentennial Era*; *Standard and Poor's Register of Corporations, Directors, and Executives*; *Who's Who in Healthcare; Personalities of America*; *Who's Who in Technology*; *Who's Who in the East*; *Who's Who in*

America; Who's Who in the World; Who's Who in Business and Finance; Who's Who Worldwide; Who's Who in the West; Who's Who in Science and Engineering; Who's Who among Human Services Professionals Worldwide Platinum Edition; Who's Who in California; Who's Who Registry Platinum Edition; One Hundred Business and Community Leaders in San Diego; and *Who's Who in Finance and Industry.*

Other honors have included selection for the "Top 25" in *Health Week* in May 1989 and the "Big Hitters" list in the *San Diego Business Journal* in 1988-1989. I was a 1977 nominee for *Modern Medicine*'s Distinguished Achievement Award and received the President's Award from the American College of Legal Medicine in 1976, 1978, 1988, and 1989.

In 1975 I was elected an honorary member of the Regional Anesthesia Society and served on its board from 1976 to 1986. In 1976 I was given the Distinguished Service Award of Medical Executives, Inc.

I was featured in *Penn Medicine* in fall 1988; *Pharmaceutical Executive* in July 1989; and *Modern Healthcare*, April 9, 1990. Faulkner and Gray included me in the Healthcare 500.

In 1989 I received the Outstanding Alumni Award from Dickinson School of Law, where I was a charter member of the John Reed Society.

In 1992 I won an Innovators Award from the American College of Physician Executives and was named San Diego Entrepreneur of the Year in 1994. In 1996 I received an honorary Doctor of Laws degree from Dickinson School of Law and also the University of California, San Diego Medical Auxiliary Achievement Award. In 1997 I was given the University of California, San Diego's Civis Universitatis Award. In 1998 the University of California, San Diego made me an honorary alumnus, and in 1999 the American College of Legal Medicine gave me its Gold Medal Lifetime Achievement Award. Two years later University of the Cumberlands in Kentucky pre-

The Monroe E. Trout Premier Cares Award is given annually to the best indigent medical care program that can be duplicated in the U.S.

sented me its Servant Leadership Award. In 2003 I received an honorary degree from University of the Cumberlands and gave the commencement address.

My fraternity honored me with the national Delta Tau Delta Alumni Achievement Award in 1996 and in 2000 named me among the One Hundred Most Influential Delts of the Twentieth Century.

I have also turned down several awards because of the length of travel it would take to receive them. An example is the International Health Care Man of the Year Award in Cambridge, England. I was not able to attend the University of Pennsylvania Sesquicentennial Class of the Greek Honor Roll representing Delta Tau Delta.

I have been cited by the United States Congress, California State Legislature, and the counties of San Diego, California, and Knox, Tennessee. Recently I was asked to serve as a Patron of the Churchill Archives Centre, along with Randolph Churchill and Baroness Margaret Thatcher, among others.

I have treasured many plaques, pieces of silver and crystal, citations, and other innovative mementos of my service on many corporate and charitable boards and committees.

It also has been my honor to receive tributes by the press. I was profiled in *The San Diego Business Journal* in the November 25-December 1, 1991, issue. *Modern Healthcare* featured me on the cover on December 7, 1991. On April 9, 1990, the magazine featured American Healthcare Systems. My picture appeared on the cover of *Pharmaceutical Executive* in July 1989, and in January 1990 the magazine interviewed me on the future of healthcare. In October 1973, *Medical Economics* asked me to predict what would happen by 1978 on such vital issues as national health insurance, malpractice hazards, fee for service, and doctor distribution. The fall 1988 *Penn Medicine* profiled me in an article called "Trout's World," which featured a picture of Sandy and me flanking Barbara Bush.

Chapter 29

The Riches in Poverty

There's no shame in being poor. But for some reason we have a stigma about poverty in this country, just as we do about mental illness and other misfortunes. I've met many people who grew up in dire circumstances but became amazingly successful adults. Yet they don't want anyone to know about their early background. What a shame that is.

I'm not embarrassed that my father and I stood in line to get cornmeal during the Great Depression. We certainly weren't alone in doing what we could for basic survival. There's no way I would want to relive the adversity, but at the same time I recognize it helped lay the foundation for who I have become.

My philosophy is there's no shame in being poor; there's only shame in not helping others when you're successful. Many "strangers on the highway of life" helped put me on the road to success. Some of them–teachers like Mrs. Burgoon, who encouraged me to graduate from high school–I have recognized as mentors. Others are truly anonymous, including people who donated money for scholarships that helped me afford college and medical school.

Growing up poor gave me incentive. I didn't like being hungry, as we sometimes were in my family of two adults and fourteen children. I worked hard as a child and young adult, juggling many jobs and going to school. It didn't matter whether I was painting parking meters or serving as a parking lot attendant, making milkshakes or picking cherries, shoveling snow or digging ditches–I was determined to get ahead. Many nights as a medical student and later as a law student, I survived on four hours' sleep, what with going to class, studying, having a family, and working various odd jobs.

No matter what cards we are dealt, through fortitude and courage we can have a successful life. I'm not talking about money necessarily because there are many definitions of success. I think one of them is being of service. It's important to give back to society in whatever way we can.

I always have liked to give back through community and professional service and charitable contributions. Sandy and I have been privileged to be able to donate to and to raise funds for many worthwhile organizations and special individuals. How rewarding it is to be the stranger on someone else's highway, to help them along in whatever way they might need.

Who among us hasn't known struggle? Even Abraham Lincoln had his share of failure, and he went on to become one of the greatest presidents America has ever had. We can learn from hard times and become even stronger than before.

Having grown up in the Depression, I learned some financial habits that seem rare today. One of them concerns debt. Back then if we couldn't pay for something, we just didn't buy it. That's a great and simple way to live.

Also, I've tended to be a saver–of money and nostalgic items. I always heard "To make money you have to have money," so from early on I saved 10 percent of my salary. Sometimes that was hard because there wasn't as much disposable income for the family to enjoy immediately. But when the chance came to make investments, we had the money to do so and they proved extremely rewarding financially.

Believe it or not, I also saved my Navy uniform as well as the jacket, leather boots, and heavy beige socks I wore when I was with the Marines. The sturdy military clothes always came in handy during snowstorms in Connecticut. I did have my 1953 Navy greatcoat tailored into a civilian overcoat which I wear to this day. I never thought the coat would last more than fifty years, although it has needed some new linings in that time.

I have needed some refurbishing over the years myself. Some of the storm clouds in my life have been related to health. I have had more than twenty operations and serious diseases that most people barely survive. I want to emphasize, as both a doctor and a patient, that we not only can survive illness, but also thrive and live full, meaningful lives.

There always will be a mix of favorable and unfavorable winds blowing through our lives. Success to me is how we decide to navigate them. I guess you could say the internal compass guides our course home.

Press reports on the
murder of my brother Bill,
November 9, 1977.

2 city men charged in murder

Two Harrisburg men today remained in area prisons awaiting Nov. 23 preliminary hearings on charges of criminal homicide in connection with Wednesday's slaying of an Uptown tavern owner.

Michael Leonard Rickard, 24, of the 500 block of Wiconisco Street, was remanded yesterday to Dauphin County Prison and Thomas Alonzo Richardson, 19, of the 2100 block of North Seventh Street, was sent to Cumberland County Prison, police said.

Both men, who were arrested Thursday on unrelated armed robbery charges, were arraigned separately before District Justice Paul H. Hardy and were ordered held without bail. They are charged in connection with the killing of William Trout, 51, owner of Troutie's Bar, Seventh and Maclay Streets.

The suspects had been held in Dauphin County Prison, facing charges of armed robbery and aggravated assault involving the theft of $50 and a .32-caliber pistol from Harry Long of 512 Maclay St. a few hours before the Trout slaying, according to Det. Cpl. John R. Christian Jr.

Long was struck on the head and shot in the foot in a struggle during the robbery, Christian said.

Besides the criminal homicide charges, Rickard and Richardson each is charged with attempted robbery and six counts of aggravated assault stemming from the pistol-whipping of six of Trout's customers, Christian said.

Five of the persons assaulted were taken to local hospitals for treatment and released, and the sixth was treated at the scene. Police reports indicate Trout was shot once in the head as he lay over a shuffleboard game.

Christian said Richardson also has been charged with the Nov. 1 holdup at To-Jo's Convenient Market, 2259 N. Sixth St., and the Nov. 5 robbery of James Allen at his Jefferson Street home.

All charges filed against the two will be heard at the Nov. 23 hearing.

10—The Patriot, Harrisburg, Pa. Thursday, May 11, 1978

Convicted Killer of Bar Owner Gets 43-86

A city man convicted of slaying Uptown bar owner William Trout was sentenced by two Dauphin County Court judges Wednesday to a combined total of 43 to 86 years on eight charges.

Thomas Alonzo Richardson, 19, was sentenced by Judge William W. Caldwell on charges of third-degree murder, robbery and five counts of aggravated assault and by Judge John C. Dowling on another robbery charge.

Caldwell, as he had done in sentencing Richardson's co-defendant in the pistol-whipping of five persons in Trout's tavern, called the in-

cident "one of the most heinous and brutal crimes that has been inflicted on our citizens and community in recent years."

Richardson, of the 2100 block of North Seventh Street, was found guilty by a jury on Feb. 15 of third-degree murder in the execution-style shooting death of Trout, 50, and guilty of five counts of aggravated assault as an accomplice of Michael Leonard Rickard, 24, convicted of beating four patrons and Trout's wife on the head with the butt of a handgun.

Both men then pleaded guilty on March 14 to robbery charges in the

theft of the gun used in the slaying. The robbery at the residence of Harry Long, 512 Maclay St., and the shooting and beatings at Troutie's Bar, Seventh and Maclay streets, all occurred on the night of Nov. 9, 1977.

Rickard, who was found innocent on the murder charge but convicted on the five aggravated assaults, was sentenced on April 10 by Caldwell to 25 to 50 years.

Richardson, in a separate jury trial at which Dowling presided, was found guilty on March 15 of robbery in the theft of $100 from To-Jo's Market, Sixth and Emerald

streets, last Nov. 1.

The double sentencing Wednesday began in front of Caldwell, who imposed maximum combined 35- to 70-year terms: 10 to 20 years on third-degree murder, 10 to 20 years on robbery and 5 to 10 years each on the five aggravated assaults. Two of the 5- to 10-year sentences were made concurrent with the robbery term.

All the other sentences were ordered to run consecutively.

Richardson then was ushered to Dowling's courtroom by sheriff's deputies.

"I can't think of a situation

which more mandat ment," Dowling sai to 16 years for the on top of Caldwell's

Court-appointed ney John D. Kuhn a impose the sente with those already that "would be to tence, which makes

Kuhn asked Ca the maximum 10- on the murder co make all the other s rent.

"We're asking

Letter about my election to the Board of Directors of Sterling Drug Inc.

STERLING DRUG INC.
NINETY PARK AVENUE, NEW YORK, N.Y. 10016

ROBERT B. SIMONTON
SECRETARY

December 4, 1978

Monroe E. Trout
Sterling Drug Inc.
90 Park Avenue
New York, NY   10016

Dear Monroe:

I am pleased to confirm that the Board of Directors of Sterling Drug Inc. elected you a director of the Corporation at the regular meeting held on December 1, 1978.

With this formal notification, I enclose copies of the Certificate of Incorporation and By-laws of the Corporation.

Congratulations and my best wishes for your success in your new responsibility.

Sincerely,

Bob

RBS/evt

Enclosures

Letter from the CEO of Sterling Drug Inc., on my tenth anniversary.

STERLING DRUG INC.
NINETY PARK AVENUE, NEW YORK, N. Y. 10016

W. CLARKE WESCOE, M. D.
CHAIRMAN OF THE BOARD

1 June 1978

Dear Monroe —

Today marks your tenth anniversary with Sterling — a significant milestone for you and for the Corporation. On behalf of all your colleagues let me express our congratulations and, as well, our thanks for jobs superbly done with loyalty, devotion and dedication. In these ten years literally all facets of our operations have been touched by what you have done. You have earned from many a great deal of affection but, more than that, an enormous respect.

My years, which almost coincide with yours, have been made more lively, more stimulating and more pleasurable by our association. For that I thank you personally — as a friend and an admirer.

I look forward to many more years of close association — of hard work together — and a deepening friendship.

Lastly, please express our thanks to Jody for all the hours she spent alone when you served above the call of duty.

Sincerely,

Clarke

Letter about my promotion to vice president of Sterling Drug Inc.

HILTON HOTELS CORPORATION

OFFICE OF THE PRESIDENT
9990 SANTA MONICA BOULEVARD
BEVERLY HILLS, CALIFORNIA 90212

January 25, 1974

Dr. Monroe E. Trout
Vice President
Sterling Drug, Inc.
90 Park Avenue
New York, New York 10016

Dear Dr. Trout:

Congratulations on the recognition that has been
extended to you by Sterling Drug. The challenges
inherent in your new position, as Vice President,
are self-evident – and I'm sure they are in capable
hands.

My best wishes.

Sincerely,

BARRON HILTON
President

BH:mn

Speaking with the mayor of Dijon, France.

L'état-major « recherche » du groupe Sterling Drug à Dijon

Réception hier matin à l'hôtel de ville de Dijon par M. Robert Poujade

Du 25 au 29 mars, le centre de recherche Winthrop, à Dijon-Longvic, accueille l'état-major « recherche » du groupe Sterling Drug : le « Sterling Research Group » qui coordonne l'ensemble des activités de recherche et développement du groupe. M. le docteur Monroe Trout, président pour les affaires médicales et scientifiques, participe à ce séminaire de même que les docteurs Chakrin, président du « Sterling Research Group », Margetts, Potts, Bailey et Ross.

« C'est une manifestation tangible de l'intérêt que porte notre groupe à notre centre de recherche pour la France implanté à Longvic », indique le docteur Jean Legros, directeur du centre et directeur de la recherche biologique pour l'Europe, « intérêt attaché à la qualité du travail effectué ici ainsi qu'à son acceptabilité au plan international ».

Créé il y a 20 ans, le centre de recherche Winthrop emploie une soixantaine de personnes.

Ce séminaire permettra d'une part de faire la mise au point sur l'état actuel d'avancement des différents projets de recherche, d'autre part de définir l'orientation des axes de recherche pour le futur.

Press report on Milrinone, Sterling's heart drug.

A12 SUNDAY, MARCH 2, 2003

New drug boon to children who undergo heart surgery

BY HANNAH LOBEL
Associated Press

DALLAS — A drug used to help the heart pump blood and lower blood pressure may reduce the risk of deteriorating heart function in infants and children soon after heart surgery, according to a study published this week by the American Heart Association.

Milrinone has been used before to treat young patients who developed low cardiac output syndrome after surgery. But the study led by researchers at The Children's Hospital of Philadelphia is the first to examine the use of the drug as a preventative measure.

The researchers found infants and children given a high dose of milrinone during the critical first 36 hours after surgery were 55 percent less likely to develop the syndrome than those not given the drug.

The report was published in the journal Circulation. The study was sponsored by the drug's manufacturer, Sanofi-Synthelabo Inc.

About a quarter of infants and

put after heart surgery, but nowadays few die of it, said Gil Wernovsky, a principal investigator and the medical director of the cardiac intensive-care unit at the hospital. That wasn't the case 20 years ago, when the condition was a likely death sentence, he said.

The study also indicated that children did not face the side effects that have been reported in adults using the drug — those being low blood pressure, blood platelet abnormalities and irregular heart rhythms.

Dr. Timothy J. Gardner, a heart surgeon at the Hospital of the University of Pennsylvania, said the study shows doctors can safely address the risks of low output syndrome before "the horse is out of the barn."

"If you can find a way to sort of tide them over that low output syndrome that develops in the first day or so after surgery, then your overall success rate will be much better," Gardner said.

The study divided 238 patients at 31 hospitals into three groups that were given either a placebo or a low or high dose of milri-

less than a year old — the most susceptible group — and all were younger than 7.

About 11.7 percent of patients given a high dose of milrinone developed the syndrome, compared with 25.9 percent in the placebo group and 17.5 percent in the low-dose group.

Infants and children given the drug also were less likely to require hospitalization longer than 15 days.

Dr. Mihai Gheorghiade, who has studied the harmful effects of milrinone when used in adult patients with heart failure, said the study results appeared to be promising for infants and children.

But he warned that a larger study may be needed to ensure that the therapy is safe. Two of the patients in the study who were given milrinone died.

"Statistically, this is not significant. However, I would underline the fact that in the placebo group was zero mortality," Gheorghiade said.

Wernovsky said an outside review committee determined that the deaths were unrelated to the

Letter from Mary Lasker on the aspirin controversy.

MRS. ALBERT D. LASKER
870 UNITED NATIONS PLAZA
NEW YORK, NEW YORK 10017
TELEPHONE 758-1242

November 24th, 1977

Dear Dr. Trout,

So many thanks for the papers you sent me on the current aspirin studies. I am very much interested in this subject, as you know.

Also, so many thanks for helping me by answering my questions on Interferon.

Warm good wishes,

Yours,

Mary Lasker

Dr. Monroe E. Trout
Vice President-Director
  of Medical Affairs
Sterling Drug Inc.
90 Park Avenue
New York, New York 10016

Letter about my meeting with Chief Buthelezi of South Africa.

Lutheran
Church
in ## America

231 MADISON AVENUE
NEW YORK N.Y. 10016
Cable: Lutheran Newyork
212-481-9639 == 696-6804

Office of the Bishop
Department of Planning, Research and Evaluation

October 7, 1982

Monroe E. Trout, M.D.
Sterling Drug, Inc.
90 Park Avenue
New York, New York 10016

Dear Monroe:

Thanks for your letter and a copy of Sterling Drug's policy regarding employees in South Africa. I am sharing both your letter and a copy of the policy with Dr. Crumley and Dr. Paul Brndjar, director of our Department of Church and Society.

By the way, Paul Brndjar should be a person who ought to be involved in any meeting with Chief Buthelezi. I do know that Dr. Crumley, Paul Brndjar and other leaders from our church have been in regular contacts with church leaders from South Africa, and that Dr. Crumley has a trip to South Africa planned for next January.

As I shared in my comments at church, many of us here on the staff share your concerns about the effect of the convention's action, not only in relating to you and others who are seeking to work for justice through corporations, but also in the many meetings that are scheduled with corporate leaders who are not members of the LCA. I believe strongly that Christians have a biblical mandate to work for justice in the world. But (maybe it's my own background in business), I personally have long objected to church statements which imply that none of the leaders of corporations are Christians who are trying to live out their faith in "the market place."

I suppose philosophically we can say tht the action of the convention is one of the risks of having a democratic procedure built into the heart of the decision making and legislative processes of the church. Realistically, I hope it does not destroy the bridges we have tired to build with persons like you.

Thanks again for your letter.

Best regards,

al

Albert L. Haversat

ALH:tkl

Letter about visiting professorship honoring Lou Goodman.

F – 502 Visiting Professor
9/26/8

THE UNIVERSITY OF UTAH
MEDICAL CENTER
SALT LAKE CITY 84132

COLLEGE OF MEDICINE

DEPARTMENT OF PHARMACOLOGY

September 20, 198:

Dear Monroe:

This brief note is to acknowledge with thanks your letter of Sept. 9th and the illuminated hand-drawn plaque. I am certain Bill Riker will make excellent use of the generous gift.

It is hard to accept the fact that it is 51 years ago that I graduated fr. the University of Oregon School of Medicine and then moved on to Johns Hopkins and Yale. The years rush by.

My best regards to you and to Clarke Wescoe, and all good wishes

Cordially,

Lou Goodman

Letter about visiting professorship honoring Alfred Gilman.

ALFRED GILMAN
123 YORK STREET, 8A
NEW HAVEN, CONNECTICUT 06511

Sept. 28, 1983

Dear Dr Trout:

Upon my recent return to New Haven from my summer home, I was greeted by the Sterling Drug Visiting Professorship Plaque. It is indeed a suitable memento and one that I greatly appreciate.

As you probably know the Department selected my son as the first recipient of the visiting professorship. Al Sartorelli made a very flattering introduction including both Sterling Drug and me. The lecture was very well attended and received. All in all it was a gala week.

Please extend my thanks to Clark Wiscoe

Sincerely,

Alfred Gilman

Letter from assistant secretary of HEW inviting me to be a consultant on medical malpractice.

DEPARTMENT OF HEALTH, EDUCATION, AND WELFARE

OFFICE OF THE SECRETARY

WASHINGTON, D.C. 20201

NOV 21 1974

Monroe E. Trout, M.D.
Vice President-Director of Medical Affairs
Sterling Drug, Inc.
90 Park Avenue
New York, New York 10016

Dear Dr. Trout:

I am aware that you in the private sector have been deeply interested in and concerned about malpractice and the issues surrounding it. I am sure we would all agree that the subject needs to be addressed at the earliest opportunity with a view to developing some means for ameliorating the problems associated with it.

The Report of the Secretary's Commission on Medical Malpractice provides a useful base from which to go forward. While it is not my intention that the Federal Government should interfere with any efforts being put forth by the private sector, I am aware there are perhaps certain areas where the Government might be able to help.

With this in mind, I am inviting you to meet with me and a small group of individuals knowledgeable in the field on Wednesday, December 11, 1974, to discuss the following broad areas:

1. Assurance of availability of malpractice insurance.

2. Other means for settling disputes than the judicial process, such as arbitration.

3. Rules, regulations, definitions, and criteria being promulgated under PSRO or National Health Insurance which may broaden the base for malpractice suits.

APPENDIX C-1b

Letter from assistant secretary of HEW inviting me to be a consultant on medical malpractice.

   4. The need for legislation and/or development of
      model legislation which might be helpful in
      coming to grips with such areas as statute of
      limitations for filing suits; misuse of <u>res</u>
      <u>ipsa</u> <u>loquitur</u>; contingency fees; informed
      consent; and <u>ad</u> <u>damnum</u> clauses.

If there are other areas which you would like to bring up,
you may, of course, do so.

It is my intention that this meeting will result in suggestions and/or recommendations as to how the Federal Government
might be useful in resolving the problems of medical malpractice. I realize, of course, that representatives of the
insurance industry, the legal profession, and others will need
to be consulted for their views; and I plan to meet with them
after this initial conference.

The meeting will start at 10 a.m. in Room 5131 HEW North and
last perhaps into the early evening.

I very much hope you will be able to join me on December 11
for what I consider an important meeting for the medical
profession.

Sincerely,

Charles C. Edwards, M.D.
Assistant Secretary for Health

Letter from Caspar Weinberger.

THE SECRETARY OF HEALTH, EDUCATION, AND WELFARE
WASHINGTON, D. C. 20201

JAN 20 1975

Monroe E. Trout, M.D.
Vice President - Director of
   Medical Affairs
Sterling Drug, Inc.
90 Park Avenue
New York, New York 10016

Dear Dr. Trout:

I very much appreciated your coming to Washington to participate
in our discussion of the malpractice insurance problem. I trust
it was understood that, from our point of view, we see no broad
Federal involvement short of being prepared to face the real
emergency, should one occur, of reduction of services by doctors
for whom insurance is no longer available. Under those circumstances, obviously the health of the nation would be involved
to an extent that we would have to do whatever we could to help.

I was sorry I was unable to stay with you through the morning
as I had hoped, but I understand from Drs. Edwards and Egeberg
that there was much healthy discussion with evidence of increased
understanding as the day wore on. I look forward to hearing the
results of the National Association of Insurance Commissioners'
committee meeting in Dallas the end of this month, and I hope that
at a meeting here toward the middle of February we may hear of
more definitive plans concerning the short-term solution to this
problem and some incisive recommendations for studies, statistical
accumulation and pilot projects that will help in the long-term
solution.

I thank you again for meeting with us and look forward to our next
meeting.

Sincerely,

Caspar W. Weinberger

Secretary

Letter from Norton Mockridge about cassette series on medical malpractice.

MEDICAL ECONOMICS CASSETTE SERVICE

MEMO FROM **NORTON MOCKRIDGE, Editor**

5/20/76

Dear Monroe,

It took a little while,
but we made it!
Have been traveling a
lot — including a
months' vacation in
Mexico — but am
trying to settle down
for the summer —
Let's have lunch soon.
It's been much too long.
Will you give me a ring
when you're free?
all the best —
Norton

MEDICAL ECONOMICS COMPANY
Litton Oradell, New Jersey 07649

201-262-3030

Letter about my appointment to the Cleveland Clinic Board.

Diamond Shamrock Corporation

General Offices   300 Union Commerce Building   Cleveland, Ohio 44115   Telephone 621-6100

JAMES A. HUGHES
CHAIRMAN OF THE BOARD

October 20, 1971

Dr. Monroe E. Trout
Sterling Drug, Inc.
90 Park Ave.
New York, N. Y.   10016

Dear Dr. Trout:

This is merely a personal note as Chairman to welcome you to the Board of Trustees of the Cleveland Clinic Foundation. I think you will find the experience rewarding - at least I have.

Hope you can make the next meeting on November 8. Unfortunately, this will be the first one in several years I will miss as must be in Europe that week.

Look forward to seeing you.

Sincerely,

JAH:vs

Letter about my election to the Board of Trustees, Dickinson School of Law.

Dickinson

SCHOOL OF LAW

CARLISLE ● PENNSYLVANIA
17013

June 25, 1973

HON. DALE F. SHUGHART, President
Cumberland County Court House
Carlisle, Pennsylvania

Dr. Monroe E. Trout
81 Mariomi Road
New Canaan, Connecticut 06840

Dear Dr. Trout:

I am delighted to receive your letter of acceptance of the election to the board of trustees of
the Dickinson School of Law.

As I indicated to you earlier, we have one
definite meeting each year at commencement time,
but more recently have been having another
meeting in the fall. A meeting is planned for
this fall to cover a number of items that will
be of interest to everyone.

Kindest personal regards,

Sincerely,

Dale F. Shughart

DFS:bd

Appendix D-3

Letter about my service on the Advisory Panel of the ACME Task Force on Accreditation.

 Alliance for Continuing Medical Education

ugust 30, 1976

Monroe E. Trout, M.D.
V.P. and Dir. of Med. Affairs
Sterling Drug Inc.
90 Park Avenue
New York, New York 10016

Dear Dr. Trout:

Thanks for your willingness to participate in the work of the Alliance for Continuing Medical Education. We would like to ask you to serve on the Advisory Panel of the ACME task force on Accreditation Standards. The goal of the task force is to come up with a final recommendation on a principal strategy for implementation of the priority (plus alternatives if possible) at the second national conference of the Alliance next January.

The Advisory Panel will serve as a sounding board for the work of the task force primarily by critical review of drafts of the task force report. Members of the Advisory Panel will not attend meetings of the task force, but may be consulted by mail or phone on specific issues in which they have expertise.

Members of the task force on Accreditation are listed on the enclosed sheet, along with the statement of the priority as given at the first national conference of ACME. All the task forces met in July and August, and shortly thereafter should be generating a preliminary statement that will be sent to Advisory Panel members.

If you are unable to serve on the Advisory Panel, please let Lew Miller know within the next 10 days. Otherwise we shall assume that you are willing to serve in this capacity.

Sincerely,

William C Felch MD

William C. Felch, M.D.

Lewis A. Miller

Lewis A. Miller

Key Objective: /st
To identify, and promote the implementation of, a rational, pluralistic, and coordinated system of continuing medical education, for the purpose of enabling practicing physicians to be optimally effective in the delivery of patient care.

Administrative Office: c/o Miller and Fink Corporation, 16 Thorndal Circle, Darien, CT 06820 (203) 655-8951

Letter about my election to the Board of Trustees, Albany Medical College.

The Albany Medical College
of Union University
Albany, New York 12208

OFFICE OF THE CHAIRMAN OF THE BOARD
THE NEIL HELLMAN MEDICAL RESEARCH BUILDING

February 28, 1977

Dr. Monroe Trout
Vice President, Director of Medical Affairs
Sterling Drug, Inc.
1450 Broadway
New York, New York

Dear Dr. Trout:

      I was delighted to learn from Stuart Bondurant and Matt Bender of your willingness to serve on the Board of Trustees of the Albany Medical College. At its meeting of February 25, 1977, the Board unanimously and enthusiastically elected you to membership. Stuart will be in touch with you to arrange for an orientation session and to give you the dates of the future meetings of the Board. I look forward to meeting you and working with you.

      Sincerely,

      Andrew Fisher

AF:jw

Letter about my service on the Professional Advisory Board of Control Data.

8100-34th Avenue South
Mailing Address/Box O
Minneapolis, Minnesota 55440

William C. Norris
Chairman of the Board &
Chief Executive Officer

CONTROL DATA CORPORATION

March 29, 1978

Monroe E. Trout, M.D.
Vice President, Director of Medical Affairs
Sterling Drug, Inc.
Ninety Park Avenue
New York, New York 10016

Dear Dr. Trout:

Thank you for your letter of March 15th, conveying your idea
of educational entertainment. I believe you are quite right,
particularly as it concerns the younger age groups.

I am aware that Gerry Smith reviewed his present thinking with
the Professional Advisory Board at your last meeting. We are
considering an employee HMO, with family enrollment. Some
educational courseware should be tailored toward the younger
members of a family group. It would be most appropriate to
include your idea as we address courseware needs for the younger
family members, and we will see that this is taken into account.

Interfacing the basic PLATO system to a computerized learning
system, terminating in a home television set, may be a bit more
difficult. Still, your idea has merit and your thoughts relative
to this as a total part of our activities warrant consideration.

The feedback I am receiving continues to indicate the value of
the Professional Advisory Board to our overall direction. The
perspective we gain through the collective and individual inputs
of Board members is significant and appreciated.

Best regards.

Sincerely yours,

William C. Norris

William C. Norris

Letter about my election as board member of Sterling Drug Inc.

THE DICKINSON SCHOOL OF LAW
CARLISLE, PENNSYLVANIA 17013

William L. Wilks
Dean

December 11, 1978

Monroe E. Trout, M.D.
Sterling Drug Company, Inc.
90 Park Avenue
New York, New York 10016

Dear Monroe:

Why do you continue to reap honors, appointments
and awards? Now you are on the Sterling Board of Directors
and I am writing you congratulations again. They have,
of course, chosen a man they should have chosen many moons
ago.

From now on, just assume I am congratulating you
and I will just write you when you foul up and do something
despicable.

Very truly yours,

William L. Wilks
Dean

WLW/ss

Letter about my election to the board of the Circle in the Square Theatre.

▢ CIRCLE IN THE SQUARE

A non-profit theatre founded in 1951

Theodore Mann
Artistic Director

Paul Libin
Managing Director

Board of Directors

John C. Russell
Chairman of the Board

Sheldon Atlas
Colleen Dewhurst
G. Morris Gurley
Dustin Hoffman
Paul Libin
Lucille Lortel
Theodore Mann
Arthur Olick
Harold Reed
George C. Scott
Hedwig A.
    Van Ameringen
Lewis M. Weston

E. Colin O'Leary
Theatre School Director

Mary K. Levenstein
Theatre School Director Emeritus

May 9, 1985

Monroe E. Trout, M.D.
Senior Vice President
Medical and Scientific Affairs
Sterling Drug Inc.
90 Park Avenue
New York, New York 10016

Dear Monroe:

It gives us great pleasure to welcome you to the Board of Directors of Circle in the Square Theatre. You have been approved as a member of the Board by unanimous vote of the other Directors.

There will be a meeting of the Board of Directors on Thursday, May 16, 1985 at 5:00 P.M. The meeting will be held in the offices of Circle in the Square, at 1633 Broadway. We look forward to seeing you.

We are pleased to announce that our next production will be George Bernard Shaw's ARMS AND THE MAN, directed by John Malkovich and starring Kevin Kline and Raul Julia. The first preview performance will be May 10. Please note on your calendar that Opening Night will be May 30. We very much hope that you can join us for that event.

Sincerely,

THEODORE MANN
Artistic Director

PAUL LIBIN
Managing Director

TM/PL: dch

1633 Broadway on 50th Street west of Broadway, New York, N.Y. 10019
Executive Offices: 212 581-3270 Box Office: 212 581-0720

Letter from the chairman of the board of Morehouse School of Medicine.

MOREHOUSE
SCHOOL OF MEDICINE

September 4, 1986

Monroe E. Trout, M.D.
Vice Chairman
Board of Trustees
Morehouse School of Medicine
81 Mariomi Road
New Canaan, Connecticut 06840

Dear Monroe:

Congratulations on your new position. I am not at all surprised that American Healthcare Systems, Inc. recognize and appreciates your leadership ability and talent!

You must know that I will vigorously attempt to dissuade you from reducing your position, or very important role, in the life of the Morehouse School of Medicine. Consideration of "conflict of interest" play no role here when dealing with a forthright and honest individual such as yourself.

We will continue to make as few "time" demands, as possible, on your career, yourself, and your family, but I will continue to insist on your involvement, advice and counsel in the interest of the Morehouse School of Medicine.

Sally joins me in warmest regards to your family.

Sincerely,

Clinton E. Warner, M.D.
Chairman

CEW/sad
cc Louis W. Sullivan, M.D.

Letter about my election to the Health Council of the Committee for Food & Shelter, Inc.

File — Comm. Food + Shelter
Sept. 21 —
2-4 PM

RECEIVED
JUN 1 5 1987

June 11, 19876

The Committee For Food & Shelter, Inc.

1518 K St., N.W., Suite 206
Washington, D.C. 20005
202 638-1526

Board of Directors

Clifford L. Alexander, Jr.
Chairman

Susan Baker
Vice Chairman

Eileen M. Evans
Secretary

Susan Kudlow
Treasurer

Ann L. Allen
Robert M. Beggan
John D. Driggs
Tipper Gore
Margaret M. Graham
David C. McCourt
John J. McManus
Lt. Col. Ernest A. Miller
Robert M. Mosbacher, Jr.
Jay S. Reibel, MD
Betty Roberts
Rabbi Martin Siegel
W. Clement Stone

Debora D. Kramer
Executive Director

Monroe Trout, M.D.
President and CEO
American Health Care Systems, Inc.
1205 Prospect, Suite 520
La Jolla, California 92037

Dear Dr. Trout:

Your acceptance of the Committee for Food and Shelter's invitation to serve on its Health Council has been enthusiastically received. Our efforts on behalf of the homeless will benefit greatly from your expertise. Robert A. Mosbacher, Jr., has agreed to serve as the Council Chairman.

The first meeting of the Health Council is scheduled for June 22, 1987, from 2 - 4 p.m., 2105 Rayburn House Office Building. The Rayburn HOB is located near the Capitol South metro stop. Enclosed are copies of the meeting agenda, a brief background paper and profile of the homeless along with a list of Council members.

We appreciate your interest in this important undertaking, and I look forward to working with you.

Sincerely,

Sarah Becker
Director, Council Program

SRB:aw

Enclosures (4)

APPENDIX D-10

Letter about my appointment to the San Diego County Healthcare Reform Commission.

County of San Diego

RECEIVED

APR 24 1992

J. WILLIAM COX, M.D., Ph.D.
DIRECTOR
(619) 236-2237

DEPARTMENT OF HEALTH SERVICES

1700 PACIFIC HIGHWAY, SAN DIEGO, CALIFORNIA 92101-2417

STEVEN A. ESCOBOZA
ASSISTANT DIRECTOR
(619) 236-7633

April 23, 1992

Monroe Trout, M.D., J.D., Chairman
  of the Board of Directors
American Healthcare Systems
12730 High Bluff Drive, Suite 300
San Diego, Ca. 92130-2099

Dear Dr. Trout:

RE: COMMISSION ON HEALTH CARE REFORM

As you are aware, on February 4, 1992 (3), the Board of Supervisors
of the County of San Diego adopted a resolution which created the
Commission on Health Care Reform. The purpose of this deliberative
body includes an examination of the conditions which contribute to
the health care crisis in San Diego and the development an
integrated set of recommendations aimed at improving the health
care delivery system.

You have been nominated to serve on this Commission and it is our
pleasure to advise you that you have been appointed. The first
meeting of the Commission shall be held on:

Monday, April 27, 1992
3:00 - 5:00 pm
County Administration Center
1600 Pacific Highway, Room 303

We appreciate your willingness to serve the residents of this
County on this important Commission and are looking forward to
working with you. If you have any questions, please contact Isabel
Perez (531-5544) or Paul Simms (285-6452).

Sincerely,

LEON L. WILLIAMS, SUPERVISOR   J. WILLIAM COX, MD, PhD, DIRECTOR
Fourth District   Department of Health Services

LLW:JWC:sp

Appendix D-11

Letter about my service on the University of Pennsylvania Nursing School Board of Visitors.

UNIVERSITY of PENNSYLVANIA

Office of the President
100 College Hall
Philadelphia, PA 19104-6380
215-898-7221

RECEIVED

AUG 20 1992

August 14, 1992

Monroe Trout, MD
American Healthcare Systems
12760 High Bluff Drive
Suite 250
San Diego, CA 92130-2019

Dear Dr. Trout:

On behalf of the University and for myself I want to thank you for your years of service on the Board of Overseers of the School of Nursing.

Because of your dedication and that of your colleagues, the board is realizing its potential as a valued advisory board, linking the campus to the world. Dean Norma Lang and I would be grateful for your continuing guidance and support; I hope that we may consult with you in the future in an informal manner as the need arises.

With kind regards and best wishes.

Sincerely,

Sheldon Hackney
President

SH/chm

Letter about my appointment to the California Business-Higher Education Forum.

UNIVERSITY OF CALIFORNIA

BERKELEY • DAVIS • IRVINE • LOS ANGELES • RIVERSIDE • SAN DIEGO • SAN FRANCISCO   SANTA BARBARA • SANTA CRUZ

RECEIVED

J.W. PELTASON
President

NOV 13 1992

OFFICE OF THE PRESIDENT
300 Lakeside Drive
Oakland, California 94612-3550
Phone: (510) 987-9074
Fax: (510) 987-9086

November 10, 1992

Monroe Trout, M.D.
Chairman of the Board
President and CEO
American Healthcare Systems
12730 High Bluff Drive
San Diego, California 92130-2099

Dear Doctor Trout:

I am please to join Chancellor Atkinson in welcoming you as a charter member of the California Business-Higher Education Forum. I look forward to working with you on what I believe is an important opportunity to make a difference to California and its future.

We have received your membership check and your personal informa-tion forms. You will receive additional information on the Forum and the initial meeting scheduled for February 11-13, 1993, at the La Quinta Hotel near Palm Desert as it is developed. Of course, any questions you have concerning the Forum or the inaugural meeting can be answered by me or Vice President William Baker, who can be reached at (510) 987-9160.

I look forward to seeing you at the opening session.

Cordially,

J. W. Peltason

cc: Chancellor Atkinson
     Vice President Baker

One hundred twenty-five years of service

Letter about my Board of Directors service with BioTransplant Inc.

BIOTRANSPLANT

INCORPORATED

RECEIVED

JUL -1 1994

Building 96, 13th Street
Charlestown Navy Yard
Charlestown, MA 02129
Tel. 617/241-5200
FAX 617/241-8780

June 28, 1994

Monroe Trout, M.D.
Chairman, President and CEO
American Healthcare System, Inc.
12730 High Bluff Drive, Suite 30
San Diego, CA 92130-2099

Dear Monroe,

Thank you for participating in our first expanded Board of Directors' Meeting this week. Your comments, questions and suggestions are very helpful and I especially appreciate the constructive spirit of the entire Board.

Regards,

Elliot Lebowitz, Ph.D.
President and CEO

EL/472

BIOTRANSPLANT

Letter about my service to find the new chancellor of UCSD.

UNIVERSITY OF CALIFORNIA

BERKELEY • DAVIS • IRVINE • LOS ANGELES • RIVERSIDE • SAN DIEGO • SAN FRANCISCO SANTA BARBARA • SANTA CRUZ

OFFICE OF THE PRESIDENT

300 Lakeside Drive
Oakland, California 94612-3550
Phone: (510) 987-9074
Fax: (510) 987-9086

May 3, 1996

Monroe Trout, M.D.
President, UCSD Foundation
Post Office Box 8052
Rancho Santa Fe, California 92067

Dear Monroe:

I am writing to thank you more formally for your valuable service as a member of
the search committee for a Chancellor of the San Diego campus. I am very pleased
that we were able to bring the search to a successful close with the appointment of
Robert C. Dynes. I know his appointment will be warmly welcomed by the UCSD
community.

Your service on the committee was appreciated greatly, and your substantial
contributions to the search process were invaluable to the work of the committee.

Sincerely,

Richard C. Atkinson
President

Letter about my service as chairman of the UCSD Foundation.

UNIVERSITY OF CALIFORNIA, SAN DIEGO UCSD

BERKELEY · DAVIS · IRVINE · LOS ANGELES · RIVERSIDE · SAN DIEGO · SAN FRANCISCO   SANTA BARBARA · SANTA CRUZ

OFFICE OF THE CHANCELLOR

9500 GILMAN DRIVE
LA JOLLA, CALIFORNIA 92093-0005
TEL: (619) 534-3135
FAX: (619) 534-6523

January 20, 1997

Dr. Monroe E. Trout
Post Office Box 8052
Rancho Santa Fe, CA 92067

Dear Monroe:

I did not want to let the opportunity pass without formally thanking you for your remarkable service as Chair of the U.C. San Diego Foundation. I deeply appreciate the outstanding leadership provided by you to the Foundation Board of Trustees. Your dedication and support for UCSD combined to provide the direction and resources necessary to advance the University's position to the front rank of American institutions of higher education.

Again, thank you for your efforts on behalf of the Foundation and the continuing friendship and leadership you provide to the University.

Warmest wishes to Sandra.

Sincerely,

Bob

Robert C. Dynes
Chancellor

Monroe I don't know where we would be without your help.

B

Letter from Congressman Brian Bilbray about my election as chairman
of Cytyc Corporation.

BRIAN P. BILBRAY
49TH DISTRICT, CALIFORNIA

COMMERCE COMMITTEE

SUBCOMMITTEE ON
HEALTH AND ENVIRONMENT

SUBCOMMITTEE ON
FINANCE AND HAZARDOUS
MATERIALS

SUBCOMMITTEE ON
OVERSIGHT AND
INVESTIGATIONS

Congress of the United States
House of Representatives
Washington, DC 20515

WASHINGTON OFFICE:

1530 LONGWORTH HOUSE OFFICE BLDG.
WASHINGTON, DC 20515
(202) 225-2040
FAX (202) 225-2948

DISTRICT OFFICE:

1011 CAMINO DEL RIO SOUTH
SUITE 330
SAN DIEGO, CA 92108
(619) 291-1430
FAX (619) 291-8956

INTERNET:

E-mail:
brian.bilbray@mail.house.gov

World Wide Web:
http://www.house.gov/bilbray/

February 24, 1998

Dr. Monroe Trout
Chairman, Cytyc Corp.
P.O. Box 8052
6135 Via Posada Del Norte
Rancho Sante Fe, CA. 92067

Dear Dr. Trout:

It gives me great pleasure to extend to you my most sincere congratulations on your election to
Chairman of the Board of Cytyc Corporation.

Cytyc Corporation is a dynamic organization with a national reputation for innovative research
and development of sample preparation systems used in medical testing. The success of the
ThinPrep System used in assisting health care providers diagnose cancers is a testament to your
outstanding participation in leadership, and commitment to excellence. The services and
products your corporation provides are indeed valuable and life changing for many Americans,
and the rest of the world as well.

Knowing of your work with UCSD and appreciating your advice and support over the past years
I am sure you will be prosperous in this new endeavor.

Congratulations and good luck.

Sincerely,

Brian P. Bilbray
Member of Congress

BB:ad

THIS STATIONERY PRINTED ON PAPER MADE OF RECYCLED FIBERS

Letter about "Patients First."

UNIVERSITY OF CALIFORNIA, SAN DIEGO

BERKELEY • DAVIS • IRVINE • LOS ANGELES • RIVERSIDE • SAN DIEGO • SAN FRANCISCO   SANTA BARBARA • SANTA CRUZ

GERARD N. BURROW, M.D.
VICE CHANCELLOR FOR HEALTH SCIENCES   LA JOLLA, CALIFORNIA 92093-0602
DEAN, SCHOOL OF MEDICINE

December 13, 1991

Monroe E. Trout, M.D., J.D.
American Healthcare Systems
12730 High Bluff Drive
Suite 300
San Diego, California 92130-2099

Dear Monroe:

I think "Patients First" is an absolutely first-rate report. I
see nothing in the report that I could not support, including the
primary care-specialty care split and experiments in
privatization of VA hospitals. In fact, in Canada the VA
hospitals were given to the university and it seems to have
worked very well.

I think that the report is particularly effective in defining the
problems and in making a number of value statements on access to
health care with which I completely agree.

I as mentioned, I will persue efforts to see whether we can have
this discussed at some kind of public forum.

Thanks very much for sharing it with me.

Warmly,

Gerard N. Burrow, M.D.
Vice Chancellor and Dean

PS we enjoyed having a
chance to talk with you
& Sandy at the hosp. top party

Letter about my invitation to Russia to participate in a healthcare conference.

MLᕼH Main Line Health, Inc.
Fidelity Court, 259 Radnor-Chester Road, Radnor, PA 19087, 215-254-8840, FAX 215-254-2993

George H. Schmitt, President

October 3, 1990

Monroe Trout, M.D., President
American Healthcare Systems
12760 High Bluff Drive, Suite 250
San Diego, CA 92130-2019

Dear Monroe:

The esteem in which you are held in the health care
industry is once again revealed by your invitation
to Leningrad and Moscow later this month to serve on
a health care commission. Events in eastern Europe
and Russia are leading to an opportunity for individuals
such as yourself to make a real difference in the future
of those countries. It's a very exciting prospect,
and I cannot think of a more appropriate or well informed
emissary for health care.

This is truly an honor for you and American Healthcare
Systems, Monroe, and, as an AmHS shareholder, we are
extremely proud.

Cordially,

George

GHS:msr

Bryn Mawr Hospital • Lankenau Hospital • Paoli Memorial Hospital
Bryn Mawr Rehabilitation Hospital

Letter about my participation in U.S.-Mexico Conference on Healthcare.

Institute of the Americas

RECEIVED

AUG - 1 1994

La Jolla, July 28, 1994

Dr. Monroe E. Trout   *Via fax: (619) 481-8919*
Chairman, President & CEO
American Healthcare Systems
12730 High Bluff Dr., Ste 300
San Diego CA 92130 -2099

Dear Monroe:

I wish to thank you for your outstanding presentation at the "Health Care in Mexico" conference. As I said in introducing you, there are many important lessons Mexican hospitals can learn from American health care systems experiences. Several Mexican participants expressed interest in learning more about your approach and may very well be in touch.

We are very pleased with the outcome of the conference, particularly the quality of the presentations and the tremendous interest of the participants. This was the first conference of its kind in the United States and everyone seemed to be appreciative of the fact that they were able to participate in it. The diversity of interests among those present impressed me, as well as the Mexican participation. It is clear that we touched upon a timely subject that deserves further work.

On a more personal note, I want to offer my best regards and wishes as you approach your retirement. I know U.C.S.D. will try to keep you busy in your important positions here. Thank you for your advice concerning the University. I am planning to seek a meeting with the Dean of the Medical School later this summer to propose some joint activity in health care policy and Mexico. I hope that such a project will again give us an opportunity to work together in the near future.

Warm regards to you and Sandy,

Ambassador Paul H. Boeker
President

P.S.: Our friend Carlos Menem of Argentina will be visiting us September 30. I hope you and Sandy can join Peggy and me in greeting him that evening.

10111 North Torrey Pines Road
La Jolla, Ca 92037 U.S.A.
Telephones: (619) 453-5560 • (619) 277-0600 • Fax (619) 453-2165

Letter to the editor about my contributions to healthcare in San Diego, CA.

January 29, 1997

To the editor:

Neil Morgan wrote recently of managed care, hospital mergers and other vital health care issues facing San Diegans today. He described an environment that appears muddled and lacking in leadership, direction or attention to the community's needs.

At the risk of sounding overly optimistic, I would like to share a slightly different point of view from the trenches. It's true that throughout the nation, the health care industry has been undergoing radical, tumultuous transformation. The public and private sector alike, from private insurance payers to indigent care providers, are experiencing the shock waves of change, and efforts are under way, at all levels of government and industry, to respond. No single entity is to blame for the situation, or for the fact that no easy course out of these difficult times has yet been charted.

By most measures, San Diego is at the head of the curve in terms of experiencing these pressures, and facing these challenges. In recent years, local health care leadership has taken aggressive action to respond to change. Not all efforts have achieved the intended results, but we have made a great deal of progress. I believe that we have forged a better understanding of the roles played by the many players who provide various components of health care. And we have collaboratively explored creative solutions that in years past would not have been considered possible.

Community involvement has been vital to this effort. For example, at UCSD we benefit greatly from the participation of nationally respected experts such as Monroe Trout, whose stellar career and accomplishments in health systems management has garnered the attention of Presidential administrations. His commitment to the San Diego region, his guidance as we have undertaken our own restructuring efforts, and his willingness to participate in the local dialogue have kept our efforts moving forward. With the continued leadership and tenacity of individuals like Dr. Trout, I believe we have made strides toward solutions that will work in San Diego, and our community will become a model for the nation in providing affordable, quality health care for all in our community.

Sincerely,

John F. Alksne, M.D.
Vice Chancellor for Health Sciences
UCSD

APPENDIX E-5

Letter about my service as chairman of the San Diego Healthcare Commission.

Answered 11/26/95

YALE UNIVERSITY SCHOOL OF MEDICINE

GERARD N. BURROW, MD
DEAN

November 3, 1995

Mr. Monroe Trout
P.O. Box 8052
6135 Via Posada Del Norte
Rancho Santa Fe, California 92067

Dear Monroe:

    I have just returned from the meeting of the Association of American Medical Colleges where I saw a number of old friends from San Diego and they had nothing but praise for the Trout Commission.

    They also told me that you were strongly recommending that the possibility of a merger between the university and the children's hospital be re-examined. I spent about a third of my time while I was in San Diego trying to effect that merger and we came so close I am convinced the longer people talk about it, it is less likely that it is going to happen. I still have warm feelings for San Diego. If there is anything I can do to help with the pediatric merger, I would of course be delighted. I realize that ex-Deans like ex-CEOs are probably not welcomed in those situation, but if I can be helpful, let me know.

    I am beginning to wonder whether there is something wrong with me, but after eight years as a dean, I still enjoy it. The challenges are enormous, but the opportunities are limitless. Ann and I send our very best to you and Sandy. I have been to San Diego several times but it has been in and out. If I get some time to stay, I'll give you a call.

Warmly,

Gerard N. Burrow, M.D.
Dean

GNB/hem

Letter about "Patients First," our commission's report on reforming healthcare.

Glaxo Inc.

Charles A. Sanders, M.D.
Chief Executive Officer

December 20, 1991

Dr. Monroe E. Trout
Chairman and Chief Executive Officer
American Healthcare Systems
12730 High Bluff Drive, Suite 300
San Diego, CA 92130-2099

Dear Monroe:

Thank you very much for your letter of December 6 and the enclosed health care reform proposal entitled, "Patients First". My colleagues and I are delighted to have it and will take the opportunity in the next several weeks to study it. I commend you on developing this very timely proposal. Health care reform has to be at the top of our domestic agenda.

Let me also tell you how much we appreciate your interest and support in regard to our various Washington efforts. I'm hopeful that in the next several months we will be able to come to a more equitable arrangement for all concerned regarding the Medicaid rebate program.

Best personal wishes. I look forward to seeing you soon. May I also wish you a wonderful Christmas and a happy New Year.

Sincerely,

Charlie

CAS/er

cc: R. Ingram
     M. Dardess (w/proposal)

Letter about "Patients First," our commission's report on reforming healthcare.

Bristol-Myers Squibb Company

345 Park Avenue New York, NY 10154-0037 212 546-2777

Richard L. Gelb
Chairman and
Chief Executive Officer

December 20, 1991

Monroe E. Trout, M.D.
Chairman of the Board and
 Chief Executive Officer
American Healthcare Systems
12730 High Bluff Drive
Suite 300
San Diego, CA 92130-2099

Dear Monroe:

Thank you for your letter of December 6th. I
look forward to reading the report on short- and
long-term health care reform developed by AmHS.
Health care reform is clearly a major issue of our
time.

My best wishes for a happy and healthy holiday
season.

Sincerely,

Richard L. Gelb

RLG/tf

Letter about "Patients First," our commission's report on reforming healthcare.

WILMINGTON, DELAWARE 19898

CHAIRMAN OF THE BOARD

RECEIVED
JUN - 3 1993

May 28, 1993

Monroe E. Trout
Chairman, President & CEO
American Healthcare Systems
12730 High Bluff Drive - Suite 300
San Diego, CA 92130-2099

Dear Monroe:

Thanks so very much for sending me a copy of your Health Care Reform proposal a few weeks ago. It is a very thoughtful plan and very clear. Such specific action would begin to resolve our problem.

Since then, I've had the opportunity to dialogue with Mrs. Clinton on her proposal and so far it sounds pretty scary to me. Let's hope that before anything is resolved by the Congress, we all get a chance to add some more realism to it.

I hope all is well with you and look forward to staying in touch. All the best.

Sincerely,

E. S. Woolard, Jr.

ESW:jh

Better Things for Better Living

Letter about the debate over the Hillary Clinton healthcare plan.

Johnson&Johnson

ROBERT E. CAMPBELL
VICE CHAIRMAN
BOARD OF DIRECTORS

NEW BRUNSWICK, N. J. 08933

August 5, 1994

RECEIVED

AUG 10 1994

Monroe E. Trout, M.D.
Chairman, President & CEO
American Healthcare Systems
Suite 300
12730 High Bluff Drive
San Diego, CA 92130-2099

Dear Monroe:

Thank you for your letter regarding the NBC Special on Health Care. As you know, the RWJ Foundation had provided the funds, but NBC was solely responsible for content.

The hope was that they would produce an impartial, educational program that would provide viewers with a better understanding of the health care debate issues.

My reaction was the same as yours. I felt it was a very poor production regardless of what side of the debate you were on and that it was biased by having Mrs. Clinton in such a prime role. It was an opportunity squandered by NBC and most of the RWJ Foundation Board gave the show a low grade.

Having said that, follow-up surveys, by independent market research groups, indicate that the viewing public, in general, believed it was fair and that they learned a lot. My own feeling is that the polling just shows how little has really sunk in with the public regarding the dangers of the Clinton plan and the threats hidden in the not so fine print.

Hope to see you soon.

Best regards,

Bob

REC:jk

Letter from President George H.W. Bush about healthcare issues.

GEORGE BUSH

July 14, 1987

PERSONAL

Monroe E. Trout, M.D.
President and Chief
  Executive Officer
American Healthcare Systems
1205 Prospect, Suite 520
San Diego, California 92037

Dear Monroe:

     Thanks so much for that excellent paper, "Health
Issues 1987." I read it carefully and with sincere
appreciation to you. A few comments:

     I agree on AIDS. I am not certain about the sin tax
per se, particularly as it affects certain publications.
It seems to me there might be some real censorship problems
in determining who gets taxed and who doesn't; but as to the
thrust of your paragraph on AIDS, I do agree.

     I had not been aware of the problems for health care
connected with the immigration bill. I'll have someone
check all that out.

     Couldn't agree more on tort reform. What you tell
me is true for doctors is also true for so many other areas.
We must have tort reform, and I want to champion that.

     I agree that the Congress will make a relatively
simple catastrophic proposal unworkable or rather unafford-
able by adding so many Christmas ornaments to it.

     I won't comment on all the points made, but again, my
sincere thanks to you for a very helpful paper. Bar sends
her love along. She is working hard all around the country
on both campaigning and illiteracy -- doing a superb job.

     My thanks and best wishes.

                                   Sincerely,

                                   George Bush

Note from Barbara Bush concerning "Patients First."

THE WHITE HOUSE

January 10, 1992

Dear Monroe,

Thank you so much for the final copy of
your manuscript. Your were so thoughtful to
send it to me.

With all best wishes,

Warmly,

Barbara

Dr. Monroe Trout
Chairman of the Board
President and Chief Executive Officer
American Healthcare Systems
Suite 520
1205 Prospect
San Diego, California 92037

*You must feel great having the
manuscript finished and well finished!*

Letter to Barbara Bush about science issues used for the presidential campaign of 1988.

American Healthcare Systems™

The National Network of Premier Health Systems   San Diego • Washington, DC

Monroe E. Trout, M.D.
Chairman of the Board,
President and CEO

May 31, 1988

Mrs. George Bush
The Vice President's House
34th at Massachusetts Avenue
Washington, D.C. 20501

Dear Barbara:

    'Thought you might like these pictures for your scrapbook. George looks good in a doctor's coat.

    I was with Frank Press, President of the National Academy of Sciences, and Sam Thier, President, Institute of Medicine, last week and they thought George should give a speech devoted to science which would spell out his vision for space exploration, research and development for safer nuclear energy, a program dealing with acid rain (this would help our relations with Canada), and also the continued development of young scientists.

    When one looks at the amount of the federal budget that is spent on research and development or on scientific projects, it's staggering. Both Dr. Press, who incidentally told me he received an honorary degree with George at a university in Ohio, and Dr. Thier would be very happy to brief the Vice President on anything related to health or science on a non-partisan basis; the offer is open-ended.

    'Hope to see you this weekend in Los Angeles.

       Regards,

       Monroe E. Trout

MET/amw

Enclosure

1205 Prospect • Suite 520 • San Diego, California 92037 • 619 456-2811

Barbara Bush's reply to my letter of May 31, 1988, on healthcare issues.

BARBARA BUSH

December 23, 1987

Dear Monroe,

Thank you so much for your nice
letter. I will give your letter to
George, and we do appreciate your
being in touch.

All best wishes for the holiday
season,

Warmly,

Barbara

I hope something has happened on this by now. All 22 (?) our gang are here!!

Letter from Barbara Bush on the campaign.

BARBARA BUSH

June 15, 1988

Dear Monroe,

Thanks so much for your thoughtful
letter.

I so appreciate having the photos of
George and will certainly include them in
my scrapbook. Also, I have forwarded your
letter to George's staff with your
suggestions about science and medicine
topics that might be included in his
upcoming speeches.

We so appreciate your support and
interest.

Warmly,

Barbara

It was great to see you two at that very grand dinner in California. Thanks.

Letter from Barbara Bush on the campaign.

MRS. GEORGE BUSH

Dear Monroe — November 21, 1986

I finally sat George down and told him of all our talk. #1. You have put the bid in for Jan. 10? or 11th ?!

#2. George took down all the Heritage news. He was shocked and saddened to hear that "we sent kids over who didn't listen." He is going to look into this.

#3 We are thrilled about Leroy Zimmerman and will follow through.

#4. Please work on your two black friends and will try to meet them. Please write names and addresses and we'll wait for the opportunity to meet them.
Many thanks. Warmly —
Barbara

Letter from Barbara Bush on the presidential campaign.

BARBARA BUSH Sept. 15 = 1987

Dear Monroe— Just a note. I
loved the editorial - Very interesting.
Things are going well. The Pat
Robertson thing is scary. We all
have to work much harder. George
and I and all children are on
the road all the time. Love —
Barbara

Letter from Barbara Bush on the presidential campaign.

RECEIVED JUL 6 1987

THE VICE PRESIDENT'S HOUSE
WASHINGTON, D.C. 20501

June 26= 1987

Dear Monroe —
Many thanks for the clippings.
I was so sorry not to be with
George on the California trip - I was
giving a graduation speech in Iowa.
I joined him in Arizona. These

have been great days for campaign
building + fund raising — Ugly
days with rumors, but I hope
that's all behind us.
Best to Sandy —
Warmly —
Barbara

Press release announcing my appointment as a co-chair of Bush's
healthcare coalition for the 1992 election campaign.

DRAFT

FOR IMMEDIATE RELEASE   CONTACT: DIDI BLACKWOOD
OCTOBER 9, 1992   (202)336-7957
BQ-   RUTH MANKIN
                                          (202)336-7900

HEALTH CARE LEADERS ENDORSE BUSH

ATTACK CLINTON HEALTH CARE PLAN

WASHINGTON, D.C. -- Bush/Quayle '92 today announced the
appointment of over eight hundred physicians, health care
providers, health insurance industry leaders, pharmaceutical
company executives, hospital administrators,and other health care
industry executives to the campaign's Health Care Coalition.

Co-Chairpersons of the committee are William Frist, M.D.,
Surgical Director, Vanderbilt Transplant Center, Vanderbilt
University Medical Center; Monroe Trout, M.D., J.D., President
and Chairman of the Board of the American Health Care Systems,
San Diego, California; Dr. Theodore Cooper, CEO and Chairman of
the Board, The Upjohn Company, Kalamazoo, Michigan; Salvatore
Risalvato, Owner-Operator, Riverdale Texaco Service Station,
Riverdale, New Jersey; and Neil Chur, Chairman of the Board, Park
Associates, East Aurora, New York.

The co-chairs strongly endorsed the President's health care
plan while scoring the Clinton proposal.

In announcing his support, Dr. Frist said, "I am endorsing
President Bush because he has the health care plan that puts the
patient first. His plan calls for maintaining the high quality of
health care that Americans demand and expect. George Bush's plan
shows compassion for the people we put first: our patients."

Dr. Trout added, "George Bush has the best approach to
quality health care. His plan builds on the best of our current
system and reforms that which needs it, making health care both
accessible and affordable. Under the President's plan low and
moderate income families would have tax credits or tax deductions
to cover health insurance costs, and that means better care and
lower costs for all. Clinton's plan would put American health
care in the hands of the government -- and that's not what
Americans want. His plan may end up rationing care with his
health care caps. We need a plan of reform which emphasizes the
patient and allows the patient to make the choice, not the
government."

--more--

Letter of endorsement for Bush by Attorney General Leroy Zimmerman of Pennsylvania.

American Healthcare Systems™

The National Network of Premier Health Systems

San Diego • Washington, DC

Monroe E. Trout, M.D.
Chairman of the Board,
President and CEO

March 15, 1988

Mrs. George Bush
The Vice President's House
34th at Massachusetts Avenue
Washington, D.C. 20501

Dear Barbara:

'Have been working on Roy for some time and he was kind enough to call me to tell me about his endorsement of George. I am glad he did before "Super Tuesday". I am sending you a copy of his press release, and a copy of the letter he sent to me only because he mentioned the drug issue as a possible campaign priority.

I know you are probably tired of bouncing around the country, but I think all of your efforts are paying off. Our people at Iowa Methodist really enjoyed having George as their guest, and I am glad it turned out so well. I saw Pete Wilson on Saturday afternoon and urged him to tell Dole to withdraw from the race for the good of the party. I had lunch with Wilky Gilmore, yesterday, and he is anxious to get started in California.

With kind personal regards.

Sincerely,

Monroe

MET/amw

Enclosures

Letter from Leroy Zimmerman about his endorsement of George H.W. Bush.

COMMONWEALTH OF PENNSYLVANIA
OFFICE OF ATTORNEY GENERAL
HARRISBURG

16TH FLOOR
STRAWBERRY SQUARE
HARRISBURG, PA. 17120

LeRoy S. Zimmerman
ATTORNEY GENERAL

March 9, 1988

Dr. Monroe E. Trout
Chairman of the Board, President
 and Chief Executive Officer
American Healthcare System, Inc.
Suite 520
1205 Prospect
San Diego, CA   92037

Dear Monroe:

Enclosed is a copy of a news release which I issued on March 7, 1988. I'm happy to be a part of Vice President Bush's campaign and look forward to helping in any way I can.

As I told you during our recent telephone conversation, I feel very strongly about the importance of the drug issue and think that this should be a campaign priority.

Best wishes to you and your family for continued good health, happiness and success.

Warmest personal regards.

Sincerely,

LeRoy S. Zimmerman

LSZ/mlm
Enclosure

Best wishes to Sandy.

Press report on my candidacy for secretary of Health and Human Services (HHS).

McGRAW-HILL's

Medicine & Health

Vol. 42/No. 42   October 24, 1988

Two States Weigh Indigent Care Plans, California To Decide on AIDS Move

More than a dozen health-related initiatives will appear on ballots Nov. 8 including indigent care plans, moves to limit medical malpractice awards, and a proposal to require identification of those infected with the AIDS virus. Voters in Georgia and Missouri will decide on establishment of indigent care trust funds. The Georgia plan, sponsored by that state's hospital association, would create but not finance a fund to expand Medicaid coverage. The Georgia Hospital Assn. plans a week of radio ads before the election; members will hand out 90,000 flyers to patients. In Missouri, providers are backing creation of a $500 million trust fund to help pay for insurance against catastrophic medical bills, create a risk pool for the uninsurable, expand Medicaid coverage of the uninsured, and pay Medicare cost-sharing costs for the indigent elderly. The plan also would set aside 22 percent of the funds to up Medicaid payments to hospitals and physicians. Missouri's Medicaid program ranks 47th out of 51 in provider reimbursement. The trust fund would be filled via a new 0.6 percent statewide earnings tax raising about $300 million a year; federal Medicaid matching funds would

chip in another $200 million. Providers back the ballot plan, opposed by taxpayer and farm groups. A poll shows 63 percent of Missouri voters backing the plan. On other topics:

AIDS. Providers and gay rights groups are fighting a California ballot initiative, sponsored by Rep. William Dannemeyer (R-CA), to require doctors, blood banks, and other providers to report the names of patients and blood donors "whom they reasonably feel have been exposed to AIDS or who have tested positive for it." Another Golden State ballot plan would require testing prisoners convicted of sex-related crimes or of assaulting police, fire, or emergency medical personnel.

Malpractice. Florida voters are weighing a plan to cap noneconomic awards at $100,000. Alaskans will consider whether to eliminate joint and several liability.

Abortion. Michigan and Arkansas will vote on plans to bar use of state funds to pay for abortions unless a woman's life is endangered.

Bush Team Looks Over HHS List

A confident Bush campaign is reviewing candidates for the top HHS job. Otis Bowen, MD, intends on returning to Indiana early next year. Leading contender: Rep. Bill Gradison (R-OH), senior GOP House Ways & Means Health Subcommittee member, considered one of the main health brains on Capitol Hill. Indications are Gradison might be willing to give up his safe House seat for the challenge of running HHS. Another candidate: Monroe Trout, MD, president and CEO of American Healthcare Systems and friend of Barbara Bush. Social Security Commissioner Dorcas Hardy and Sen. Dave Durenberger (R-MN) also are being considered, but if Durenberger wins his tight Senate race he'll be more useful on the Hill; Hardy probably will wind up elsewhere. Bush wants to limit the number of Reagan people keeping the same job. HCFA Administrator William Roper, MD, might move to assistant secretary for health or under secretary.

Richard Sorian, Editor

Letter from Senator Pete Wilson about my second candidacy for secretary of HHS.

PETE WILSON
CALIFORNIA

COMMITTEES:
ARMED SERVICES
AGRICULTURE, NUTRITION, AND FORESTRY
COMMERCE, SCIENCE, AND TRANSPORTATION
SPECIAL COMMITTEE ON AGING
JOINT ECONOMIC COMMITTEE

United States Senate

WASHINGTON, DC 20510

December 12, 1988

RECEIVED
JAN 0 9 1989

The Honorable George Bush
President-Elect
The White House
Washington, D.C. 20500

Dear Mr. Vice President:

This is to commend to you the candidacy of Dr. Munroe Trout of San Diego for appointment to the office of Secretary of Health and Human Services.

Clearly, Dr. Trout, as a senior advisor to your campaign on health care issues, has proven his knowledge and leadership with respect to addressing the social service and health care needs of the Nation in the immediate years ahead.

The financing of health care will be the major focus of HHS during your Administration, and few in the Nation are as expert as Dr. Trout when it comes to understanding the complexities of our health care financing system and the related issues of quality health care. One glance at his resume speaks for itself.

In addition, Dr. Trout is a proven combination of business manager (American Healthcare Systems and Sterling Drug) and academician (M.D., J.D. and almost a dozen editorial and faculty appointments).

I believe you will find that Dr. Trout will be an active and thoughtful manager of HHS -- a man able to establish effective priorities, articulate them to the appropriate "publics", and carry them out in such a manner as to reflect credit on you and your Administration. At the same time, he will command the respect of the employees of HHS and of the general public.

I urge you to select Dr. Trout for your Cabinet; both you and the Nation will gain.

Sincerely,

PETE WILSON

PW:da

bcc: Dr. Munroe Trout √

Press report on candidates for secretary of HHS.

Washington Outlook

EDITED BY LEE WALCZAK

CAPITAL WRAPUP

A TAX
COU

With
de
Co
perts aren't
their next b
Even thou
new taxes, a
up support
Republicans
almost-painle
deficit.
The perce
would do no
major reason
an-style tax
prodigious r
would raise
housing wer
duce enough
with plenty
For years,
byist Charls
tion taxes. B
when then-W
for a VAT an
er is both p
Ernest Chris
transfer tax,
At the m
Finance Co

CAPITAL WRAPUP

HEALTH

In an attempt to heal the wounds created by the unseemly dumping of Margaret Heckler as Secretary of Health & Human Services, the Reagan Administration is considering several physicians as replacements. Among the doctors in the running: general practitioner Otis Bowen, 67, former Republican governor of Indiana and most recently chairman of a high-level HHS advisory group on medicare; William "Bud" Mayer, 62, a psychiatrist, now Assistant Secretary of Defense for Health Affairs and former health chief when Ronald Reagan served as governor of California; and Monroe Trout,

54, an internist who is a senior vice-president for medical and scientific affairs at Sterling Drug Inc. in New York.

n.) is not keen on a VAT but may give it a
he considers new taxes next year.
e VAT's obvious deficit-cutting allure, inter-
l is also being generated by a growing
e to improve the competitive position of
ustry. As is common with VAT schemes, the
d be rebated on exports, lowering the price
goods abroad, and would be added to the
imports. This has attracted trade-oriented
embers, such as Sam M. Gibbons (D-Fla.)
ard T. Schulze (R-Pa.).

ING THE PRESIDENT. The main obstacle to
backers concede, is the President. But they
cenario showing how Reagan's opposition
lt: Tax reform dies, but Reagan's desire for
t survives; next, congressional panic over
t forces Reagan to choose between a 1986
and massive defense cuts; faced with this
VAT suddenly looks less odious. "The Presi-
ld like it," says Walker, "if it were present-
y, in the right context, and by the right

elieve Treasury Secretary James A. Baker
d the idea as politically unwise, might be
along. Deputy Secretary Richard G. Dar-
rested in a consumption tax if tax reform
would need help from White House Chief of
Staff Donald T. Regan. Thus far, Regan has expressed no
great affection for a VAT. But Alfred H. Kingon, Regan's
influential domestic policy chief, is attracted to the idea. One
way to cement the President's interest might be to require
that any proposal include a binding cap on the VAT rate.
For now, the VAT remains a legislative long shot. But next
year? Next year could be a whole different story.

By Stephen H. Wildstrom, Lee Walczak, and Ronald Grover

WASHINGTON OUTLOOK

VAT to pay for the cleanup of toxic wastes (page 30). Senator
William V. Roth Jr. (R-Del.) is pushing a measure that would
impose a 10% VAT. The plan would require businesses to tote
up their gross sales, deduct all nonlabor costs, and pay a tax
on the remainder. Roth, co-author of Reagan's 1981 tax cuts,
wants the VAT to be used only to cut tax rates—a provision
most other VAT backers promise to jettison.
In addition to Roth, several other prominent Finance Com-

CAPITAL WRAPUP

HEALTH

In an attempt to heal the wounds created by the unseemly dumping of Margaret Heckler as Secretary of Health & Human Services, the Reagan Administration is considering several physicians as replacements. Among the doctors in the running: general practitioner Otis Bowen, 67, former Republican governor of Indiana and most recently chairman of a high-level HHS advisory group on medicare; William "Bud" Mayer, 62, a psychiatrist, now Assistant Secretary of Defense for Health Affairs and former health chief when Ronald Reagan served as governor of California; and Monroe Trout,

54, an internist who is a senior vice-president for medical and scientific affairs at Sterling Drug Inc. in New York.

TRADE

The Administration is threatening retaliation against European Community steel shipments to the U. S. unless the EC renews last year's voluntary export-restraint agreement. Negotiations are deadlocked, and an Oct. 31 deadline is looming. "Chances [for an accord] are less than 50-50," says a top Administration trade official. "Barring an agreement, we'll feel free to take strong unilateral action after Nov. 1."

DEFENSE

Joseph P. Addabbo (D-N. Y.), chairman of the House Appropriations defense subcommittee and a leading Pentagon critic, has been sidelined by a serious kidney ailment. That leaves Representative Bill Chappell Jr. (D-Fla.), a pro-defense conservative, in charge of the panel. So far, the subcommittee has followed Addabbo's wishes by recommending that the 1986 defense budget be held to 1985 levels. If Addabbo does not return, House Democrats probably will retain Chappell at the subcommittee's helm—but only if he agrees to keep his pro-Pentagon philosophy in check.

Press report on candidates for secretary of HHS.

> ▶ Dr. Monroe E. Trout, senior vice president for medical and scientific affairs at Sterling Drug Inc., in New York. Trout, 54, is both a physician and a lawyer.

A36 THE MORNING CALL, SATURDAY, OCTOBER 26, 1985

NATION

Wide net cast for Heckler successor

By WILLIAM KRONHOLM
Of The Associated Press

WASHINGTON — The White House has cast a wide net in its search for a successor to Margaret M. Heckler as secretary of health and human services, but a decision still appears some time away.

A source in the health care industry who maintains close ties to the White House says several candidates are being interviewed by White House personnel director Robert Tuttle and his aides, and that the list of candidates appears to be growing.

Tuttle is screening candidates before submitting a short list of top prospects to White House Chief of Staff Donald Regan, who will make a final recommendation to President Reagan, said the source, who spoke on condition of anonymity.

But none of the candidates has been interviewed by Regan yet, the source said. Of a selection, he said: "It's not imminent. It's at least another week or two or three, and it could stretch beyond that."

Asked about the delay, an administration official said, "We've got some other things that have been distracting us." The official, speaking on the condition that he not be identified, added, "It's Regan really. ... He has not interviewed anybody. That's really the biggest thing. It would move

pretty quickly" if Regan decided to get it done.

The search began in earnest Oct. 1 after Heckler, at the president's request, agreed to resign the Cabinet job and accept a diplomatic post, ambassador to Ireland. She remains as HHS secretary until confirmed in her new assignment, however.

The list of potential candidates is heavy with physicians and corporate officers, reflecting Regan's desires, the source said. A few academicians also are mentioned, but are considered dark horses in the contest. At least three women have been mentioned as prospects.

Candidates mentioned by sources in industry and on Capitol Hill include:

▶ Former Indiana Gov. Otis R. Bowen, 67, interviewed by Tuttle last week. A physician and medical school professor, Bowen was governor from 1973 to 1981 and has served on presidential commissions under both Reagan and President Ford.

He was chairman of Reagan's Advisory Council on Social Security, which in March 1984 proposed major changes in Medicare to keep the federal health insurance program for the elderly and disabled from expected bankruptcy.

▶ Dr. William Mayer, 62, now assistant secretary of defense for health. He is a psychiatrist who most recently came to public

attention as the Pentagon official handling the issue of AIDS in the military.

Mayer has been the Pentagon's chief health official since November 1983. Previously, he was head of the Alcohol, Drug Abuse and Mental Health Administration, a branch of HHS, and he earlier served as head of the California State Department of Health.

▶ Dr. Monroe E. Trout, senior vice president for medical and scientific affairs at Sterling Drug Inc., in New York. Trout, 54, is both a physician and a lawyer.

Trout is chairman and chief executive officer of the American Hospital Supply Corp. Bays, 51, is a member of the federal Prospective Payment Assessment Commission, which evaluates Medicare payment policies, and served on the executive committee of Reagan's Private Sector Survey on Cost Control, usually known as the Grace Commission.

However Bays has asked that his name be withdrawn from consideration.

▶ Dr. William Walsh, who heads Project Hope and who headed Reagan's 1980 transition task force on health. One source said Walsh has told the White House he does not want the HHS job, but agreed to an interview with Tuttle at Regan's request.

▶ Los Angeles surgeon Tirso del Junco, a longtime Reagan supporter and former

▶ Anne Dore McLaughlin, now undersecretary of interior, the department's No. 2 spot, where she has a reputation as an able administrator who often is used as a trouble-shooter. She has served as director of public affairs for both the Environmental Protection Agency and the Treasury Department.

▶ Michael Novak, a resident scholar and theologian at the conservative American Enterprise Institute. Novak has written more than a dozen books on welfare reform and social policy.

▶ Rita Ricardo Campbell, a senior scholar at the Hoover Institute, a conservative think tank in California, who headed a task force on Social Security during Reagan's 1980 transition period.

▶ James K. Cavanaugh, a health specialist who served in the White House under Presidents Nixon and Ford.

▶ Anne L. Armstrong, former co-chairman of the Republican National Committee and a former ambassador to Great Britain.

None of the candidates has emerged as a front-runner for the post, although Bowen, Mayer and Trout are mentioned as strong contenders.

"If you had to pick a name off the list,

Letter from Louis Stokes for my candidacy for secretary of HHS.

LOUIS STOKES
21ST DISTRICT, OHIO

COMMITTEE ON APPROPRIATIONS

SUBCOMMITTEES:
LABOR/HHS-EDUCATION
HUD/INDEPENDENT AGENCIES
DISTRICT OF COLUMBIA

PERMANENT SELECT COMMITTEE
ON INTELLIGENCE

CHAIRMAN
SUBCOMMITTEE ON BUDGET AND
PROGRAM AUTHORIZATION

Congress of the United States
House of Representatives
Washington, DC 20515

2304 RAYBURN HOUSE OFFICE BUILDING
WASHINGTON, DC 20515
(202) 225-7032

DISTRICT OFFICE:
ROOM 2847
NEW FEDERAL OFFICE BUILDING
1240 EAST 9TH STREET
CLEVELAND, OH 44199
(216) 522-4900

CLEVELAND HEIGHTS OFFICE
2140 LEE ROAD
SUITE 211
CLEVELAND HEIGHTS, OH 44118
(216) 522-4907

December 10, 1985

Dr. Monroe Trout
Senior Vice President
Sterling Drug Inc.
Ninety Park Avenue
New York, New York 10016

Dear Dr. Trout:

Thank you for your kind letter in regard to my efforts to support your nomination as Secretary, U.S. Department of Health and Human Services.

Although you were not nominated, I continue to believe that you would have made an excellent Secretary, sensitive to the very grave health concerns in the black community. I wish you continued success in your current position and in any future endeavors.

Please do not hesitate to contact me if I can ever be of assistance to you.

Sincerely,

LOUIS STOKES
Member of Congress

LS/cls/bt

Letter from the president of the National Medical Association about my candidacy for secretary of HHS.

National Medical Association

1012 Tenth Street, Northwest · Washington, D.C. 20001
(202) 347-1895

Edith Irby Jones, M.D.
President
2601 Prospect Street
Houston, Texas 77004
(713) 529-3145

November 27, 1985

Monroe E. Trout, M.D.
Senior Vice President
Medical and Scientific Affairs
Sterling Drug, Inc.
Ninety Park Avenue
New York, New York 10016

Dear Dr. Trout:

Thank you for your letter of November 18, 1985.

I do hope you continue to give your services to have improved health care for all. Yes, I had hoped that this would be as Secretary of Health and Human Services. I recognize my vision is limited and acquiesce to the forces of the universe with "something better for you". Your contributions to medical education and health care have not gone without appreciation and recognition by many.

God bless you with continued abundance of supply and concern to continue to join with us to have quality health care accessible and available to all.

Sincerely,

Edith Irby Jones, M.D.

EIJ/brr

Letter from Cleveland, Ohio, Mayor George Voinovich about my candidacy for secretary of HHS.

City of Cleveland

GEORGE V. VOINOVICH, MAYOR

ALL-AMERICA CITY

October 25, 1985

The Honorable George Bush
Vice President of the United States
Executive Office Building
Washington, D.C. 20501

Dear Vice President Bush:

Recently, it was brought to my attention that Dr. Monroe Trout is being given consideration for the post of Secretary of Health and Human Services. We are extremely familiar with Dr. Trout's ability and management experience, and believe that he would do an outstanding job as Secretary of Health and Human Services.

His appointment would be warmly received by the medical community of Greater Cleveland.

I think Barbara is acquainted with Dr. Trout, and I'm sure that he would do an outstanding job for the country.

Looking forward to seeing you in early November, I am

Sincerely,

George V. Voinovich, Mayor
City of Cleveland

GVV/kc

cc: William S. Kiser, M.D., Chairman of the
    Board of Governors & Chief Executive Officer
    The Cleveland Clinic Foundation

Letter of support for my candidacy for secretary of HHS.

PLEASE RESPOND TO
WASHINGTON OFFICE
☐ 1210 LONGWORTH HOUSE OFFICE BUILDING
WASHINGTON DC 20515
(202) 225-3801

DISTRICT OFFICE
☐ 10 PARK PLACE SOUTH
SUITE 210
ATLANTA GA 30303
(404) 688-8207

WYCHE FOWLER JR
5TH DISTRICT GEORGIA

OCT 24 1985

COMMITTEE ON
WAYS AND MEANS

Congress of the United States
House of Representatives
Washington, DC 20515

October 22, 1985

Mr. Donald Regan
Chief of Staff
The White House
Washington, D.C. 20500

Dear Mr. Regan:

Dr. Monroe E. Trout is currently being considered for the position of Secretary of the Department of Health and Human Services, and I encourage you to recommend that he be appointed to the Cabinet in this capacity.

Dr. Trout has both an M.D. degree and a J.D. degree as well as extensive experience as Senior Vice President of a major drug company, Sterling Drug, Inc. He has served our nation in the Navy and the Navy Reserve, and was a Regimental Surgeon with the Marines.

I am familiar with Dr. Trout's work through his involvement with the Morehouse School of Medicine in my Congressional District in Atlanta. A Member of the Board since the School of Medicine was founded in 1980, Dr. Trout has served as Vice Chairman of the Board of Trustees since 1981. He has helped secure corporate support for the medical school and has played an instrumental role in its growth and development. While living hundreds of miles away from Morehouse, Dr. Trout has never missed a Board of Trustees meeting, and his dedication to the goal of educating physicians to meet the needs of the underserved has never waned.

I believe Dr. Trout will bring a similar commitment to the job of Secretary of Health and Human Services, and under his leadership the Department will undoubtedly be efficiently run and effectively managed.

I urge you to select Dr. Trout for Secretary of HHS. If I can provide any additional information, please do not hesitate to let me know.

Sincerely,

WYCHE FOWLER, JR.
Member of Congress

APPENDIX F-20

Letter of support for my candidacy for secretary of HHS.

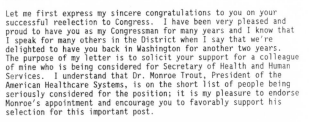

Larry L. Mathis
President
Chief Executive Officer

Methodist

The
Methodist
Hospital
System

6565 Fannin
Houston, Texas 77030
(713) 790-3366

November 22, 1988

RECEIVED
NOV 2 8 1988

The Honorable Bill Archer
U. S. House of Representatives
1135 Longworth House Office Building
Washington, D.C. 20515-4307

Dear Bill:

Let me first express my sincere congratulations to you on your
successful reelection to Congress. I have been very pleased and
proud to have you as my Congressman for many years and I know that
I speak for many others in the District when I say that we're
delighted to have you back in Washington for another two years.
The purpose of my letter is to solicit your support for a colleague
of mine who is being considered for Secretary of Health and Human
Services. I understand that Dr. Monroe Trout, President of the
American Healthcare Systems, is on the short list of people being
seriously considered for the position; it is my pleasure to endorse
Monroe's appointment and encourage you to favorably support his
selection for this important post.

As President and Chief Executive Officer of The Methodist Hospital
System, I serve as a member of the board of directors of American
Healthcare Systems (AmHS), an alliance of 32 of the nation's leading
not-for-profit healthcare systems, of which The Methodist Hospital
System is a member and Monroe is President. As a member of the
AmHS executive committee, I have been fortunate to work with Monroe
Trout and I have developed enormous regard for this man. His
judgment, his experience, and his stature, both as an attorney and
a physician, are respected in both the not-for-profit and
for-profit sectors of the healthcare industry. His extensive
talents and abilities make him imminently qualified to direct the
federal government's health and human services programs. From my
observations of Dr. Trout and my experiences working with him, I
believe he will be an outstanding choice to serve the country in
this important capacity.

I hope you will endorse Dr. Trout for this federal appointment and
please let me know if I can do anything else to advance his
selection; I certainly will be happy to do so.

Sincerely,

Larry L. Mathis
President
Chief Executive Officer

LLM:bk

bcc: Monroe Trout, M.D.
      Jim Scott

Invitation to join President Bush's finance committee.

THE FUND FOR AMERICA'S FUTURE

VICE PRESIDENT GEORGE BUSH
Founder and Honorary Chairman

ROBERT MOSBACHER
Finance Chairman

May 27, 1985

Monroe E. Trout, M.D.
81 Mariomi Road
New Canaan, Connecticut   06840

Dear Doctor Trout:

    Barbara Bush told me of your interest and willingness to help the Fund for America's Future. The Fund for America's Future will be the Vice President's principle vehicle to aid candidates for high office throughout the Nation in 1986. Right now, our main concern is to raise the funds necessary to enable the Vice President to maximize his and Barbara's unique position in supporting candidates next year.

    I know that the Vice President and Barbara are very pleased to have you on their team. If you wish to make a contribution, please use the enclosed envelope and reply card. If you would like to help raise money for the Fund, I would be pleased to discuss the details with you, either in person (should you be in Washington, D.C.), or on the telephone. Please feel free to call me at (202) 337-2601.

    On behalf of the Vice President, thank you for offering your help to the cause.

Sincerely,

Frederick M. Bush
Finance Director

FMB/cjb
Enclosure

2828 PENNSYLVANIA AVENUE, SUITE 400, WASHINGTON, D.C. 20007

Paid for by The Fund For America's Future.
Roy G. Hale, *Treasurer*

Letter from John Gavin, ambassador to Mexico.

EMBASSY OF THE
UNITED STATES OF AMERICA
MEXICO

OFFICE OF THE AMBASSADOR

October 22, 1985

Monroe E. Trout, M.D.
Senior Vice President
Sterling Drug Inc.
90 Park Avenue
New York, New York 10016

Dear Dr. Trout:

It was a pleasure to meet you last week on the flight to New York.

Should you visit Mexico, I hope you will look me up. In the meantime, I trust that your visit to Washington will have had a successful result.

Cordially,

John Gavin

Card and note from Barbara and George Bush after his victory in 1988.

The exhilaration of victory is matched only by the deep appreciation we feel for your friendship and support from start to finish.

Now the work begins to see our dreams for America fulfilled. We are confident and ever grateful that you'll be with us in this quest.

Barbara Bush   George Bush

10-8-88

Dear Monroe —

The statistics on minority employment etc. are very helpful. (letter to BPB — 9-21) Thanks so my much.

Rush, rush — G

Invitation from Congressman William Lowery.

CONGRESS OF THE UNITED STATES
WASHINGTON, D. C. 20515

BILL LOWERY
CALIFORNIA

The Honorable and Mrs. Bill Lowery

invite you to attend a

Inaugural Reception

proceeding the swearing-in of

George Herbert Walker Bush

and

James Danforth Quayle

Friday, January 20, 1989

1:00 - 3:00 p.m.

438 Cannon House Office Building
Washington, D.C. 20515

R.S.V.P.
(202) 225-3201

Letter from Sam Thier on AIDS.

NATIONAL ACADEMY OF SCIENCES
INSTITUTE OF MEDICINE
2101 Constitution Avenue, Washington, D.C. 20418

December 13, 1988

The Honorable George Bush
President-elect
Office of the President-elect
1825 Connecticut Avenue, N.W.
Washington, DC 20270

Dear Mr. President-elect:

During your term in office, AIDS will claim over 200,000
American lives. It is estimated that 1 million to 1.5 million
Americans, mostly young adults, are infected; in the absence of
effective therapy, most will die. Your Administration can take
several actions to slow the spread of this unprecedented epidemic
and limit its damaging effects on this and other countries. The
Institute of Medicine and National Academy of Sciences have
prepared the enclosed white paper to help you meet this
challenge.

The white paper draws from the Institute of Medicine and
National Academy of Sciences study, <u>Confronting AIDS: Update
1988</u>, issued last June. The AIDS Oversight Committee, a panel of
nationally recognized professionals, conducted that study and
would be glad to serve you in any further advisory capacity. The
Presidential Commission on the Human Immunodeficiency Virus
Epidemic, as you know, also issued its report last June, and the
broad concurrence of the two reports gives added weight to their
findings. Until the newly legislated national commission on AIDS
is established, the IOM/NAS committee is the only standing
committee of national stature charged with assessing the nation's
progress against the AIDS epidemic.

The program detailed in the white paper entails actions by
various individuals. However, you and your Secretary of Health
and Human Services can take the lead early in your terms of
office by providing overarching direction for all segments of the
government and the private sector.

<u>Presidential actions should include the following</u>:

o   Use the newly legislated national commission on AIDS to
     develop a forceful and coherent national policy.

Letter from Sam Thier on AIDS.

The Honorable George Bush
December 13, 1988
Page 2

    o   Encourage the enactment of legislation to protect HIV-infected persons from discrimination in the private and public sectors.

    o   Express your strong support for an aggressive, unambiguous education program (as is occurring in Western Europe) about behavior changes necessary to avoid HIV infection. Use your influence to ensure that government at all levels provides funds for appropriate education in the schools and messages in the media.

    o   Express your belief that testing for HIV infection should only be conducted when the purpose of the testing is clear, and when the test results allow effective and humane interventions that would not have been possible in their absence.

    o   Recognize this country's special responsibility in international efforts to control the spread of HIV infection.

Your Secretary of Health and Human Services should be directed to:

    o   Develop a comprehensive, private-public (federal, state, and local) national plan for delivering and financing care for HIV-infected and AIDS patients.

    o   Initiate a forceful program for the prevention and treatment of drug abuse and prevention of the related spread of HIV infection.

    o   Bolster efforts in surveillance, case reporting, and the gathering of information about risk behavior.

    o   Ensure that biomedical research (including drug and vaccine development and regulation) continues to follow productive paths.

A crucial element in the task ahead is the tone set by the President. Vigorous measures are required to control the disease and to improve the social conditions (poverty, drug abuse, lack of education, etc.) that sustain it. The nation's leader, speaking from his unique position to inspire action against the

Letter from Sam Thier on AIDS.

The Honorable George Bush
December 13, 1988
Page 3

disease among all the people, must balance this call to action
with a concern for the civil rights of all.

Americans have generated an enormous fund of knowledge about
AIDS. We know its cause, we can test for the presence of HIV in
the body, and we know what measures would, if successfully
applied, slow its spread. Furthermore, the scientific
understanding that lays the groundwork for the development of
effective vaccine and drug treatment grows daily. Yet despite
these triumphs, we have not successfully confronted the epidemic.
Your Administration inherits the opportunity to harness our
knowledge and turn the tide against AIDS.

Yours sincerely,

Samuel O. Thier
President
Institute of Medicine

Frank Press
President
National Academy of Sciences

Letter from Otis Bowen nominating me for the AIDS Commission.

THE UNDER SECRETARY OF HEALTH AND HUMAN SERVICES
WASHINGTON, D.C. 20201

June 9, 1987

The Honorable Gary L. Bauer
Assistant to the President
    for Policy Development
The White House
Washington, D.C. 20500

Dear Gary:

     Please find enclosed the curriculum vitae of Monroe E.
Trout, M.D., J.D., whom I heartily endorse for consideration as a
member of the President's Commission on AIDS. Dr. Trout is a
highly respected physician and administrator who has been deeply
involved in research and development programs for the last 10
years.

     Dr. Trout is presently the president and chief executive
officer of American Healthcare Systems. This organization
represents 174,000 hospital beds in the United States. He
anticipates his hospitals will be significantly impacted by this
dreaded disease. The insight and expertise which he would bring
to the President's Commission cannot be overestimated.

     Dr. Trout is well known throughout the medical field as well
as the healthcare field. He would bring significant knowledge
and hands-on experience to the President's Commission on AIDS.

                                        Sincerely,

                                        /s/

                                        Otis R. Bowen, M.D.
                                        Secretary

bcc: Dr. Trout

Board Resolution on my retirement from American Healthcare Systems.

Monroe E. Trout, M.D., J.D.
Board Resolution

WHEREAS, Monroe E. Trout, M.D., J.D., has distinguished himself throughout his career as a compassionate and accomplished humanitarian with a universally recognized aptitude for health care, business and innovation; and

WHEREAS, as head of American Healthcare Systems Dr. Trout has served as chairman of the board and chief executive officer of the nations largest not-for-profit, multihospital system alliance; and

WHEREAS, under his leadership, Dr. Trout streamlined and strengthened the governance process to facilitate decision making and give AmHS management the authority to make judgements required for the efficient daily operations of the company.; and

WHEREAS, Dr. Trout clarified AmHS focus, strategic direction and purpose to ensure achieving its goals as well as improving its financial picture, stopping the losses and spearheading ambitious profitable programs including a Shareholder-owned self assurance program, the AmHS Excess Liability Insurance Program, to provide long term availability of coverage and limits at stabilized premiums; and

WHEREAS, during Dr. Trout's tenure, AmHS Purchasing Partners L.P. developed strategic corporate partnerships with the leading organizations in the health care field to address cost containment issues while delivering the highest quality health care products and services; and

WHEREAS, Dr. Trout led the development of innovative long term corporate partnerships; and

WHEREAS, Dr. Trout initiated numerous profitable AmHS investments in varied health care firms, improved the price and quality of products and services provided to AmHS Shareholders; and

WHEREAS, Dr. Trout provided for expansion of its shareholder membership to broaden its base and give a stronger geographic representation in areas in which it was minimally represented; and

WHEREAS, Dr. Trout promoted the creation of the annual AmHS Cares Award which honors innovative programs nationally that improve access to health care for the medically disadvantaged; and

WHEREAS, Dr. Trout has been a leading advocate for health care reform and spearheaded AmHS issuance of PATIENTS FIRST, one of the most comprehensive proposals ever developed to restructure the American health care delivery system and a major philosophical basis for the Cooper-Grandison Bill; and

WHEREAS, Dr. Trout is chairman of the Board of Trustees of the University of California, San Diego Foundation and serves on the California Business Higher Education Forum Board; UCSD Thornton Hospital Board of Advisors; ACSD Board of Medical Advisors; and UCSD CONNECT Steering Committee; and

WHEREAS, Dr. Trout has received praise and accolades from the medical and business communities, the health care industry and educational institutions on local, regional, national and international levels; and

WHEREAS, under Dr. Trout's leadership, AmHS has become the most profitable integrated health care system alliance in the country and one of the largest in the world; therefore be it

RESOLVED, on the occasion of his retirement, that American Healthcare Systems and its board of directors recognize Monroe E. Trout, M.D., J.D. for his substantial contributions to AmHS, health care and community; and be it further

RESOLVED this day in the Executive Session of the Board of Directors of AmHS, the 13th of October, 1994, that Monroe E. Trout, M.D., J.D., be made CHAIRMAN EMERITUS of American Healthcare Systems upon his retirement.

Poem written by John Gailey III, general counsel, on my retirement from West Pharmaceutical Company Board of Directors.

What Can You Say 'Bout Monroe?

By John R. Gailey III

What can you say 'bout Monroe?
A lawyer by trade
A rich man, self-made
There's no doubt he's got lots of dough.

A physician of note
(But not one to gloat)
And past AHS CEO.

He's certainly no dummy
At times, even funny
Is there anything he doesn't know?

He now lives in Knoxville
With his art and his Rockwells
Did I hear he has a Van Gogh?

His wife is named Sandy
Who claims he's quite randy
But with age just a little bit slow.

At six foot six tall
He towers o'er us all
Especially our new CFO.

His leadership prowess
Never ceases to wow us
Cowabunga! Gee Whiz! and Good Show!

No patience for gabbers
When he drops the hammer
We cry out, "Look out below!"

What can I say 'bout Monroe?
As governance king
You've taught me a thing
And I gotta tell ya
That you're a fine fella
And I hate to see Monroe go.

\\MARKETING\USERS\JGAILEY\WORDDOCS\BODMEC\Ode to Monroe.doc

Resolution of the Baxter Board on my retirement.

WHEREAS, Monroe E. Trout, you entered the working world at the age of six young years; you shoveled snow in the winter and carried ashes out from the coal furnace; you cut the lawn in the summer and trimmed the hedges to help your family survive the Depression years.

Education became your passion fueled by the admiration you felt for the physician/mayor who employed you during those early years and inspired by the junior high teacher who mentored to you. Junior high turned into high school; high school turned into a degree from the University of Pennsylvania; the undergraduate degree turned into a medical degree from Penn Medical School and the ever-present thirst for increasing knowledge led to a law degree from Dickinson College.

The United States Navy engaged you for five years as you satisfied your obligation to practice medicine in repayment for your medical school education. Upon discharge from the Navy, you walked through the door at Harrisburg State Hospital as Chief of Medicine.

The business world enticed you away from the hospital setting, where you were able to bring medical science and law together in an illustrious career as head of Government Affairs at Pfizer; Vice President for Medical and Scientific Affairs and member of the Board of Directors and Executive Committee at Sterling Drug; Chairman, Chief Executive Officer and President at American Healthcare Systems and Chairman of the Board of Cytyc Corporation.

Accomplishments are not always measured, but frequently, achievements are recognized and applauded. Bestowed upon you were:

The Alumni Award of Merit from the University of Pennsylvania
An Honorary Degree from Cumberland College
An Honorary Degree from Bloomfield College
The Salvation Army Caring Award
Bnai Brith International Health Care Award
The Gold Medal of the American College of Legal Medicine
The Life Time Achievement Award of Delta Tau Delta
Honorary Degree and The Distinguished Alumni Award from Dickinson School of Law
The University of California San Diego Universitatus Award and Honorary Alumni
Award; and
The Horatio Alger Award

Education for you has been the key to success, and with that success comes responsibility. That responsibility is fulfilled when one is "imbued with a spirit of helping others," as you have exemplified in philanthropic endeavors such as:

The Sandra and Monroe Trout Chair of Pharmacology and the Monroe E. Trout Chair
in Surgery at the University of California, San Diego;
Scholarship Endowments at Dickinson School of Law, Cumberland and Bloomfield
Colleges and Morehouse School of Medicine
The Monroe E. Trout Premier Cares Award

NOW THEREFORE, it is

RESOLVED, that we, the Board of Directors of Baxter International Inc., appreciate your dedicated nine years of service on this Board, we respect and will remember your leadership, your commitment to the shareholders of this Company, your unique blend of skills and your wisdom that you carried with you to each and every meeting and which have contributed immeasurably to the future of Baxter. We wish for you sounds of symphonies, paint on your pallet, books on your shelves, and an endless impact on society as you further the love of learning.

Remarks by Vern Loucks at the B'nai B'rith awards dinner.

WORDS OF THANKS TO MONROE TROUT

I am honored by the opportunity to express the gratitude of everyone here for your statesmanship and leadership during some of the most trying and difficult years any of us have ever known. Your wisdom and the course you steered for your part of our world showed clarity and light of vision which has defied the **_darkness_** with which the promise of reform has **_threatened_** that **_purpose_** toward which we have all devoted our lives: continued strength for the finest healthcare system in the world.

Among us, you are the most seasoned of veterans and you know first hand much of what this obsession with healthcare excellence is all about:

- Doctor
- Lawyer
- Chief of R&D
- Chief Executive of one of the great hospital systems

This collective experience is perhaps most responsible for the extraordinary sense of balance with which you have dealt so well with the enormous complexities which have weighed upon us all.

We have looked to you for guidance and you have rewarded us greatly. We thank you with all the heart and soul which, as an industry, we can command.

More important than what you have done for our healthcare world, Monroe, we are all drawn to you by the richness of your person.

You are a man we all admire -- a strong character with solid values who always stands tall with dignity and decency and all the other elements of the human spirit which rank you as a giant among us.

Ralph Waldo Emerson said: *Beauty is its own excuse for being.* Monroe, you and Sandy are beautiful people -- We wish you great happiness in the years ahead.

by
Vernon R. Loucks Jr.
Chairman and CEO
Baxter International Inc.
at The 1994 NATIONAL HEALTHCARE DINNER
Grand Hyatt Hotel, New York
on Monday, June 13, 1994

Letter from Claudine Malone about my SAIC Board service.

CLAUDINE B. MALONE
PRESIDENT

August 30, 2004

Monroe Trout, M.D.
2110 Cove View Way
Knoxville, TN 37919

Dear Monroe,

We SAIC directors miss you already and we will increasingly miss your courage, your integrity, your experience and your leadership. I have learned a great deal from you about how a director can and should carry out one's fiduciary responsibilities. My efforts are guided by your example even though I continue to fall short of the standard you have set for us all.

I was appalled that after your years of devotion to him, Bob Beyster did not appreciate your friendship, your medical support and your Board service. I hope for his sake that he will come to reflect and realize the debt of gratitude he owes to you, both personally and professionally. Your fellow directors certainly hold you in the highest regard.

Monroe, you continue to surpass yourself in my esteem. After learning that you are not only a lawyer and a medical doctor and after admiring your Board leadership, I returned home from one of my trips and found the oil painting you sent me. I was awe struck. You are a marvel! So now I add artist to your list of merit badges. I adore having the painting as a reminder of our years together. I appreciate your thoughtfulness in sending it to me. I wish you much joy in the years ahead. Thank you for all of your guidance, support and friendship.

Sincerely,

Claudine B. Malone

7570 Potomac Fall Rd. McLean, VA 22102 (703) 821-8861

Letter about my part in change of leadership at SAIC from current lead director.

A. Thomas Young

P.O. Box 518
18210 Poplar Cove Road
Onancock, VA 23417

12/14/04

Dear Monroe,

SAIC is doing well under the leadership of Ken Dalberg. We miss your wisdom and leadership — — — And _courage_ on the Board. Your extraordinary actions clearly were the catalyst that got us on course for the "New" SAIC. If you had not acted, I cannot imagine what a horrible situation we would be in today. You are a model for the characteristics of a responsible Director.

Letter about my participation in the Baxter annual meeting.

Vernon R. Loucks, Jr.
Chairman and
Chief Executive Officer

Baxter Healthcare Corporation
One Baxter Parkway
Deerfield, Illinois 60015

Baxter

RECEIVED

MAY 10 1993

May 5, 1993

Monroe, E. Trout, M.D., J.D.
Chairman, President and CEO
American Healthcare Systems
12730 High Bluff Drive
San Diego, California 92130-2099

Dear Monroe:

I don't know that there are any words that can match
the eloquence of your support on both my behalf and
Baxter's at last Friday's meeting. Needless to say,
it came at a very important time for this company -
and for me. You and I know, perhaps better than
anyone, how hard we have worked to make the
association between our two companies so very
meaningful. I hope we will always be able to earn
the kind of respect and heartfelt support which you
so elegantly set forth last Friday.

You are the very best, a great friend and I am very,
very proud to know you.

Sincerely,

VRL:eg

Letter about my participation in the Baxter annual meeting.

CAREMARK

RECEIVED

MAY - 7 1993

Caremark International Inc.

2215 Sanders Road, Suite 400
Northbrook, Illinois 60062
708.559.4600
Fax 708.559.4603

C. A. Lance Piccolo
Chairman and
Chief Executive Officer

May 3, 1993

Monroe E. Trout, M.D., J.D.
Chairman, Chief Executive Officer and President
American Healthcare Systems
12730 High Bluff Drive
Suite 300
San Diego, California 92130

Dear Monroe:

I have had the entire weekend to be reflective about your presentation at the Baxter International Shareholders Meeting.

You have brought life, definition and meaning to the word partnership. It is seldom that one meets an individual who has both the individual strength and integrity that you so ably represent.

It is an honor to know you and even though I am writing as an alumnus of the world's best healthcare company, I want you to know how much I admire what you did. There is no finer person in this world than Vern Loucks and now I know two of you.

Sincerely,

Lance Piccolo

LP:js

Letter about my participation in the Baxter annual meeting.

THE UNIVERSITY OF IOWA
HOSPITALS AND CLINICS

Office of the Director and Assistant to
The President for Statewide Health Services
200 Hawkins Drive
Iowa City, Iowa 52242-1009

319/356-2265

May 4, 1993

Monroe E. Trout, M.D., J.D.
Chairman, Chief Executive Officer
    and President
American Healthcare Systems
12730 High Bluff Drive
Suite 300
San Diego, CA 92130

RECEIVED

MAY 10 1993

Dear Monroe:

    Just a short note to express sincere appreciation for your splendid remarks at the Annual Meeting of Baxter Shareholders last Friday. I thought your commentary was most cogent and beautifully timed. As you probably noted, after you spoke, the momentum started to turn toward support of Vern Loucks and the programs of Baxter. As one member of the Board, I would like to thank you sincerely for taking the time to travel to Chicago to be with us and for your very thoughtful remarks to the shareholders.

    Best wishes to you and your system for continued success in the years ahead.

Sincerely,

John W. Colloton
Director and Assistant to the President
    for Statewide Health Services

JWC:lj

Letter from a young Marine whom we helped get over a bad period.

CHARLES F. PADGET

RECEIVED
DEC -1 1992

November 24, 1992

Monroe E. Trout, M.D.
Chairman of the Board
President
Chief Executive Officer
American Healthcare Systems
12730 High Bluff Drive
Suite 300
San Diego, CA 92130-2099

Dear Dr. Trout:

On behalf of my entire family, I wanted to express our deepest gratitude for all that you have done for us over the past several weeks. Moreover, I only wish I could properly convey to you what the gift as provided by you and Mrs. Trout has meant to this family. Honestly, at that point of time, I don't think we could have survived without it.

Additionally, I enjoyed meeting Ms Cheri Caviness, and appreciated her time in explaining her perspective on how one successfully locates employment, proper interview techniques, and what she personally looks for in a candidate applying for employment with American Healthcare Systems. Having recently utilized this information, it appears that my search for employment may not last as long as I first anticipated.

Again, Dr. Trout, words alone cannot express our gratitude and we wish both you and your family the best during the upcoming holidays.

Very truly yours,

Charles F. Padget
Charles F. Padget

cfp

4827 Gardenia Street • Oceanside, California 92057 • (619) 945-5402

Letter about my chair in Surgery at UCSD.

J. W. Peltason
President
University of California

May 31, 1995

Dear Monroe:

It is my distinct pleasure and honor to tell you that at its May meeting, the Board of Regents approved the establishment and naming of the Monroe E. Trout Chair in Surgery on our San Diego campus; congratulations. This action is intended to reflect the respect and esteem in which you are held by the University community.

The Regents, Chancellor Atkinson, and I are delighted to have the privilege of recognizing in this special way your commitment to and support of the University of California and most especially our San Diego campus. We are proud of your association with the University of California.

My best to Sandy.

Cordially,

cc: Chancellor Atkinson

Dedication for the house Sandy and I had built in Appalachia.

DEDICATION OF SCOTT & HEATHER GRIMES HOME
OCTOBER 3, 2006
11:00 A.M.

Welcome and Recognition of Dr. and Mrs. Monroe Trout	Dr. Jim Taylor *President*
History of Mountain Outreach	Mr. Marc Hensley *Mountain Outreach Director*
Song: Blessed Be The Name	Mountain Outreach *Summer Team*
Poem	Ms. Sarah Whitaker *Mountain Outreach Student Staff*
Introduction of the Grimes Family	Ms. Ranessa Capps *Mountain Outreach Student Coordinator*
Remarks	Dr. Monroe Trout
Litany of Dedication	Mr. Marc Hensley
Prayer of Dedication	Ms. Tracey Smith *Mountain Outreach Student Staff*

...ON

...mpletion of this home for

...home constructed by the
...r caring and compassionate

...we give thanks for the admin-
...erlands who saw a need and

PEOPLE: We give thanks for leaders through the years who have guided Mountain Outreach with enthusiasm and commitment.

LEADER: As we consider the present, we give thanks for Dr. and Mrs. Monroe Trout, who unselfishly gave to make this Grimes home possible.

PEOPLE: We give thanks for the caring concern of Monroe and Sandra Trout and their generous gift which made the construction of the Grimes home possible.

LEADER: As we consider the future, we are mindful of the 123 homes that have been constructed in the past 24 years.

PEOPLE: We give thanks for the student volunteers, church groups, faculty, staff and administrators who have served His ministry and pray that others will feel the call of God to serve in the future.

UNISON: With gratefulness for the past and enthusiasm for the future, we dedicate the Grimes home.

Letter about our scholarship support for the Horatio Alger Award.

H. WAYNE HUIZENGA
200 SOUTH ANDREWS AVENUE
FT. LAUDERDALE, FLORIDA 33301

305/627-5022

August 10, 1995

Mr. Monroe E. Trout
Chairman Emeritus
American Healthcare Systems
Box 8052
Rancho Santa Fe, CA 92067

Dear Monroe:

I was delighted to hear from Terry Giroux that you recently joined the Chairman's Club to support the scholarship program of our Horatio Alger Association.

I wanted to express my appreciation for your having made this commitment as it is a significant financial commitment and demonstrates your continuing belief in and support of the programs of our Association.

I look forward to seeing you soon and working with you on many other Horatio Alger Association projects.

Sincerely,

H. Wayne Huizenga

HWH/dar

Letter about Monroe E. Trout Premier Cares Award, which I initiated in 1992.

C. R. Bard, Inc.
730 Central Avenue
Murray Hill, NJ 07974

William H. Longfield
President and
Chief Operating Officer

BARD

January 19, 1994

Monroe E. Trout, M.D.
Chairman, President and
  Chief Executive Officer
American Healthcare Systems
12730 High Bluff Drive
Suite 300
San Diego, CA 92130

Dear Monroe:

Bob Johnson has just told me about the very kind way you recognized Bard and the other companies that joined us in contributing to the AmHS Cares Award.

I know you know we did not do this for the recognition, but because we felt it was a tremendously well done endeavor by AmHS for some very deserving recipients, and we hoped that a few more dollars would help you do even more. Apparently that was the case, and believe me we are thankful to AmHS for letting us participate.

I continue to progress after my surgery and should soon be able to travel and look forward to visiting with you.

Sincerely,

William H. Longfield

st

Letter from the president of Bloomfield College about my being named to the
Power Thinkers list by McGraw-Hill.

Bloomfield College

3/25/96

Dear Monroe,

I've finally decided not to make a California trip this spring, though a trip in early summer is still a possibility,

more likely to drop your name when I'm in someplace over my head.

My best regards to Sandy. Congratulations to both of you.

Very truly yours,

Jack

Letter from Mayor Mike Ragsdale about the Knoxville Opera Rossini Festival.

OFFICE OF COUNTY MAYOR, MIKE RAGSDALE

400 Main Street, Suite 615, Knoxville TN 37902

April 19, 2004

Jack McElroy, Editor
Knoxville News Sentinel
2332 News Sentinel Drive
Knoxville, TN 37921-5761

Dear Jack:

This weekend is Knoxville was filled with many outstanding festival activities...one of which was the successful Rossini Festival Italian Street Fair. This event continues to grow and draw increased attendance each year. It has been sponsored by Sandra and Monroe Trout for its three inaugural years and this past Saturday Dr. Trout announced that he and Sandy have committed to sponsoring the 2005 Rossini Festival.

Events such as the Rossini Festival play a significant role in the revitalization of downtown Knoxville. We owe Sandra and Monroe Trout a "thank-you" for making this event possible. I for one am looking forward to Rossini 2005.

Best regards,

Mike Ragsdale
Knox County Mayor

Letter about the B'nai B'rith award.

UNION UNIVERSITY
SCHENECTADY, NEW YORK 12308-2311

OFFICE OF THE VICE CHANCELLOR
(518) 370-6687

UNION COLLEGE, 1795
ALBANY MEDICAL COLLEGE, 1839
ALBANY LAW SCHOOL, 1851
DUDLEY OBSERVATORY, 1852
ALBANY COLLEGE OF PHARMACY, 1881

May 6, 1991

Dr. Monroe Trout
12730 High Bluff Dr.
Suite 300
San Diego, CA 92130-2099

Dear Monroe,

Sincerest congratulations on the recognition accorded by the B'nai B'rith International -- the 1991 National Healthcare Award! Reading the brief biography included with the announcement was inspirational, especially as the treatment touched upon, because of space limitations, only some of your involvements and achievements. The mention of Danocrine did however, stimulate reflection on some pleasant and satisfying moments of association.

Congratulations again and best wishes for many more years of accomplishment and recognition together with derivative gratification.

Respectfully,

Robert L. Friedlander, M.D.
Vice Chancellor

RLF/bsm

Letter about my service on Arizona State's Board of Visitors.

Arizona State University

College of Business
School of Health Administration and Policy
Tempe, Arizona 85287-4506
602/965-7778
FAX: 602/965-5539

May 15, 1991

Charles S. Lauer, Dinner Chairman
B'Nai B'rith International
National Healthcare Award Dinner
Honoring Dr. Monroe E. Trout
823 United Nations Plaza
New York, New York 10017

Dear Mr. Lauer:

Due to my son's graduation from high school, I regret that I will
not be able to attend the B'nai B'rith National Healthcare Award
Dinner honoring Monroe Trout. I want to share with you, and
hopefully through you with Monroe, my thoughts about him on the
occasion of his recognition by your organization.

I first met Monroe over twenty years ago - when he was President
of the American College of Legal Medicine. At that time I was at
N.Y.U. writing a dissertation on individuals cross-educated in
law and medicine. Monroe, having graduated from both law school
and medical school was then President of the American College of
Legal Medicine and pursuing a very successful career at Sterling
Drug. What made Monroe very unusual was his clarity of thought
about where medicine was going and how someone with training in
two professions could make a very unique contribution to health
care. Monroe Trout is a role model for bridging academic
disciplines and professional communities.

When Monroe moved to California I was pleased to renew our
acquaintance. At that time we were forming an advisory committee
for the School of Health Administration and Policy at Arizona
State University. Under the leadership of the late David Kinzer,
this group was charged with reviewing the strategic direction of
the School, providing advice to the director, and working to
ensure that the School gained national recognition. Monroe has
been thoroughly unselfish in his commitment to our school. His
depth of understanding of the health care industry has led us to
clarify our thinking on many issues. With tact and diplomacy, he
challenges our assumptions and, with great expertise, leads us
back onto very productive pathways.

Obviously Monroe Trout is a very important person to our field.
The faculty of the School of Health Administration and Policy and
colleagues on the David Kinzer Panel of Visitors congratulate
Monroe on the occasion of his recognition by B'nai B'rith.

Sincerely,

Eugene S. Schneller, Ph.D.
Professor and Director

cc. Ben Forsyth, M.D. (Senior Executive Assistant
             to the President)
    Larry Penley, Ph.D. (Interim Dean, College of Business)
    Members of the David Kinzer Panel of Visitors

APPENDIX K-3

Letter about my B'nai B'rith International Healthcare Award.

Helge H. Wehmeier

President and Chief Executive Officer

Agfa Corporation
100 Challenger Road
Ridgefield Park NJ 07660
NJ (201) 440-2500
NY (212) 971-0260

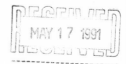
MAY 17 1991

May 13, 1991

Monroe E. Trout, M.D.
Chairman of the Board
President and CEO
American Healthcare Systems
12730 High Bluff Drive
Suite 300
San Diego, CA 92130-2099

Dear Monroe:

Let me congratulate you on receiving the prestigious 1991 National Healthcare Award.

Since I will be traveling to Europe on June 4th, I would like to express my sincere regret that I will be unable to attend this important event, recognizing your vast contribution to National Healthcare.

Again, you have my warm congratulations and best wishes for your continued success.

With best personal regards,

Helge H. Wehmeier /sg

HHW/sg
(signed in Mr. Wehmeier's absence)

Letter about my B'nai B'rith International Healthcare Award.

MICHAEL S. ROSKOTHEN
COLGATE - PALMOLIVE EUROPE
BD. DE LA WOLUWE 58
1200 BRUSSELS
BELGIUM

8 May 1991

Mr. Monroe E. Trout, M.D.
Chairman of the Board,
President and CEO
AMERICAN HEALTHCARE SYSTEMS
12760 High Bluff Drive
San Diego, CA 92130-2019

Dear Manroe,

My warmest and heartfelt congratulations to your elevation
as International Healthcare Award winner of the year 1991.

B'nai B'rith International have taken a wise and right
choice and recognized your outstanding contributions both
as a person and a healthcare leader.

Unfortunately Ute and myself cannot be with you on June 3
in New York as I have already a one-year old speaking en-
gagement in Europe.

Our best regards to you and Sandy.

Michael S. ROSKOTHEN

Letter about my B'nai B'rith International Healthcare Award.

Kidder, Peabody & Co.
Incorporated

20 EXCHANGE PLACE
NEW YORK, N.Y. 10005

RECEIVED JUN 2 5 1991

Gerald H. McGinley
SENIOR VICE PRESIDENT

(212) 510-5376

June 20, 1991

Dr. Monroe E. Trout
President
American Helath Care Systems
12760 High Bluff Drive
Ste. 250
San Diego, Ca 92130

Dear Monroe,

What a thoughtful guy to include me among your family of friends at the recent B'nai B'rith Healthcare Award Dinner.

Typical of you, your acceptance speech showed you to be the great guy you are. All that talent in one package, but still modest and very caring. Not many successful people have those qualities.

Again, congratulations! Please give Sandy a big hug and my warmest regards to you.

Gratefully,

APPENDIX K-6

Letter from Eddie Cohen about my chairmanship of a B'nai B'rith fundraising dinner.

B'NAI B'RITH INTERNATIONAL

OFFICE OF SPECIAL EVENTS

823 United Nations Plaza • Suite 400 • New York, NY 10017

TEL (212) 490-3290   FAX (212) 687-3429

RECEIVED

JUN 24 1994

EDWIN COHEN
National Director

June 20, 1994

Dr. Monroe E. Trout
Chairman of the Board/President
   and Chief Executive Officer
American Healthcare Systems
12730 High Bluff Drive, Suite 300
San Diego, CA 92139

Dear Monroe:

Thank you for all your efforts on behalf of our dinner in honor of Chuck.

To start with, Chuck would never have said "yes" if you had not agreed to serve as chairman. You helped generate a great deal of support, and did an outstanding job as toastmaster.

I appreciate all the help you have given me, as well as, the financial support we have received from AHS.

With kindest personal regards.

Sincerely,

Eddie

Edwin Cohen

Letter about one of my published papers.

NEW YORK LAW SCHOOL

57 WORTH STREET
NEW YORK, N. Y. 10013

OFFICE OF THE DEAN

March 12, 1976

Monroe E. Trout, M.D., J.D., F.C.L.M.
Vice President
Sterling Drug, Inc.
90 Park Avenue
New York, New York

Dear Monroe:

Congratulations on your excellent article, "New Recommendations to Update Malpractice Legislation," which appeared in the February, 1976 issue of The Journal of Legal Medicine.

Cordially yours,

E. Donald Shapiro
Dean

EDS/dr

Letter about my service as an editor of *Legal Aspects of Medical Practice*.

Legal Aspects of Medical Practice
Publication of the American College of Legal Medicine

777 Third Avenue, New York, N.Y. 10017 • Phone 212-838-7778

DON GUSSOW
Chairman and Editor in Chief

December 28, 1978

Monroe E. Trout, M.D.
Senior Vice President
Medical and Scientific Affairs
Sterling Drug Inc.
90 Park Avenue
New York, New York 10016

Dear Monroe:

As a founding father of LEGAL ASPECTS OF MEDICAL
PRACTICE most assuredly, as you say, you have a
fondness in your heart for this magazine and what
we are trying to do with it for the medical profession.

So while I am naturally sorry to see you leaving the
editorial board (albeit for good reason), I do know
that we can expect your interest and support in the
months ahead.

Best regards.

Sincerely,

Don Gussow

DG:mm

cc: James Zimmerly

APPENDIX L-3

Letter about my service as a reviewer for the *Annals of Internal Medicine.*

Independence Mall West, Sixth Street at Race, Philadelphia, PA 19106-1572, Telephone 215 351 2400 or 800 523 1546, Fax 215 351 2644

Annals of Internal Medicine
Published by the American College of Physicians

Frank Davidoff, MD, FACP
Editor

September 17, 1996

Monroe E. Trout, AB, MD, JD
Box 8052
Rancho Sante Fe, CA 92067

Dear Doctor Trout:

I write to thank you for the exceptionally fine quality of your
reviewing for *Annals of Internal Medicine* during 1995. As noted in
the 15 December 1995 issue of the journal where we acknowledged the
help of all reviewers over the past year, the strength of *Annals*
depends in large measure on our reviewers' abilities and efforts.
As editors, we weigh your comments carefully. We particularly
appreciate having reviewers point out important facts and
perspectives we didn't notice when we read a paper.

While a superb review is the product of both expertise and
commitment, it is also a remarkably anonymous accomplishment. The
author of a paper may appreciate the help a good critique provides,
but under the present peer review system the author rarely knows the
identity of the reviewer. And departmental chairs, division chiefs,
and tenure and promotion committees are often totally unaware of the
amount and quality of this important academic work.

Not all reviews and reviewers are of the same high quality.
The quality and timeliness of your reviewing for *Annals* placed the
work you did for us in the top 30% of all reviews in 1995. We want
you to know this, and we thank you. Because we are interested in
giving more credit to reviewers like you who provide exceptional
service to medical science in this important role, we strongly urge
you to send a copy of this letter to whomever you think should see
it.

Again, many thanks for your fine help. Not only have the editors
and authors benefited, but the journal's readers and, ultimately,
our patients have too.

Sincere regards,

Frank Davidoff, MD, FACP

FD/rb

Letter from the CEO of the Cleveland Clinic about a paper I wrote on leadership.

FLOYD D. LOOP, M. D.
THE CLEVELAND CLINIC FOUNDATION
ONE CLINIC CENTER
9500 EUCLID AVENUE
CLEVELAND, OHIO 44195-5066

April 30, 1990

Monroe E. Trout, M.D.
American Healthcare Systems
1205 Prospect
Suite 520
San Diego, California 92037

Dear Dr. Trout:

I appreciate your paper on leadership succession.
It gets right to the point and, as I settle into
this job, contains some of the best advice I have
received so far. I have saved it and plan to
reread it again and again.

Last week I met with Gary Aden and we had a good
discussion. I hope to become personally involved
with American Healthcare Systems.

Best wishes,

Floyd D. Loop, M.D.

FDL/lam

APPENDIX L-5

Letter about my service to Drew University.

CHARLES R.
DREW
UNIVERSITY OF MEDICINE & SCIENCE   KING/DREW MEDICAL CENTER

November 14, 1996

Monroe Trout, M.D., LL.B., J.D.
Box 8052
Rancho Santa Fe, California 92680

Dear Dr. Trout:

Thank you for speaking to the Board of Directors and the Executive Council of the Charles R. Drew University of Medicine and Science at our Third Annual Retreat.

Your presentation on "Effectuating Strong and Successful Campaigns" was very inspiring. Your expertise and professionalism was highly praised by all in attendance. We are very grateful to you and look forward to expanding our network of benefactors.

We are excited about the ideas you have given us and anticipate putting them into action.

Once again, thank you for participating in our Retreat.

Sincerely,

Robert L. LeMaile-Williams, M.D., M.P.H.
Retreat Co-Chair

Matthew Jenkins, D.V.M.
Retreat Co-Chair

101 North La Brea Avenue, Suite 610   Inglewood, California 90301   Telephone: (310) 671-4886   Fax: (310) 671-6989

Letter from FDA executive about Dr. Alksne's alleged malpractice in the San Diego *Union-Tribune*.

AMERICAN COLLEGE OF LEGAL MEDICINE

Executive Office ■ 611 East Wells St. ■ Milwaukee, WI 53202-3810
(414) 276-1881 ■ (800) 433-9137 ■ FAX (414) 276-3349

March 23, 1994

RECEIVED
MAR 28 1994

Monroe E. Trout, M.D., J.D., F.C.L.M.
President and Chief Executive Officer
American Healthcare Systems, Inc.
12730 High Bluff Drive
Suite 300
San Diego, CA 92130-2099

Dear Monroe,

Thank you very much for participating in the ACLM annual meeting in Anaheim. Our March 10 panel on new developments in Food and Drug Law was a good one. We had a large block of time to occupy and we occupied it well.

I heard many favorable comments about our session, including the format, the audience participation and the preparation and knowledge of our speakers. In fact the only complaint I heard was that time did not allow us to cover the remainder of the topics that we had prepared (but, then we had no idea there would be so much audience participation).

Your perspectives as the head of American Healthcare Systems, as a past President of ACLM, as the past chief physician of a major drug manufacturer, and as one who has been active in American politics were central to the issues before our panel.

I received your letter of March 17 and I will pass on the San Diego Union-Tribune article to my colleagues at FDA. I look forward to seeing you at Bloomfield College.

On behalf of the American College of Legal Medicine and myself, thank you.

Sincerely yours,

Peter H. Rheinstein,
M.D., J.D., M.S., F.C.L.M., F.A.A.F.P.

Monroe E. Trout, M.D., J.D.
Papers published, accepted for publication, or read

1. "Gonococcal Endocarditis," *Journal of Military Medicine* (1960).
2. "Care of the Aged," National Geriatrics Society, honorable mention (1962).
3. "Abortion Laws Need Therapy," *Temple Law Quarterly* (winter 1964).
4. "Genesis of a Drug," read at symposium sponsored by the Pittsburgh Institute of Legal Medicine, Philadelphia (November 1966).
5. "FDA Law," *Hospital Formulary Management* (December 1966).
6. "Medical-Legal Development of a New Drug," read at symposium sponsored by the Institute of Continuing Legal Education (ICLE), University of Michigan (April 1967). Published in *Drug Liability Seminar*. (ICLE, December 1967).
7. "LSD and the Law," *Hospital Formulary Management* (September 1967).
8. "Legal Hazards of Prescribing," *Patient Care* (December 1967).
9. "Medical Witnesses–A Review," read at the American College of Legal Medicine Annual Meeting, Atlantic City (June 1967). Published in *Cleveland Marshall Law Review* (May 1968).
10. "The Medical Witness and the Law," delivered at the Symposium on Cross-Examination of Medical Experts, Practicing Law Institute, New York City (September 1968).
11. "The Genesis of a Drug," delivered at the Symposium on Drug Liability Litigation, Practicing Law Institute, Las Vegas (November 1968).
12. "Blood Transfusions," *Dickinson Law Review* (winter 1969).
13. "Therapeutics," *Medico-Legal Annual*. (Appleton, Croft, Century, 1969).
14. "The Physician and the Lawyer," presented to combined meetings of the Seneca County, Ohio, Medical Society and Bar Association (September 1969).
15. "Drugs in the Seventies," delivered at symposium sponsored by the New York University Medical School, Department of Pharmacology (March 10-12, 1970).
16. "Psychiatric Terms," published in booklet, *Drugs,* Lutheran Church in America (1970).

17. "Marihuana," published as position paper in booklet form, Lutheran Church in America (1970).

18. "Medico-Legal Implications of Careless Adverse Reaction Reporting: Case Reports of Alleged Pentazocine Dependence," read at Second World Congress on Medical Law, Washington, D.C. (August 20, 1970). Published in *Hospital Formulary Management* (October 1970).

19. Review of *Pharmacological Treatment in Burns* by A. Bertelli and L. Donati, *Hospital Management* (1970).

20. "Impact of Drugs on Business and Society," delivered to the Industrial Relations Association, New York City (October 13, 1970).

21. "Product Liability," delivered at Dickinson School of Law, Carlisle, PA (October 16, 1970).

22. "Problems in Drug Research and Development," delivered at Wayne State Medical School (October 24, 1970). Published in *Intersections of Law and Medicine*, chap. 8. (ICLE, 1972).

23. "Adverse Reaction Reporting," delivered at University of Pittsburgh and Duquesne University (November 20, 1970). Published as chapter in *Exploring the Medical Malpractice Dilemma* (1972).

24. "A Rational Approach to Drug Therapy," *Patient Care* (October 31, 1970).

25. "Drug Abuse," address to students at Upsala College, NJ (February 10, 1971).

26. "Remarks on Pentazocine," *Proceedings* of NAS-NRC Annual Meeting on Drug Dependence (1971).

27. "Role of the Physician in Industry on Problems of Drug Abuse," delivered to combined meeting of industry, FDA, and Justice Department officials, New York City (February 24, 1971).

28. "Euthanasia," delivered to the Pastors Institute, Waltham, MA (April 26, 1971).

29. "Newer Concepts in Medical Malpractice," delivered at Dickinson School of Law (October 15, 1971).

30. "Errors in Therapy," *MXR* (December 1971).

31. "FDA-Pharmaceutical Relations," delivered at Columbia College of Pharmacy, New York City (December 21, 1971).

32. "Drug Abuse," delivered to St. Luke's School, New Canaan, CT (January 10, 1972).

33. "Free Clinic Responsibilities," delivered at Annual Meeting of Free Clinics Association, Washington, D.C. (January 6, 1972).

34. "Hexachlorophene," delivered to American Medical Association Commission on Cutaneous Health, New York City (April 21, 1972).

35. "Medical Malpractice," delivered to Medical Law Commission of New York City Bar Association (May 2, 1972).

36. "Informed Consent," delivered to the International College of Surgeons Annual Meeting, Lake Geneva, NY (July 8, 1972).

37. "Comments on Hexachlorophene," *Pediatrics Supplement* (March 1973).

38. "The Anesthesiologist's Legal Responsibility in Blood Transfusions," *Forensic Science* (September 1972): 133-145.

39. "Drug Abuse–National and International Control," delivered at Symposium on Medicines in Our Times, University of Pretoria Medical School, South Africa (October 16-20, 1973). *Proceedings* published in *Journal of Legal Medicine* (March-April 1973): 55-60.

40. "Is Unjustified Surgery the Cause of Increased Malpractice Actions?," (M. Rockmore column), *White Plains Reporter,* 7 August 1972.

41. "Malpractice Dilemma: Did These Doctors Settle Too Soon?" (my response to the question), *Medical Economics* (September 1972).

42. "Medical Malpractice," telesessions cassette, no. 1 (summer 1972).

43. "pHisoHex in Perspective," Albany Medical College Postgraduate Medicine Symposium on Drugs, the Mother, and Child (December 6, 1972).

44. Malpractice Cassette Series, *Medical Economics* (1972-73).

45. "Arbitration on Malpractice," delivered before American Arbitration Association luncheon, New York City (December 20, 1972).

46. "Defending Freedoms" (editorial), *Journal of Legal Medicine* (May-June 1973): 6.

47. "Ideas Whose Time Has Come" (medical education), presented to Federation of State Medical Boards (February 9, 1973). Also in *Federal Bulletin* (July 1973).

48. "Medical Malpractice in the U.S.," presented to New South Wales Medical Legal Society, Sydney, Australia (March 1, 1973). Published in *Proceedings*.

49. "Responsibilities of Physicians and Lawyers," delivered to combined Shelby County Medical and Bar Societies, Memphis. Also presented to Memphis State School of Law (April 15, 1973).

50. "Marihuana Today," *Journal of Legal Medicine* (May-June 1973): 44-46.

51. "Therapeutics," to be published as book chapter.

52. "Hexachlorophene in Perspective," delivered to the American College of Clinical Pharmacology, Atlantic City (April 28, 1973). Published in *Journal of Clinical Pharmacology* 13 (November-December 1973): 451.

53. "Therapeutic Freedom," delivered to Third World Congress on Medical Law, Ghent, Belgium (August 22, 1973). Published in *Journal of Legal Medicine* (September-October 1974): 40-42.

54. "On Hexachlorophene" (letter to the editor), *Medical Tribune* (April 1973).

55. "Implementation of the Recommendations of the Secretary's (HEW) Commission on Medical Malpractice at the State Level," delivered at the Cleveland Clinic Symposium on Implementation of the Recommendations of the Secretary's Commission on Malpractice (September 6, 1973). Published in *Journal of Legal Medicine* (November-December 1973): 32-35.

56. "Observations on the Medical Malpractice Commission Report," delivered to the American College of Surgeons, New Brunswick, NJ (September 22, 1973).

57. Review of *Testifying in Court* by J.E. Horsley, *Journal of Legal Medicine* (January-February 1974): 63.

58. "Whither Malpractice," *Hospital Formulary Management* (July 1973).

59. "Take the H out of HEW" (editorial), *Journal of Legal Medicine* (September-October 1973).

60. "Physicians' Liability in Drug Therapy Cases," delivered to the Armed Forces Institute of Pathology Symposium on Medical Malpractice (October 18, 1973). Published in *U.S. Medicine* (November 1973).

61. "Package Inserts and Informed Consent" (editorial), *Journal of Legal Medicine* (January-February 1974): 6.

62. "Liability and Malpractice Affecting Free Clinics." In *Free Medical Clinics: Innovations in Health Care Delivery*, J. Schwartz. (Health, Education, and Welfare, 1973).

63. *Medical Economics*, 50th Anniversary Issue on Look into Future– Comments on Malpractice (October 1973).

64. "Blood." In *International Anesthesiology Clinics*. Vol. II, no. 4 (1974).

65. Query and Comment, *Journal of Legal Medicine* (January-February 1974): 16.

66. "The International Convention on Psychotropic Substances" (editorial), *Journal of Legal Medicine* (May-June 1974): 6.

67. "Should Prison Research Be Barred?" (editorial), *Journal of Legal Medicine* (September-October 1974): 6.

68. Query and Comment, *Journal of Legal Medicine* (November-December 1974): 13.

69. Review of *The Abortion Controversy* by Sarvis and Rodman, *Journal of Legal Medicine* (November-December 1974): 62.

70. "On Immunization Warnings" (editorial), *Journal of Legal Medicine* (April 1975): 7.

71. "Malpractice Insurance: Claims-made Policies Pose a New Dilemma," *Journal of Legal Medicine* (June 1975): 33-34.

72. Review of *How to Help Your Doctor Help You* by J. Gaver, *Journal of Legal Medicine* (June 1975): 54-55.

73. "New York State Malpractice Legislation," *Journal of Legal Medicine* (July-August 1975): 26-27. Reprinted in *New York State Journal of Medicine* (February 1976): 302-303.

74. "Malpractice Prevention," *Journal of Legal Medicine* (September 1975): 22-23.

75. "Medical Liability Crisis," delivered at the American Association of Clinical Urologists meeting, Miami Beach (May 9, 1975).

76. "The Malpractice Crisis," delivered at New Castle Country Medical Society meeting, Wilmington, DE (April 15, 1975) and at the Monmouth County Medical Society meeting, Long Branch, NJ (April 23, 1975).

77. "Medical-Legal Implications of Prescribing," delivered at Cleveland Clinic Symposium (September 8, 1975). Published in *Hospital Formulary Management* Vol. II, no. 2 (February 1976): 89-90.

78. "Malpractice Today," delivered at Cleveland Clinic Symposium (September 9, 1975). Published in *Hospital Formulary Management* (February 1976).

79. "Medical Ethics in Research," delivered at American Medical Writers Symposium in Philadelphia (October 2, 1975). Published in *Connecticut Medicine* (March 26, 1976).

80. "State Laws May Ease Malpractice Ills," *Patient Care* (January 15, 1976): 18-34. Co-authored with Ball, Bernzweig, Egeberg, Hastings, Klein, Welch, and Wolske.

81. "New Recommendations to Update Malpractice Legislation," *Journal of Legal Medicine* (February 1976): 9-13.

82. "Patient Package Inserts," delivered at the National Conference on Medical Devices and Drugs, New York University Public Liability Institute, et al. (March 26, 1976). Published in *Proceedings*.

83. "Ethics of Clinical Research," delivered at the Legal Medicine Symposium, Armed Forces Institute of Pathology, Veterans Affairs, Department of Medicine and Surgery, and the American College of Legal Medicine, Washington, D.C. (December 9, 1975).

84. Review of *Parikh's Simplified Textbook of Medical Jurisprudence and Toxicology for Classrooms and Courtrooms* by C.K. Parikh, *Journal of Legal Medicine* (June 1976): 32-33.

85. Review of *Ethical Constraints and Imperatives in Medical Research* by M. Visscher, *Journal of Legal Medicine* (July-August 1976): 30-31.

86. "Surgical Malpractice Prophylaxis," delivered at Crozier-Chester Medical Center, Chester, PA (May 4, 1976).

87. "Immunizations: A Societal Dilemma," *New York Law Journal* (July 1977).

88. "The Courts and the Practice of Medicine" (editorial), *Journal of Legal Medicine* (October 1976): 2.

89. "Palaver over Patient Package Inserts," *Patient Care* (February 1, 1977): 22-49.

90. "Drug Licensing," *Food Drug Cosmetic Law Journal* 32, no. 2 (February 1977): 63-66. Reprinted in *Hospital Formulary Management* 12 (May 1977): 342.

91. "Question of Confidentiality" (letter to editor), *Journal of Legal Medicine* 5 (April 1977): 32.

92. "Cancerphobia" (editorial), *Journal of Legal Medicine* 5 (May 1977): 4.

93. *Rights and Responsibilities in Drug Research.* (Washington, D.C.: Medicine in the Public Interest, Inc., 1977), 84 pp.

94. "Generic Substitution Laws–Physician's Liability," *Journal of Legal Medicine* 5, no. 7 (July 1977): 14-16.

95. "Damages Denied in Tay-Sachs Case," *Journal of Legal Medicine* 5, no. 9 (September 1977): 55-56.

96. "Ideal Drug Coverage under NHI," delivered to HEW Invitational Conference on Drug Coverage under National Health Insurance, Washington, D.C. (October 5, 1977). Published in *Proceedings*.

97. "Malpractice Prophylaxis," delivered to Grand Rounds, Harrisburg

State Hospital (October 14, 1977) and Cornell Medical School Grand Rounds (October 19, 1978).

98. "Professional Liability Prophylaxis," delivered to American College of Surgeons Annual Meeting, Dallas (October 18, 1977). Published in *Bulletin of the American College of Surgeons* 63, no. 7 (July 1978): 6-9.

99. "Medical Legal Aspects of Adverse Reactions," Albany Medical School (October 27, 1977).

100. Invited participant to WHO Conference on Trends and Prospects in Health Care, "Drug Research and Development," Geneva, Switzerland (December 8-9, 1977). Published in *Proceedings*.

101. "DES Case Decided for Defendant," *Legal Aspects of Medical Practice* 6, no. 5 (May 1978): 43.

102. "National Health Insurance and the Patient," *Hospital Formulary* 1, no. 3 (March 1978): 213-216.

103. "When Can a Child Consent to Treatment?," *Legal Aspects of Medical Practice* 6, no. 9 (September 1978): 31-34.

104. "Complications of Medical Devices," delivered at Symposium on Unexpected Complications in Medical Care, Stockholm, Sweden. Published in *Skandia Int'l. Symposia*, Stockholm (1979): 127-136.

105. "Drug Regulatory Reform Act of 1978." Testimony before U.S. House of Representatives Sub-Committee on Health and Environment, (June 14, 1978). Published in *Congressional Record*.

106. "Generic Drugs–A Bane or a Boon to Physicians and Consumers?," *Drug Therapeutics* (1980): 209-218.

107. *Report of Joint Commission on Prescription Drug Use* (January 23, 1980). Twelve volumes.

108. "Postmarketing Drug Surveillance," delivered to PMA Medical Section, Washington, D.C. (November 19, 1979).

109. "New Drug Development," Cornell Medical School pharmacology lecture (December 13, 1979).

110. "Drug Therapy," Morehouse College of Medicine Dean's Hour, Atlanta (May 21, 1980).

111. "Drug Research," Fu Wai Hospital, Peking, China (February 21, 1980).

112. "The Genesis of a Drug," Dickinson School of Law (October 17, 1980).

113. "AAAS," Toronto, Canada (January 8, 1981).

114. "Enterprise Liability," American College of Legal Medicine meeting, Corona, CA (May 1981).

115. "Reye's Syndrome and Aspirin," *Hospital Formulary Management*, (July 1981): 773-774.

116. "The CUNY–Industry Forum Series: Forum on the Pharmaceutical Industry," Research Foundation of the City University of New York 2, no. 3 (May 1985).

117. "Some Thoughts on Medical Liability," *The Bulletin of the American College of Surgeons* 71, no. 3 (March 1986): 12-13.

118. "What National Multi-hospital Organizations Look for in Joint Ventures with Suppliers," delivered for Prudential-Bache, Dallas (April 3, 1987).

119. "Risk Management," delivered for PIMA, Santa Barbara (July 21, 1987).

120. "Growth of Group Purchasing," interview: Monroe Trout, *Topics in Hospital Pharmacy Management* (August 1987): 40-47.

121. "Profile of American Health Care Systems," *Medical Practice Management* 3, no. 1 (summer 1987): 37-42.

122. "Interview: AmHS' Trout: 'Never Forget the Patient'," *Hospitals* (September 5, 1987): 73-74.

123. "The Impact of Alternative Health Care Delivery Systems on Physicians and Hospitals," delivered at the Ninth Annual H. Horton Roundtree Distinguished Lecturer in Health Law, Ninth Annual Health Law Forum, East Carolina University School of Medicine, Greenville (September 23, 1987).

124. "Future Challenges for Physicians and Hospitals," delivered at:

   a. Evangelical Health Systems' Annual Governance Retreat, Chicago (September 24, 1987).

   b. Southwest Community Health Services' Fall Leadership Retreat, Ruidoso, NM (October 10, 1987).

   c. Baystate Health Systems' Fall Retreat, Bolton Landing, NY (October 24, 1987).

125. "The Future of Health Care," delivered at Goldman, Sachs & Co., Second Annual Health Care Conference, Napa Valley, CA (October 20, 1987).

126. "National vs. Regional Health Care Systems," delivered at the Foundation of the American College of Health Care Executives Eastern Conference, Boston (November 10, 1987).

127. "AIDS and Access: Taking the Long View," *Healthweek* (December 23, 1987): 26.

128. "The Future of Health Care," delivered at Health Care Executive Association of San Diego County meeting, San Diego (January 20, 1987).

129. "AmHS Claims to Be Biggest in Its Field," San Diego *Union-Tribune*, 5 February 1988.

130. "Insider Interview: Monroe E. Trout, M.D.," *HealthWeek* (February 28, 1988): 26-27.

131. "Future Challenges for Physicians and Hospitals," delivered at Rushmore Health System's Planning Retreat (March 2, 1988).

132. "Nationwide Health Care During Recessions...and How This Would Affect Suppliers," delivered for Prudential-Bache, Dallas (March 24, 1988).

133. "Strategic Direction and Future Trends with Multi-hospital Systems," delivered at Healthcare Manufacturer's Marketing Seminar, Philadelphia (May 4, 1988).

134. "Health Campaign Issues–The Republican Perspective," delivered at:

   a. AHA Fifth Annual Symposium Quality: Achieving the Competitive Edge, Washington, D.C. (May 23, 1988).

   b. Rancho Santa Fe Women's Republican Club, San Diego (September 16, 1988).

135. "Cost Containment and Quality Management," delivered at American College of Legal Medicine workshop, San Diego (July 22, 1988).

136. "AmHS Update," delivered at:

   a. Yankee Alliance's Annual Meeting, Boston (September 23, 1988).

   b. Presbyterian Health Care System's Annual Meeting, Austin (September 30, 1988).

137. "Integrity Is the Real Bottom Line," *Trustee* (December 1988): 11.

138. "Hospitals Ponder How to Counter Negative Image," *HealthWeek*, Forecast 1989 insert (December 27, 1988): 6.

139. "Development and Use of Pharmaceutical Products." In *Legal Medicine*. (C.C. Mosby & Co., 1988), 507-533.

140. "Bush Administration to Target Healthcare Issues," *Health Industry Today* (January 1989): 4-5.

141. "The First Annual Multi-hospital Invitational Symposium on

Information Systems," keynote address, Sheldon Dorenfest & Associates, Ltd., Chicago (March 7, 1989).

142. "AmHS: The Power and Limitations of Alliances," delivered at the University of Minnesota (September 27, 1989).

143. "The Future of Health Care," delivered to Bethesda Hospital System, Cincinnati (December 5, 1989) and to Forbes Hospital System, Pittsburgh (December 6, 1989).

144. "Prophesy on the Next Decade of the Pharmaceutical Industry," *Pharmaceutical Executive* (July 1989).

145. "Drug Therapy," in *Legal Medicine Primer*.

146. "Rationing Healthcare," Society of Medical Administrators, Key Largo (January 15-18, 1990).

147. "AmHS' Impact on Medical Care," Robert Wood Johnson Fellows, Washington, D.C. (January 30, 1990).

148. "Participation in the Venture Market as an End User," Biomedical Business International, Newport Beach, CA (March 13, 1990).

149. "The Rationing of Healthcare," American College of Legal Medicine, Orlando (March 15, 1990).

150. "Leadership Succession," AHA Multi-hospital System Symposium, Scottsdale, AZ (March 28, 1990).

151. "The Rationing of Healthcare," delivered to Harrisburg Polyclinic Hospital (April 5, 1990) and to Harrisburg State Hospital, Harrisburg, PA (April 6, 1990).

152. "Leadership Succession," AHA Annual Convention, Education Session for Senior Management (July 31, 1990).

153. "Improved Quality Measures and Better Data Are Essential Prerequisites to Purchaser Decisions about Providers Based on Differences in Quality," Joint Commission on Accreditation of Healthcare Organizations, Washington D.C. (September 17, 1990).

154. "The Alliance Challenge: Balancing Costs, Quality, and Delivery," SMS Annual Health Executives Forum, Scottsdale (October 9, 1990).

155. "Healthcare Rationing," *ACLM Newsletter* (February 1991): 13-14.

156. "Managing Alliances," *Frontiers of Health Service Management* (spring 1991): 32-34.

157. "Comment on Global Marketing," *Pharmaceutical Executive* (February 1991): 50.

158. "Exec-Turned-Patient Gets Overdose of Managed Care," *Modern Healthcare* (March 11, 1991): 23.

159. "Future of Healthcare," medical staff, Harrisburg State Hospital, Harrisburg (April 26, 1991).

160. "Alliances," University of Minnesota, Minneapolis (November 7, 1991).

161. "Patients First," co-author, AmHS Institute, Washington, D.C. (December 1992).

162. "Patients First," a plan for healthcare reform in the U.S., Annual Meeting of the California Society of Plastic Surgeons, Newport Beach (March 9, 1992).

163. "Patients First," a plan for healthcare reform in the U.S., Kiwanis Club of San Diego, San Diego (March 10, 1992).

164. "Patients First," a plan for healthcare reform in the U.S., University of California, San Diego, Medical Center Board of Advisors, San Diego (March 13, 1992).

165. "Patients First," a plan for healthcare reform in the U.S., American College of Legal Medicine, San Diego (March 28, 1992).

166. "Healthcare Reform: Keep the Baby, but Try Fresh Bath Water," *San Diego Business Journal*, San Diego (April 20, 1992).

167. "Healthcare Reform," annual medical staff meeting and dinner, San Diego (June 3, 1992).

168. Lecture on legal medicine, University of California, San Diego medical students, San Diego (July 6, 1992).

169. "Long-Term Structural Changes Key to Reform," *San Diego Business Journal*, San Diego (July 13, 1992).

170. "A Vision of a Healthier America," presented to San Diego County Commission on Healthcare Reform (July 15, 1992).

171. "Patients First," a plan for healthcare reform in the U.S., California Ambulatory Surgery Association, Newport Beach (September 17, 1992).

172. "Patients First," a plan for healthcare reform in the U.S., Downtown Rotary Club, San Diego (September 24, 1992).

173. "Information Systems in the Health Care Industry," Satellite TV Network, National Library of Medicine (October 22, 1992).

174. "Patients First," a plan for healthcare reform in the U.S., Medical Executives, New York City (November 11, 1992).

175. Discussion on Healthcare Reform, KNSD Television, Channel 39, San Diego (February 21, 1993).

176. "Let's Put the Patients First," *Journal of Phi Rho Sigma* 88, no. 2: 1.

177. "Healthcare Must Go under the Knife in Order to Achieve Recovery," *San Diego Business Journal* (May 17, 1993): 23.

178. Explanation of the need for healthcare reform and responses to questions from listeners, WTHI Radio, Terre Haute, IN (October 18, 1993).

179. "Role of Strategic Alliances in Healthcare Reform," Conference on Strategic Alliances, University of North Carolina at Chapel Hill (November 11, 1993).

180. "The Big Picture: Executive Overview," *Business Travel News* (November 29, 1993): 6.

181. Panel member defining the status of healthcare reform followed by questions from the audience, Alumni Advocacy Program, University of California, San Diego (January 4, 1994).

182. Addressed CONNECT luncheon on healthcare reform, University of California, San Diego (March 9, 1994).

183. "Drugs and Devices in the News: Perspective of the Healthcare Institution," Thirty-fourth Annual Conference on Legal Medicine, Anaheim, CA (March 10, 1994).

184. Addressed Foster Higgins Insurance Company's Board of Directors on healthcare reform, Los Angeles (March 24, 1994). Article on address appeared in Los Angeles County Medical Association's *LACMA Physician* (May 2, 1994).

185. Addressed Federation of American Health Systems on healthcare reform, Orlando (April 13, 1994).

186. "Impact of the Pharmaceutical Industry on the Quality of Life," Bloomfield College, Bloomfield, NJ, on the occasion its 125th anniversary (April 21, 1994); University of California, San Diego alumni, San Diego (May 6, 1994); and BioInternational '94, Houston (May 10, 1994).

187. "Strangers on the Highway of Life," commencement address, Bloomfield College, Bloomfield, NJ (May 1994).

188. "The Future of Healthcare," SAIC Board of Directors (June 7, 1994).

189. "Reducing the Costs of Healthcare," Institute of the Americas (July 19, 1994).

Letter about my participation in the U.S.-Russian Conference on Healthcare.

Research Health Services System

2302-2310 E. Meyer Blvd., A-10
Kansas City, Missouri 64132

816-276-9167

E. Wynn Presson
President

OCT 5 1990

September 28, 1990

Dear Monroe,

Congratulations on being chosen as one of the ten Americans to attend the US/USSR Leadership Conference in Lenningrad and Moscow! What a tremendous teaching and learning experience tnis will be for everyone involved.

I'll be anxiously awaiting to hear about some of the stories when you return.

Sincerely,

E. Wynn Presson

EWP:sak

Monroe E. Trout, M.D.
Chairman of the Board
President & Chief Executive Officer
American Healthcare Systems
12730 High Bluff Drive, Suite 300
San Diego, California 92130-2099

Research Health Services System

University of Pennsylvania Alumni Award of Merit.

THE

UNIVERSITY OF PENNSYLVANIA
STUDENT AWARD OF MERIT

HAS BEEN GRANTED TO

Monroe E. Trout

Class of 1953, College.

Chairman of the Undergraduate Council as well as of the Interfraternity Council, a member of Friars Senior Society and Phi Kappa Beta Junior Society, and one of the Dean's Advisory Council in the College, you have shown effective and commendable leadership that should serve you and your University in good stead throughout your association with Pennsylvania affairs.

THE GENERAL ALUMNI SOCIETY

SECRETARY

PRESIDENT

January 17, 1953

Letter about my honorary degree from Dickinson School of Law.

Peter G. Glenn
Dean and Professor of Law

THE DICKINSON SCHOOL OF LAW

February 26, 1996

(717) 240-5208
Fax: (717) 243-4366
Internet: pglenn@dsl.edu

Dr. Monroe E. Trout
American Healthcare Systems
12730 High Bluff Drive
Suite 300
San Diego, CA 92130-0568

Dear Monroe:

It is with great pleasure that I write to confirm the invitation of our Board of Trustees and Faculty for you to receive an Honorary Doctor of Laws Degree from The Dickinson School of Law at our Commencement Ceremony at 10:00 A.M. on June 1, 1996. We will be delighted to honor you for your many professional and personal achievements.

We look forward to having you join us to receive the diploma and hood emblematic of the Honorary Doctor of Laws Degree. The Commencement Weekend festivities will begin on Friday, May 31, with our annual Senior Class Dinner attended by graduating students, their friends and families, and our trustees, honorary degree recipients, faculty, staff and honored guests. We would be pleased to have you and as many of your family and friends as you would like join us for the Friday evening activities and, of course, for the Commencement Ceremony on Saturday, at which we can, if you wish, provide special reserved seating for your family and friends.

We will be happy to make housing reservations for you for the weekend. Please confirm, at your convenience, that you will be able to attend to accept the award and, when it later becomes convenient, please let us know how many of your family members and friends will join us for all or part of the weekend.

We are pleased and proud to have you as part of our Dickinson Law School family.

With best regards,

Sincerely,

Peter G. Glenn

150 SOUTH COLLEGE STREET, CARLISLE, PENNSYLVANIA 17013-2899 (717) 240-5000

Letter about my honorary degree from Cumberland College.

CUMBERLAND COLLEGE

6191 College Station Drive
Williamsburg, Kentucky 40769-1372
Phone (606) 539-4201
Fax (606) 549-2820
E-Mail presoff@cumberlandcollege.edu
Office of the President

January 10, 2003

Dr. Monroe Trout
2110 Cove View Way
Knoxville, Tennessee 37919

Dear Dr. Trout,

The date has been set! We will award your honorary doctorate degree on Saturday, May 10, 2003, during our annual Commencement which begins at 10:00 a.m.

As soon as possible, please send me a list of the names and addresses of the persons you would like for us to invite to the ceremony.

Commencement generally lasts around one and one-half to two hours, depending on the number of graduates. If you would like to respond after being presented your degree, certainly you may do so. That is left entirely up to you.

We are excited about this opportunity to honor you. You should plan to arrive in my office on the morning of the 10th no later than 9:30 a.m. This will give us time to robe and to practice the hooding.

Between now and May, please let me know if you have any questions or concerns.

Sincerely,

Jim Taylor
President

JT/rc

cc: Emily Meadors
     Don Good
     Shannon Warmoth

Letter about my honorary degree from Bloomfield College and commencement address.

Need gown & cap

BLOOMFIELD COLLEGE

Office of the President

April 21, 1994

Monroe E. Trout
Chairman of the Board
President and CEO
AmHS
12730 High Bluff Drive
Suite 300
San Diego, California 92130-2099

Dear Monroe,

I want to reiterate my invitation to you to speak at our Commencement Thursday morning, May 26, and I want to add another element to it: to accept an honorary Doctor of Laws as well. I've just finished speaking to the Trustees who were present this morning and to the other members of the Executive Committee, and they agree wholeheartedly with Richard Guarino and me: you are a superbly qualified candidate with a keen appreciation of our mission.

I know how short this notice is: I would have extended the invitation five years ago if we had met then.

You were a thought-provoking and inspiring presence today. I thank you warmly for that.

Sincerely yours,

John F. Noonan
President

Letter about my election as an honorary alumnus of UCSD.

UNIVERSITY OF CALIFORNIA, SAN DIEGO   UCSD

BERKELEY • DAVIS • IRVINE • LOS ANGELES • RIVERSIDE • SAN DIEGO • SAN FRANCISCO   SANTA BARBARA • SANTA CRUZ

OFFICE OF THE CHANCELLOR

9500 GILMAN DRIVE
LA JOLLA, CALIFORNIA 92093-0005
TEL: (619) 534-3135
FAX: (619) 534-6523

April 28, 1998

Monroe Trout, M.D.
P.O. Box 8052
Rancho Santa Fe, CA 92067

Dear Monroe:

I am delighted to learn that you have been selected by the Alumni Association as this year's Honorary Alumnus. This selection recognizes the significant service and contributions you have rendered this University as an exemplary volunteer.

It will be a pleasure for me to participate in the celebration acknowledging your distinction on June 13. In appreciation for your significant commitment to this institution as Chair of the UC San Diego Board of Trustees, and for your service on advisory boards of both the Medical Center and Thornton Hospital, the University community and I consider it an honor to pay tribute to you.

I applaud your many contributions to this University, and heartily endorse your selection as this year's Honorary Alumnus. Congratulations!

Sincerely,

Robert C. Dynes
Chancellor

Appendix M-7

Letter about my Civis Universitatus Award from UCSD.

 The UC San Diego Foundation

University of California, San Diego
9500 Gilman Drive • La Jolla, California 92093-0940
(619) 534-6385 • Fax: (619) 534-8160

June 9, 1997

Dr. Monroe E. Trout
P. O. Box 8052
Rancho Santa Fe, California 92067

Dear Monroe:

It is my pleasure to confirm that you have been nominated to receive the UC San Diego Foundation's 1997 *Civis Universitatis* Award in the category of outstanding UC San Diego Foundation Trustee. As you are well aware, the presentation of this award signifies that we are inducting you into our community of scholars in recognition of the crucial role you have played in expanding the University's programs and missions.

You are most deserving of this honor, Monroe, and I look forward to being able to present you with the award on June 27 at the Foundation's 25th anniversary dinner.

On a personal note, may I express my deep appreciation to you and Sandra for your commitment, service and generosity to UCSD.

Sincerely,

Bob

J. R. Beyster
Chair

c: Chancellor Robert C. Dynes
    Winifred A. Cox
    Richard S. Podgorski

Letter about my award as San Diego Entrepeneur of the Year in 1994.

Johnson & Higgins of California
2029 Century Park East
Los Angeles, CA 90067
Phone   310 552 8950

John A. McMahon
Managing Principal and Executive Vice President

June 27, 1994

RECEIVED

JUN 28 1994

Monroe E. Trout, M.D.
Chairman of the Board
President and Chief Executive Officer
American Healthcare Systems
12730 High Bluff Drive, Suite 300
San Diego, California 92130-2099

Dear Dr. Trout,

Congratulations on earning the Entrepreneur of the Year
Lifetime Achievement Award. Very impressive and
absolutely deserving.

We are very proud of our relationship with you personally
and AmHS. You and your staff have accomplished what
many have attempted, but virtually none have achieved.

Sincerely,

John A. McMahon

/r

Letter about my receiving an award for healthcare innovation.

CRITICARE SYSTEMS, INC.

RECEIVED

OCT 21 1992

October 8, 1992

Monroe E. Trout, M.D.
Chairman of the Board, President
   and Chief Executive Officer
American Healthcare Systems
12730 High Bluff Drive (Suite 300)
San Diego, CA 92130-2019

Dear Monroe:

I would like to take this opportunity to congratulate you and
American Healthcare Systems for being honored by the American
College of Physician Executives for health care innovation. I
can't think of anyone more deserving than you for this award.
Everybody at Criticare is very proud of your accomplishments.

Looking forward to seeing you at the ASA, I remain,

                              Sincerely,

                              Gerhard J. Von der Ruhr
                              President

GvdR/jn

MAILING ADDRESS: P.O. BOX 26556 ● MILWAUKEE, WI 53226
SHIPPING ADDRESS: 20900 SWENSON DRIVE ● SUITE 398 ● WAUKESHA, WI 53186
TELEPHONE: (414) 797-8282 ● **TELEX:** 5106012199 ● **TELEFAX:** (414) 797-8491

Resolution of the California Assembly on our receiving The Salvation Army Tradition of Caring Award.

CALIFORNIA LEGISLATURE

Assembly

RESOLUTION

By the Honorable Susan A. Davis
Seventy-sixth Assembly District; Relative to commending

Dr. and Mrs. Monroe Trout

Whereas, Dr. and Mrs. Monroe Trout have been selected as the 1996 recipients of the "Tradition of Caring" Award from The Salvation Army, Headquarters, Sierra Del Mar Division, in San Diego, in recognition of the vital role that they have played in improving the quality of life for humankind; and

Whereas, Monroe and Sandra Trout participate with and support many local charitable and civic associations and organizations in the area, and they have distinguished themselves by founding the Morehouse School of Medicine and endowing scholarships at Morehouse, Dickinson Law School, and Bloomfield College; and

Whereas, Dr. Trout, who is Chairman Emeritus of American Healthcare Systems, worked his way through medical school and later earned a law degree from Dickinson College, and served nearly 25 years as a senior executive specializing in medical and scientific affairs for two of the nation's largest pharmaceutical companies; and

Whereas, He has served on more than 45 boards of major corporations, foundations, and universities during his career, and his greatest supporters have been his wife, Sandra, and his two sons, Timothy William and Monroe, Jr.; and

Whereas, Because education unlocked the door to his future, Dr. Trout has dedicated himself to opening windows of opportunity for others, and he has endowed a chair in pharmacology at the University of California, San Diego; and

Whereas, As respected civic leaders, Monroe and Sandra Trout have provided dynamic role models for all people who believe strongly in their obligation to improve the quality of life for future generations; now, therefore, be it

Resolved by Assembly Member Susan A. Davis, That Dr. and Mrs. Monroe Trout be congratulated on their selection as the 1996 recipients of the "Tradition of Caring" Award from the Salvation Army, Headquarters, Sierra Del Mar Division, in San Diego, commended for the significant contributions that they have made to the people of the local community, the state, and the nation, and extended sincere best wishes for continued success in the future.

Members Resolution No. 761

Dated this 24th day of April, 1996

Susan A. Davis
Honorable Susan A. Davis
76th Assembly District

San Diego County Board of Supervisors citation for my service as co-chairman of the San Diego County Healthcare Reform Commission.

County of San Diego
California
PROCLAMATION

PROCLAMATION
presented by
Supervisor Leon L. Williams
relative to commending
MONROE TROUT, M.D., J.D.
Member of the San Diego County
Commission on Health Care Reform

WHEREAS, the health of County residents is impacted by a multiplicity of problems such as access, costs, and unfunded State and Federal mandates; and

WHEREAS, the lack of proper health care hinders the economic development and progress of this entire County; and

WHEREAS, the solutions for health care reform lie in our ability to implement effective partnerships with both the private and public sectors of our diverse community; and

WHEREAS, the Board of Supervisor established the Commission on Health Care Reform as a vehicle to discuss the role of government in meeting its responsibilities for protecting the public's health and bringing coordination to a fragmented health care system; and

WHEREAS, the Commission on Health Care Reform represents a private-public partnership which is both business friendly and family centered; and

WHEREAS, the members of the Commission on Health Care Reform were successful in building consensus on complex health issues and developing a Managed Care Medi-Cal delivery model entitled "Healthy San Diego"; and

WHEREAS, it is essential that all citizens of San Diego County be aware of the impact their behavior can have on reducing the cost associated with health care; NOW THEREFORE

BE IT PROCLAIMED By Supervisor Pam Slater and the Board of Supervisors of the County of San Diego on this Third Day of January, 1995, that they commend MONROE TROUT, M.D., J.D. for his outstanding contributions to the Commission on Health Care Reform and improving the quality of health care provided to the residents of San Diego County.

Supervisor 1st District

Supervisor 2nd District

Pamela Slater
Supervisor 3rd District

Leon Williams
Supervisor 4th District

John MacDonald
Supervisor 5th District

Tennessee Colonel appointment as appreciation for chairing a debate on medical malpractice by the presidents of the American Medical Asscociation and the American Bar Association.

THE STATE OF TENNESSEE

By His Excellency

Winfield Dunn
Governor

To the Honorable   MONROE TROUT, M. D., J. D.

W HEREAS, reposing special trust and confidence in your patriotism, valor and fidelity, I do by these presents constitute and appoint you

COLONEL

Aide de Camp, Governor's Staff

to rank as such from the date of this commission and to hold such office under the conditions prescribed by law.

Given under my hand and the Seal of the State of Tennessee at the Capitol in Nashville, this 14TH day of MARCH *in the year of our Lord, one thousand nine hundred and* SEVENTY-THREE *.*

Governor

Adjutant General   Secretary of State

Appendix M-13

Letter about my Gold Medal Award from ACLM.

AMERICAN COLLEGE OF LEGAL MEDICINE

Executive Office • 611 East Wells Street • Milwaukee, WI 53202
(414) 276-1881 • (800) 433-9137 • **fax** (414) 276-3349
website http://www.aclm.org
e-mail info@aclm.org

**1998-99 ACLM
Executive Committee**

President
John A. Anderson
MD JD FCLM
Atlanta, GA

President-Elect
Edward David
MD JD FCLM
Bangor, ME

Treasurer
Jack W. Snyder
MD JD MPH PhD FCLM
Philadelphia, PA

Secretary
Fillmore Buckner
MD JD FCLM
Seattle, WA

Past-President
Martin B. Flamm
MD JD FCLM
New Orleans, LA

Board

Genifer Y. Chavez
MD JD MPH MA FCLM
Tucson, AZ

Philip S. Cifarelli
MD JD FCLM
Santa Ana, CA

Alan L. Dorian
MD DSc FCLM
Marathon, FL

Louis M. Dyll
JD MD FCLM
Dallas, TX

Robert H. Gans
MD LLB FCLM
Beverly Hills, CA

Jay A. Gold
MD JD MPH FCLM
Madison, WI

Theodore R. LeBiang
JD FCLM *(ex officio)*
Springfield, IL

Michael M. Raskin
MD JD MS MPH FCLM
Tamarac, FL

Bruce H. Seidberg
DDS MScD JD FCLM
Jamesville, NY

Philip A. Shelton
MD JD FCLM
West Hartford, CT

Daniel R. Shirey
JD MD MBA FCLM
Evansville, IN

Dan J. Tennenhouse
MD JD FCLM
Mill Valley, CA

Clark Watts
MD JD FCLM
Austin, TX

Richard Wilbur
MD JD FCLM
Lake Forest, IL

Miles J. Zaremski
JD FCLM

November 17, 1998

Monroe E. Trout, MD JD FCLM
P.O. Box 8052
6135 Via Posada del Norte
Rancho Santa Fe, CA 92067

Dear Monroe:

It is my distinct pleasure to inform you of your selection by the Board of Governors to be the recipient of the Gold Medal of the American College of Legal Medicine. This medal is the highest award the College can bestow on one of its members and is being presented to you in recognition of the outstanding and distinguished service you have provided ACLM over the years.

The Gold Medal will be presented at the Annual Banquet to be held in conjunction with the 1999 Annual Conference of the American College of Legal Medicine at the Westin Canal Place in New Orleans, Louisiana, March 11 – 13, 1999. I look forward to the Gold Medal Ceremony where I can join the rest of your peers in acknowledging your many contributions not only to the College, but also to the entire field of Legal Medicine.

Again, please accept my personal congratulations on achieving this well-deserved recognition.

Sincerely,

John A. Anderson, MD JD FCLM
President

Press release about my election as a member of the Society of Medical Administrators.

AmHS®
American Healthcare Systems

The National Network of Premier Health Systems

Anna-Marie Webber

News Release

Contact: Jack A. Bernard

Phone: (619) 456-2811

May 10, 1989

AMERICAN HEALTHCARE SYSTEMS'® TROUT HONORED WITH APPOINTMENT TO SOCIETY OF MEDICAL ADMINISTRATORS

SAN DIEGO -- Monroe E. Trout, M.D., chairman of the board and chief executive officer of American Healthcare Systems (AmHS®), has been elected to the Society of Medical Administrators, one of the oldest and most prestigious healthcare professional associations in the United States. The organization, founded in 1909, is restricted to include only a total of 50 members, each of whom has distinguished himself or herself in the healthcare field.

Over the last eighty years, the Society's members have been leaders in key healthcare and professional organizations throughout the country. Members have served as assistant secretaries of the Department of Health & Human Services and also as presidents of the American Hospital Association, the Association of American Medical Colleges, the Council of Teaching Hospitals and other groups which have had great impact upon the progress of healthcare in the 20th century.

"The American healthcare system is the envy of the world, but we can still improve upon it. The Society of Medical Administrators is a leader in the struggle for the betterment of healthcare for all Americans," said Trout. "I am awed by the history of the organization and by the notable achievements of the Society's past and present members."

Trout became AmHS president and CEO in October 1986. AmHS is one of the largest healthcare networks in the nation, representing more than 1,000 not-for-profit healthcare facilities in 43 states and Washington D.C., with combined revenues of more than $13 billion.

In addition, Trout serves as chairman of the board for AmHS Institute, a Washington, D.C.-based representational and education organization and AmHS Capital Corporation (AmHSCC®), a captive finance company.

Prior to joining AmHS, Trout was senior vice president, medical and scientific affairs, for Sterling Drug, Inc. He was responsible for worldwide research and drug regulatory affairs, among other activities. He also has held positions with Winthrop Laboratories, Chas. Pfizer & Co., Harrisburg (Pennsylvania) State Hospital and Dickinson School of Law.

Trout received his bachelor's degree in 1953 and his medical degree in 1957, both from the University of Pennsylvania. He earned law degrees (L.L.B., 1964; J.D., 1969) from Dickinson School of Law in Pennsylvania.

###

Letter about my Delta Tau Delta Fraternity Alumni Achievement Award.

Delta Tau Delta Fraternity

President
Jeff Heatherington

January 30, 1996

Monroe E. Trout, MD
Box 8052
6135 Via Posada Del Norte
Rancho Santa Fe, CA 92067

Dear Monroe:

Over the years many Delts have achieved great distinction for outstanding accomplishments in their chosen fields of endeavor. Their accomplishments have reflected honor on Delta Tau Delta. In 1966 the Fraternity established the Alumni Achievement Award to recognize these brother Delts. These awards have been presented to a total of only 156 Delts out of some 78,000 living Delts.

We are pleased to advise you that you have been nominated and unanimously approved by the Arch Chapter to receive this distinguished award as one who is a leader in your profession. The awards will be presented at the Karnea banquet on Saturday evening, August 17, 1996, at the Grand Hyatt Hotel in Washington, DC.

We hope your schedule will permit your attendance at the Karnea, particularly at the Saturday evening banquet to accept from your Fraternity this award and the acclaim which you have earned. No response at the banquet is allowed. We believe your achievements speak for themselves. If you are unable to attend, the award will not be presented until you can be present to accept.

To allow ample time for arrangements, including preparation of the award and appropriate news releases, we would appreciate a reply **no later than April 1, 1996** as to your availability to be present for this occasion.

Fraternally,

Jeff Heatherington
International President

JH:pe

2121 S.W. Broadway, Suite 300, Portland, Oregon 97201 • (503) 222-2779 - Office • (503) 283-0986 - Home • (503) 222-2392 - Fax

UCSD Honorary Alumnus Award.

Dickinson School of Law Honorary Degree.

The Dickinson School of Law

Monroe E. Trout

MONROE E. TROUT, you are honored today for your distinguished career in health care and for your dedication to helping others.

As one of 14 children born to a Harrisburg family, you rose from humble beginnings, becoming the first in your family to graduate from college. With the help of academic scholarships and part-time jobs, you worked your way through the University of Pennsylvania, graduating in 1953. You earned your M.D. degree from Penn's medical school after securing a Navy tuition grant.

Following your internship and residency in the U.S. Navy, you pursued an intense interest in politics and public affairs by enrolling in The Dickinson School of Law while simultaneously serving as chief of the EKG and Medical Department of Harrisburg State Hospital and as a member of the Harrisburg Polyclinic Hospital staff. You graduated from law school in 1964.

After holding a number of high level positions with pharmaceutical companies, you became president of American Healthcare Systems in 1986 and its chairman a year later.

Considered a pre-eminent authority on a range of health care issues, you have lectured at universities throughout the United States and in Asia, Australia, Europe, and Africa. You have written more than 150 scholarly papers and book chapters.

Active in many community service and charitable organizations, you are a Fellow and former president of the American College of Legal Medicine. You were instrumental in helping to found the Morehouse College of Medicine, the nation's only African-American medical school established in this century.

Though retired from AHS, you remain active as a member of boards and committees, and even government agencies and departments solicit your counsel. Your service has earned you numerous accolades and awards, including the B'nai B'rith International's Healthcare Award, the Salvation Army Caring Award, the Horatio Alger Award, and the Law School's General Alumni Association's Outstanding Alumni Award.

As a trustee emeritus of The Dickinson School of Law and a former special lecturer in Legal Medicine, you have served your law school well.

We are honored to bestow upon you the degree of Doctor of Laws, Honoris Causa.

President Robert M. Frey

Dean Peter G. Glenn

Letter from Jack Horsley about my Horatio Alger Award. Also received a similar letter from Leroy Zimmerman, former attorney general of Pennsylvania.

answered 7/11/95

JOHN H. ARMSTRONG
JOHN P. EWART
RICHARD F. RECORD, JR.
STEPHEN L. CORN
RICHARD C. HAYDEN
ROBERT G. GRIERSON
GREGORY C. RAY
PAUL R. LYNCH
KENNETH F. WERTS
JOHN L. BARGER

MARK R. KARPUS
BEVERLY J. RING
JOSHUA N. ROSEN
KATHLEEN M. STOCKWELL
RICHARD A. TJEPKEMA
REONA J. JACK
SAM A. LIMENTATO

CRAIG & CRAIG
ATTORNEYS AT LAW
1807 BROADWAY AVE.
P.O. BOX 689
MATTOON, ILLINOIS 61938-0689
TELEPHONE (217) 234-6481
FACSIMILE (217) 234-6486

227½ SOUTH 9TH ST.
P.O. BOX 1545
MT. VERNON, ILLINOIS 62864-1545
TELEPHONE (618) 244-7511
FACSIMILE (618) 244-7628

JACK E. HORSLEY
OF COUNSEL

CRAIG VAN METER
(1895-1981)

FRED H. KELLY
(1894-1971)

ROBERT M. WERDEN
(1908-1969)

GEORGE N. GILKERSON
(1911-1985)

PLEASE REPLY TO:

P.O. BOX 689
MATTOON
61938-0689

July 4, 1995

Monroe E. Trout, J.D., M.D.
Post Office Box 8052
6135 Via Posada del Norte
Rancho Santa Fe, California 92067

My Dear Friend:

Mary Jane and I were overwhelmed with the distinction incident to your being awarded the honors at the Horatio Alger Awards. I have just returned from vacation. Our vacation time started on Friday morning, June 16th, but we "puttered" with our final arrangements and departure because we wanted to be sure to be home to see the Awards presentation and hear your acceptance. As I told you, we were fortunate because it was aired on CBS from 7:00 to 8:00 p.m. and on ABC from 8:00 to 9:00 p.m, Central Time. So we were able to see the complete ceremony twice. And seeing you was certainly the high point.

Although we have been friends for a quarter of a century and in former years we saw each other often and pleasurably, I had no idea of the credit involved in your rise from a disadvantaged childhood into one of our most distinguished citizens. It made me truly proud.

In addition to the kudos I expressed when I telephoned you after we had seen the show, I want now to record my admiration and extend again in writing my hearty congratulations. Best wishes always my Friend!

Sincerely,

Jack

Jack E. Horsley

JEH/sc

Press report on my activities.

NEW CANAAN ADVER

NEW CANAAN, CONNECTICUT, THURSDAY, FEBRUARY 4, 19

New Canaan neighbors

Councilman, doctor, lawyer, corporate chief

By SUSAN KENNEDY

What does it take to become a household word? Most never do. Some never try. Some don't try and do anyway. It just sort of happens.

In New Canaan, Monroe Trout is a household word. He didn't try. He didn't have to.

Being a medical doctor and a corporate lawyer and six feet five inches tall, Monroe is a rather spectacular man. In recent years through his work on the New Canaan Town Council, he also has become a rather controversial man.

MY ONLY CONTACT with Monroe Trout until recently had been seeing him at basketball games and reading about him in the newspapers and not knowing what to expect, except a crick in my neck. I walked up to a one-on-one conversation at a holiday party with slight awe. "Awe . . . no . . . what am I going to say to HIM?"

One of my dumber questions. Monroe Trout is easy to talk to. Great at listening and funny.

Monroe Trout is from Harrisburg, Pa. He's the son of Florence Kashner Trout of Satellite Beach, Fla. and the late David Trout. David Trout was, before the Depression of the thirties, a cabinetmaker.

Then, because people weren't buying the artistry, David became a full-time carpenter to support his 14 children. As the fifth of 11 sons, Monroe falls somewhere in the middle.

At William Penn High in Harris-

Monroe Trout . . . hooked on activity   —Bukovcik Photo

idea of mild involvement is a most interesting one. See for yourself.

After med school, the Navy and the Marines and the leper colony —

have the tallest one," Monroe recalls.

Well, the tallest one was Miss Sandra Lemke, a Wisconsin co-ed

They both are a little shy and quiet and have a most refreshingly reserved opinion of teir importance.

Until 1968, Monroe Trout, sr., was the head of Pfizer's government operations and assitant to the v.p. of pharmaceutical operations. This took him to Washington three days a week and though the "climate" suited him, he wanted to return to the medical side.

In 1968 he left Pfizer for Sterling Drugs (Bayer, Lysol, Mydol, Phillips, Stridex, just to name a few) where today he's sr v.p. and director of medical and scientific affairs and responsible for Sterling's three major research branches. The "real excitement," he says, is in pharmaceutical drugs and research fronts about to be broken.

Why not a private practice? Dr. Trout feels "What I'm doing now can help more people."

But he couldn't stay out of Washington. In 1970 President Nixon appointed Monroe to the Commission on Drugs. He also serves on the Committee on Pharmaceutical Drug Use under Ted Kennedy. "I'm his token Republican," Monroe laughed.

Back to education. Monroe is a trustee of Albany Medical Center, Cleveland Clinic and Dickinson College. In 1975 he helped found the Morehouse School of Medicine (an all-black medical school). Today he's vice chairman of the board. He's taught all over the world and worked with governments all over the world.

ONE OF HIS DELIGHTS is taking the family with him on these trips

Press report on my activities.

Monroe Trout . . . hooked on activity — Bukovcik Photo

ing the artistry, David became a full-time carpenter to support his 14 children. As the fifth of 11 sons, Monroe falls somewhere in the middle.

At William Penn High in Harrisburg, Monroe became the student and lifelong friend of Latin teacher Elva Lippe.

"She was an incredible woman," Monroe remembered. "Teaching was her life and she taught me that education is the most important thing in the world. I've tried to instill those teachings in our children. I hope I have."

Elva Lippe, Dr. Trout's educational inspiration, still holds the high honors record at Dickinson College in Carlisle, Pa.

AFTER GRADUATING from the University of Pennsylvania with a dual major of chemistry/English, Monroe received his degree from the University of Pennsylvania Medical School in 1957. He enlisted in the Navy and interned at Great Lakes Naval Hospital; and then did his residency in internal medicine at Portsmouth Naval Hospital.

Then Lt. Commander Trout spent his remaining enlistment with the Marines in the Philippines, in Korea and in a leper colony in Okinawa.

Though medicine and law were his courses of formal study, Monroe always had a deep-seated interest in politics and the Republican party . . . stemming back to 1944 when his "godfather," Howard Milliken, ran for his first term as mayor of Harrisburg. Monroe, then 13 years old, worked on his campaign.

He worked for Congressman Kunkle and then in the sixties he and Ray Schaffer wrote speeches for William Scranton during his campaign for governor. At one point in Monroe's life he admitted he considered running for Congress himself.

"I like the idea of having an impact in areas I know best," he said, "but also know I can have that impact without getting deeply involved to the exclusion of all else."

Monroe Trout's career bears witness to that philosophy though his idea of mild involvement is a most interesting one. See for yourself.

After med school, the Navy and the Marines and the leper colony — leprosy, he told me, is a disease of the nerves and takes years to contract, Dr. Trout went back to Harrisburg.

He's also a walking wealth of not only information but great stories. We got to talking about Paul Hornung, an idol of Monroe's. To recap: "When I was in med school I worked my way through by being among other jobs proctor in the football dorm. One of my patients at the hospital was a little boy who was dying of leukemia and who happened to love football, especially Paul Hornung.

"NOTRE DAME was coming to play Penn and I got permission to take the boy to the game. I spoke to the captain of our team about talking to Hornung to see if he would say 'hello' to the little guy when we were at the game.

"He did a lot better than that. After the game, Paul Hornung came across Franklin Field, hoisted this kid onto his shoulders and marched him into the Notre Dame locker room with all the TV cameras going. Everyone was sure he was David Eisenhower.

"Then, as Terry Brennan held him, all the players came over and signed the game ball and gave it to him. This little boy didn't have a father and his mother never came to see him and he loved football. Paul Hornung gave him a wonderful gift."

Monroe's little friend died about a month after this game.

Of Mr. Hornung he said, "I think Hornung is the greatest as a human being. You never saw a little boy so happy in your life. I'll never forget it."

GOOD THINGS happen to Monroe during football season. At another Big 10 game, Penn vs. Wisconsin, Monroe and two friends had blind dates. "All I said was please let me have the tallest one," Monroe recalls.

Well, the tallest one was Miss Sandra Lemke, a Wisconsin co-ed. Sandy and Monroe Trout were married in June, 1960. By 1961 the young doctor was practicing in Harrisburg and by 1964 he was chief of medicine of a 2,700-unit facility for the aged . . . Harrisburg State Hospital.

At the same time, he was driving 48 miles round-trip everyday to teach a course on legal medicine at Dickinson and decided "it was foolish to travel all that way to teach for an hour so I started taking courses." Three years later Monroe Trout, the only professor/student at Dickinson Law School, was graduated with his third degree.

The year 1964 brought Monroe to Pfizer and the Trouts to New Canaan. By now they numbered three. Monroe Eugene Trout, jr., NCHS '79, is today a sophomore at Harvard (he was deemed a Harvard Fellow before he left high school) and a member of the Harvard basketball team.

[Here's an aside, all you basketball freaks: NBC has chosen Harvard/Princeton (tentatively) as its Game of the Week to be televised on February 13.]

Monroe, jr. is on the dean's list, starts on varsity basketball team and, best of all, has found time and love for an 11-year-old boy in the "Big Brothers" program. His father said, "Ian really looks up to Monroe." Monroe Trout, jr., is six-eight, but you can't joke about something as touching as a 20-year-old who realizes just how lucky he is and then does something about it.

On the home front there is big Tim Trout (he arrived in 1966). Tim is a sophomore at NCHS where he's an honor student, on the j.v. and varsity basketball teams and a state swimming champion.

Yes, the Trout kids are super achievers, but New Canaan has a generous share of those. The thing that sets these young men apart from many is the kind of people they are.

all-black medical school). Today he's vice chairman of the board. He's taught all over the world and worked with governments all over the world.

ONE OF HIS DELIGHTS is taking the family with him on these trips though he admits "the boys are getting a little jaded . . . they prefer fishing in Wisconsin to Europe, but Sandy and I always have a great time."

Sandy Trout, her husband lovingly says, "has done it all . . . she's probably been publicity chairman of every organization you can name." Well today I can name Woman's Club, Sports Council, Basketball Parents and Woman's Republican Club.

They love the theatre, tennis, paddle, and Penobscot Bay in Maine. Monroe loves just sitting, reading, working crosswords and doing some pretty respectable landscape painting. No, he does not admit to sleeping.

When he retires, he's going to teach in a law school or a medical school.

Four years ago, Monroe was elected to the Town Council. Since then, especially around budget time, Monroe has a way of getting himself quoted. Sometimes not too accurately. I went to a couple of those meetings and heard his plea for cutting down on some waste and alternative cost-effective methods and then I read and heard that he was "anti-education."

Good grief! Have you stopped beating your wife? Well, he'll be at it again come March and the budget meetings and you'll undoubtedly be hearing about it.

All this comment brought only this from Monroe: "I ran for the Town Council because I wanted the job. I thought I could do a good job. I'm doing it the way I see it. I don't think excellence necessarily depends on spending lots of money. My stand isn't going to win me any popularity contests, but I can't change it."

Popularity contests are funny things. But in Monroe Trout's case, I can positively say that if you knew him, you'd vote for him in a minute.

Letter from Ed Hollowell about my lecture at East Carolina Medical School.

HOLLOWELL & ASSOCIATES, P.A.
ATTORNEYS AT LAW

EDWARD E. HOLLOWELL
MARC W. INGERSOLL
JOAN M. MITCHELL
BARRY H. BLOCH *
H. LAWRENCE WARNER, JR. **

ALSO LICENSED IN OHIO *
ALSO LICENSED IN PENNSYLVANIA **
ALSO LICENSED IN DISTRICT OF COLUMBIA **

MICHAEL C. HALE
OF COUNSEL

RECEIVED
DEC - 8 1993

OFFICES
2840 PLAZA PLACE, SUITE 300
CROSSPOINTE PLAZA
RALEIGH, NORTH CAROLINA 27612

MAILING ADDRESS
POST OFFICE BOX 31208
RALEIGH, NORTH CAROLINA 27622-1208

TELEPHONE (919) 783-5657
N.C. WATS (800) 662-7403
TELEFAX (919) 787-1833

November 30, 1993

Monroe E. Trout, M.D., J.D.
Chairman of the Board
President and Chief Executive Officer
American Healthcare Systems
12730 High Bluff Drive, Suite 300
San Diego, California 92130-2099

Dear Monroe:

I received a copy of your letter to Marvin, and I support your elevation to emeritus status in the College.

Monroe, you have always been a very special friend. You were kind to serve as the H. Horton Rountree Distinguished Lecturer in Health Law at our Annual Health Law Forum of the School of Medicine of East Carolina University, and I have your picture, along with Judge Rountree and Dean Laupus hanging on my wall.

You are a "giant" in medical law, and I wish that you were in North Carolina so that you could associate with us when you retire from American Healthcare Systems.

I look forward to seeing you at the Annual Meeting of the College next year.

With best wishes for continued success in your endeavors, I remain

Sincerely,

Edward E. Hollowell

EEH/jsd

President's Award, ACLM.

Letter about my serving on the boards of the San Diego Community Foundation and San Diego Museum of Art.

JOSEPH W. HIBBEN
SUITE 550, 1205 PROSPECT STREET
LA JOLLA, CALIFORNIA 92037
(619) 459-8233

May 3, 1996

Dr. Monroe E. Trout
P.O. Box 8052
Rancho Santa Fe, CA   97067

Dear Monroe:

The comments that you and your wife made at the Salvation Army luncheon honoring you both were significant and helpful, so I made some brief notes. I was very pleased to be there, and would like to congratulate you again on this well deserved honor.

Your comments about your new responsibilities in Seattle fascinated me. I know that with your help, this company will be an outstanding success benefiting untold numbers of people.

Mary L. Walshok, whom you know at UCSD, is Chairperson of the Governance Committee of the San Diego Community Foundation. This committee is concerned with public awareness influencing attitudes of potential donors and beneficiaries alike. It is also concerned with the standing reputation and integrity of Governors who constitute the Board.

This rapidly growing foundation manages and dispenses income as grants from assets currently exceeding $140,000,000. It is almost certain that Sol Price and Irwin Jacobs will establish the Symphony Endowment at the Community Foundation to ensure its perpetuity. Sol has used the Foundation several times for other charitable purposes. As you probably know, UCSD has received a number of grants and the funding of several chairs through the Community Foundation.

Mary Walshok has asked me to urge you to favorably consider accepting a position as member of the Governing Board. Meetings are monthly, and terms are normally one year, renewable for three years.

Strangely perhaps, Lynn Gildred, President of the Board of Turstees of the San Diego Museum of Art has asked me to request that you accept a position as Trustee in that institution. I can assure you that a special audit recently completed by Price Waterhouse proves nothing wrong has been done by this institution or its top employees. Their endowment of $32,000,000 is all from private resources.

If you have questions, please call me at 459-8233 during normal business hours.

Thank you so much for reading this letter.

Best regards,

Joseph W. Hibben

Proclamation issued by Knox County Mayor Mike Ragsdale.

Proclamation

By Executive Order of the
Honorable Michael R. Ragsdale, Knox County Mayor
it is hereby proclaimed:

MONROE TROUT DAY

Whereas,   Monroe and Sandy Trout have shown outstanding community leadership throughout the region for the past decade; and

Whereas,   Their contributions have supported many great causes including the arts, cultural events, and educational initiatives benefiting our entire region; and

Whereas,   Monroe Trout is a true patriot and appreciates the sacrifices of all veterans; and

Whereas,   He has given six paintings to the Ben Atchley State Veterans Home paying tribute to each branch of the U.S. Military; and

Whereas,   Knox County wishes to honor Monroe Trout; his devotion to veterans of the U.S. Military and to his fellow patriots has been immeasurable, and his presence in Knox County has benefited this community greatly.

NOW, THEREFORE, I, MICHAEL R. RAGSDALE, KNOX COUNTY
MAYOR, do hereby proclaim March 11, 2007 as

MONROE TROUT DAY

In Knox County, and urge all citizens to join me in this observance.
Let all within the reach of this proclamation heed its directive(s).

His Honor the Knox County Mayor *Michael R. Ragsdale*
Michael R. Ragsdale

County of Knox
Knoxville, Tennessee

Be at war with your vices, at peace with your neighbors, and let every new day find you a better man. *–Benjamin Franklin*

Make sure what you do today is important, for you have given up a day of your life to do it. *–Anon.*

God gave us two ears and one mouth because listening is twice as hard as talking. *–Anon.*

Being hungry is a good motivator.

Honor your teachers. They are the best thing that ever happened to you.

If you are one of fourteen children, you are never late for meals.

Education is never out of date.

Tennis is for exercise. Only a few get to Wimbledon.

Any college is better than none.

Don't take yourself too seriously because no one else does.

Any college is suitable because they all will teach you more than you can learn.

Avoid hospitals unless you are visiting.

Don't ever lie on your resume because some day it will ruin you.

Enjoy fine art, and you will enjoy the essence of life.

Art is for the masses, not just an opiate for the elite.

Cacophony is music only if you are a teenager.

Civilizations are judged by how they treat the poor and downtrodden and how they treat the arts.

Don't just manage–lead.

Walking a mile a day is better than eating an apple a day.

Don't talk about your health problems unless you want to hear someone else's.

Health is more important than money.

Getting old isn't healthy.

Life is too short to make enemies.

You are only as old as you think you are.

AIDS is a societal problem, not a social problem.

Obesity is a disease caused by overeating.

Don't celebrate too soon. You may live to regret it.

Friends are more important than another drink.

Success is measured by the number of strangers you have helped on the highway of life.

Exercise is better than going to a doctor.

There is more to life than football.

True friends are for keeps; others are to be pitied.

You can have a big house and a big heart.

The Knoxville Opera Rossini Festival is to Knoxville
what the Spoleto Festival is to Charleston.

Make me glad and I will remember.
Make me mad and I will forget.

Grandchildren are the joy of life.
It's too bad you can't have them sooner.

Ballets are for sissies until you marry a ballerina.

Work is a vacation.

Money buys everything but good health and happiness.

Beware of people who want to manage your money.

INDEX